P9-EFJ-517

Surviving
STREET
PATROL

DISCARD

Surviving
STREET
PATROL

STEVE
ALBRECHT

The Officer's Guide to Safe and Effective Policing

PALADIN PRESS
BOULDER, COLORADO

Surviving Street Patrol: Realistic Officer Safety Solutions
by Steve Albrecht

Copyright © 2001 by Steve Albrecht

ISBN 10: 1-58160-129-8
ISBN 13: 978-1-58160-129-9
Printed in the United States of America

Published by Paladin Press, a division of
Paladin Enterprises, Inc.
Gunbarrel Tech Center
7077 Winchester Circle
Boulder, Colorado 80301 USA
+1.303.443.7250

Direct inquiries and/or orders to the above address.

PALADIN, PALADIN PRESS, and the "horse head" design
are trademarks belonging to Paladin Enterprises and
registered in United States Patent and Trademark Office.

All rights reserved. Except for use in a review, no
portion of this book may be reproduced in any form
without the express written permission of the publisher.

Neither the author nor the publisher assumes
any responsibility for the use or misuse of
information contained in this book.

Visit our Web site at www.paladin-press.com

ACC Library Services
Austin, Texas

Table of Contents

Foreword

I first met Steve Albrecht back in 1988. At that time Steve had not yet written his acclaimed text *Streetwork: The Way to Police Officer Safety and Survival* (Paladin Press, 1992). Since that time, I've come to know him as a consummate professional, and my respect for him as a police officer/supervisor/writer has grown proportionately with the years.

Undoubtedly, the lessons learned from *Streetwork* have found their way into department and academy curriculum in both basic and recruit school programs over the last dozen years.

There has never been a more important time in law enforcement for *Surviving Street Patrol: The Officer's Guide to Safe and Effective Policing.* Today's criminal element is bolder and more violent than ever before. Their willingness to take you on knows no boundaries or limits, and the granite walls of the National Law Enforcement Officers' Memorial bear the evidence of their ruthlessness.

The concepts, techniques, tactics, and strategies found in *Surviving Street Patrol* offer some solutions to this ever-growing problem. Rookie and veteran officers alike will benefit from the insight and advice offered on such complex issues as "Police Officer-Hostage," "SWAT Calls," "Ground Fighting," and "*CONTACT & COVER* Revisited."

Surviving Street Patrol was designed to be an off-the-shelf reference text that will benefit every aspect of the law enforcement profession. Academy instructors and field training officers (FTOs) will find it an invaluable resource text for their lesson plan development. Public Information Officers (PIOs) will find the chapters on the media a tremendous asset, since police press briefings have become almost as dangerous as the streets.

Patrol officers and detectives will gain from the knowledge contained in the chapters titled "Rape Investigations in Patrol," "Armed Robbers: Their Motives and Methods," "Responding to Workplace Violence Incidents," and "The Police Response to Domestic Violence in the Workplace."

Even first and second-line supervisors will find practical answers to complex questions in chapters such as the two entitled "Professional Courtesy."

No other police manual has served as such a concise, one-stop reference source wherein police professionals can access information on such provocative topics as "Militias in Our Midst," "Police and Customer Service," and "The Art of Blending." But *Surviving Street Patrol* was written primarily for the street cop, and that's where its real value lies.

Steve has spent the better part of his adult life in law enforcement, initially as a full-time street cop and later as a reserve sergeant, all with the San Diego, California, Police Department (SDPD). His service included time as an investigator with the SDPD Domestic Violence Unit, and he continues to work with the San Diego County District Attorney's Stalking Strike Force. Now he has put that vast experience to work in an easy-to-read, well-researched amalgamation of relevant topics that should become a part of every cop's library.

Surviving Street Patrol should have been written years ago. In my mind, it is one of the most important reference books on street patrol to have come down the pike in the last five years.

—David M. Grossi, Senior Instructor
Calibre Press, Inc.
Street Survival Seminars

Preface

As usual, these are interesting times to be a street cop. It's hard to recall a time in recent history when the law enforcement profession has received such public and media scrutiny. It seems everyone has an opinion about how, where, when, and why we do our jobs.

Just in the few months it took me to prepare this book for print, I've heard about two officers from my former police department in San Diego getting shot and wounded as they were responding to a call in a hotel bar. They killed the armed suspect after a blazing gunfight in the crowded lobby. The only good to come from this incident was that it served to put a near halt to the constant stream of news stories wherein the media and "outraged citizens" groups labeled San Diego Police Officers as "trigger-happy." (Are you listening, New York and Los Angeles?)

In the past few months, I've read or heard about two ambushed officers in Long Beach, California—one who survived a gang-related hit and one who did not. I've followed a story about a white supremacist who placed a home-made bomb near a cop's house. (Thank God it was manufactured by an idiot, so it failed to detonate.) I've seen the angry reactions to more than one controversial and difficult New York City police shooting. And yet, through all this, cops around this country continue to do their jobs, mostly by sucking it up and strapping it on.

It's a sad but true fact that it takes the injury or death of one or more cops to remind citizens, the media, watchdogs, and other "experts" who watch and comment about our profession, that street policing is dangerous or, more accurately, life-threatening or life-ending.

It's a shame we have to lose brother or sister officers, deputies, or agents to pursuit-based car crashes, close-quarter knife battles, or bullets big or small before people reacquaint themselves with the simple fact that neither serious crooks nor stupid crooks always comply.

In this profession of "public behavior control," it would be easier and we would be more likely to go home in one piece if everybody stopped when we said stop, gave up when we asked, and didn't use their weapons, bodies, or cars to try to kill us. But that's not reality, so we can't ever stop paying strict and careful attention to our safety.

This book should serve as a learning tool for those street cops out there, who, regardless of the size of their beat, agency, county, or city, are just trying to do the right thing. This text is for the "patrol dogs" who work for large and small police and sheriffs' departments, for those corrections-based deputies who are preparing to go back into the field after a stint turning keys, and for others in law enforcement who use different titles, all to describe the same job.

You're all cops to me, regardless of where you work, how long you've been on the job, or the color of your patrol cars, uniforms, or badges.

I've used the terms "cops" or "police officers" to cover everyone who holsters a handgun and goes out to do a job that most people wouldn't touch with a fire-breathing nightstick.

And even though I'm now retired from police work, you'll notice my frequent use of "we" and "us" to talk about tactical principles in general or things I have seen, heard, or done in the field. I wrote every one of these sections when I was either a full-time officer, a reserve officer, a reserve sergeant, or a crimes-against-persons investigator. Rather than go back and change every section to a past-tense description, I've left it as it was when I wrote it. After all, being a cop is like being a Marine; you never *really* stop being a law enforcement officer, do you?

Here's to the attitude that says, "I'm a street warrior and a street survivor, in and out of uniform, on or off the job, for the rest of my life."

—Steve Albrecht
San Diego, CA

"A" Is for Aggressive
Avoiding In-the-Line-of-Duty Deaths

Nearly 10 years ago, two agents from the FBI conducted an in-depth study of cop killers in custody. They were attempting to discover why some officers were killed in certain situations, why the crooks acted as they did, and how other officers might benefit from this information.

The researching agents admitted that before interviewing the 50-plus cop killers they were tempted to bring certain preconceived notions into the report, mainly that most of those killed would be, as they termed it, "rough, needlessly aggressive [officers] who could be described in terms of the 'John Wayne' or 'Jane Wayne' syndrome. . ."[1]

Their belief tended toward the idea that it is the so-called tough cop who got killed while the more careful, prudent officer survived. In reality, their study revealed the opposite. To quote from the study, "Many of the slain officers were known as friendly, hard-working, service-oriented people who were described by colleagues as 'laid back' and 'easy-going.' They also had a tendency to use less force than other officers and didn't always strictly follow departmental procedures."

Further, the officers "tended to use less force than other officers in similar circumstances, and often considered force only as a last resort. They were more service-oriented and tended to gravitate toward the public relations aspects of law enforcement work."

Other notable findings from the FBI study suggest that the slain officers made many tactical errors that gave their killers the opportunities they were waiting for, such as not approaching them tactically, failing to take control of the situation with command presence, failing to get more Cover Officers, searching poorly, or, sadly, even failing to wear body armor.

Knowing all these street survival "musts" as we do now, it's easy to start pointing fingers and making sweeping generalizations that start with, "If only they had . . ." and end with ". . . they might be alive today."

Every situation is different, and each officer will react to how he or she perceives the situation. What might be no big deal to you could cause another officer to get on the radio and ask for immediate help. And what one officer might use as a force option, another would not even consider.

I believe the study demonstrates a simple principle: Cops who handle dangerous situations with we might call "controlled aggression" survive those situations. Those who go out of their way to make parts of the arrest process more comfortable for the crook (e.g., avoiding the crotch area during a search was mentioned in the study as a reason so many crooks were able to hide their weapons until they could use them to kill) suffer mightily for their politeness.

Perhaps all this can be best evaluated on a spectrum, with the hard-as-nails cop on one end and Good Ol' Officer Friendly on the other. As I read this study of the deaths of 54 cops, the Officer Friendly types ended up deader faster than their less amiable colleagues did.

All this is not to say, of course, that you can use good officer safety as your excuse for being rude to every contact. But in this era of community-oriented policing, let's not forget that some street people see a cop's being "too nice to them" as an invitation to take control of the contact, attack, or ambush the officer who has traded his or her good police sense for a desire not to "inconvenience" the suspect.

I believe that many law enforcement officers already exhibit just the right level of no-nonsense command presence to keep the street thug in his place without creating a nonstop string of Internal Affairs complaints. These officers know how to take control of the psychological and physical parts of the contact so that if it escalates, they are already in a tactical position and can fight back.

As an example, on some high-risk contacts with hinky street types, some officers routinely use the back of their cage car to interrogate people so as to develop probable cause to arrest. Similarly, some officers will handcuff squirrelly contacts when emotions are running high and the officers have arrived at a jumbled mess where all the players and related information are not known.

It should be easy to justify in a "Detention Only" report why the situation, the suspect's words or actions, or those of his cohorts, caused you to (good report-writing lingo here) "legally and temporarily detain him in a safe and secure manner." As we all know, it's always easier to remove handcuffs from a now-cooperative person that it is to affix them to a noncooperative one.

If you set an early standard of authority that says, "I will not take any crap from you," perhaps it will supress a crook's neurotic impulses to assault or murder you. Remember, not everybody likes us, nor will they ever, and we shouldn't go about our workday assuming it's our job to convince every resident to join the Law Enforcement Fan Club.

Since we are in the behavior control business, it follows that there are those people who will wait for their chance to hurt us if they feel we have given them the physical or psychological opportunity.

Most of the cop killers studied in the FBI report had lengthy criminal records and were no strangers to the criminal justice system. While I'd never say that it's time to go back to the era of saps to the head and handcuffed beatings, sometimes people like those who have been in a highly structured, dominance-based environment like a county jail or a state prison need to know that those of us in uniform are still large and in charge. In other words, don't trade your life for your manners.

Notes

1. San Diego District Attorney's Office, *Law Enforcement Quarterly* (August-September 1993).

The APTRA Model
A Tactical Action Plan
for Problem-Oriented Policing

Across this country, citizens are asking their local law enforcement agencies to try harder to take back the streets from crime. Some members of the community are now seeing cops as their partners. In groups or alone, they say, "How can we help you close down this house that's full of drug dealers?" or "What can we all do to get transients, graffiti taggers, problem liquor stores, rowdy bars, or abandoned cars out of our neighborhoods?"

And with this new trend toward law enforcement and the community working more like partners and less like adversaries in some cities, much of the responsibility for initiating "problem-oriented policing" (POP) projects starts at the patrol level.

Patrol supervisors now go straight to their officers and say, "Here's a police-related problem on your beat. Take this initial information, gather more, apply every resource you can think of, and come back to me when it's fixed." And equally, patrol officers are coming to their bosses and saying, "Here's a crime problem that's got our attention. Will you give us the time, support, equipment, or manpower to work on it as a POP project?"

As a supervisor or a patrol officer, your future success in your department may depend on your ability to solve these complex or crisis-generated problems as they are thrust upon you. It's also no real secret that the best way to look good at promotional or specialized-unit interviews is to have a healthy stack of completed POP projects to your credit.

While many departments cite POP projects as the next wave in law enforcement, some agencies lack a proven model for effective case management. With that in mind, I'd like to suggest one, based on my experiences in the private sector helping companies solve their own event-specific crisis management problems.

It's called the APTRA model, and it can help you better organize your time, thoughts, and actions, on paper, in your head, and on the streets:

ANTICIPATE
PLAN
TRAIN AND PRACTICE
REVIEW
ACT, REACT, ADJUST, AND MOVE FORWARD

In terms of solving tough problems, I've always held the rock-solid belief that there is a time to energize and go forward and a time to retreat and regroup, but there is never a good time to sit and wait for bad things to get better.

Military generals all agree: even a less-than-perfect plan is better than no plan at all. Action and reaction should be what guide you, not vague hopes of a miraculous recovery, apathy based on fear or ignorance, or any false sense that you can or should try to outlast a serious problem without intervening or getting more help.

The APTRA Model offers one cornerstone for you as a POP project problem-solving technique. Applied in its complete form, with vigorous work on your part to match it to the needs of your POP project, it will serve you well.

If this were a perfect world, the five steps of the APTRA Model would solve all of our POP problems and help you manage and cover all of your police or community-related crises with guts, tact, and wisdom. Unfortunately, stuff happens. No matter what POP problem faces you, no matter its size or complexity, and no matter how hard you work to follow these steps, something still may go wrong. The key to your success lies in your ability to never give up and never give in. Better to put some plan of yours into immediate action and follow it than to flail around with nothing to do or nowhere to go.

ANTICIPATE

Too many supervisors and officers make their POP project decisions in what might be called "the echo of the gunfire," meaning that they only respond after something bad has happened to cause them to move. That's not a good time to be thinking about the problem for the first time. Decisions you can make today about something that might happen tomorrow, next week, next year, or, with luck, never, are a lot stronger than decisions you're forced to make in the heat of the moment, when all around you are losing their heads. Much of your early POP project management thinking starts with your ability to move outside your comfort zone for as long as it takes to solve the problem at hand. Yes, it can be difficult to take busy patrol time to talk to dozens of neighbors about a problem house, it can be time-consuming to spend your pre- or post-shift hours on the phone with one city or state agency after another, and it can be frustrating to work for weeks or months while seemingly nothing good happens to advance your POP project to completion.

These tasks can certainly take you away from your day-to-day activities, which, for most patrol officers, consist of serving the needs of their beats. But the more thinking and working you can do early on, the farther ahead you can move once you get rolling.

PLAN

Good plans make POP projects easier to manage from point to point, especially when dealing with citizens and neighborhood groups. People who want to feel more involved with you need things to do. When you create plans that people can know, review, implement, and offer suggestions for and improvements to, it sends a strong message to the community that says, "As a law enforcement agency, we are *very* interested in what goes on around here. We are *very* interested in the ongoing safety and protection of this area. And as a police department, we are *very* interested in your ideas, feedback, and suggestions that will help us all stay on track."

Your plans will certainly depend on the needs of your POP project and your patrol area, but all of them should cover ways to move the project forward, even if only in seemingly small steps. Remember, most crime or neighborhood problems are solved through cumulative efforts. The little things add up to the big things.

How well you respond in the early going sets the stage for your next moves. Your ultimate goal, besides those relating to the safety of all police personnel and civilians involved, should be to complete the project as methodically, quickly, legally, and efficiently as possible.

TRAIN AND PRACTICE

Since most POP projects relate to some form of criminal, civil, or behavioral problems, it's not surprising that you sometimes will need to gather up the troops, load up your cars with gear, and start making arrests. In narcotics POP projects, as an example, this can be especially dangerous.

Before you commit bodies and equipment to your POP project, get together and discuss your tactical approach, intervention methods, arrest procedures, and withdrawal plans. Most POP projects involving real crooks and their friends take place in what might best be called "hostile areas." It always helps for everyone to have the lay of the land in their heads before they get on scene.

Some people think walk-throughs, dry runs, or chalk talks are a waste of time. Experience probably will tell you that the people who say, "Don't worry about me, I'll know what to do when the time comes, I don't need to review it all again," are usually the ones who mess up first, worst, and longest.

It's okay to find these practice sessions and possible scenarios uncomfortable; it's not supposed to be fun, it's supposed to train you how to react when suspects are bailing out of skylights and basements.

REVIEW

The after-action process following your POP arrests or related enforcement activities should cover three distinct areas: an ongoing review of your department policies and procedures to clarify the rules of your organization and to make sure you are staying within legal guidelines, a post-incident review of your training and practice procedures to make sure you've covered every contingency—yours or the suspects'—and a post-incident review of your tactics during your arrests or enforcement activities.

Good cops always review their actions and activities in the aftermath of any serious or significant law enforcement problem. They ask themselves and each other the following:

- Did we solve the problem by doing the right things?
- What did we do right or wrong?
- What were our strong points or weak points?
- What were we prepared for or what surprised us?
- How well did we work, as individuals or as a team?
- What was our biggest area of threat or liability?
- How well did we communicate with our sergeants, lieutenants, captains, or related specialized units?
- Any telephone calls or announcements we should have made?
- If necessary, how well did we handle the media?
- Did we protect our officers and citizens as best as possible?
- How should we adjust our contingency plans for an even better response in the future?

ACT, REACT, ADJUST, AND MOVE FORWARD

Going back to the idea that even a spotty plan is a good plan, there is more strength, power, and control in action than in reaction. This is not to say you should charge around like a maniac, but neither should you sit passively and wait for small POP problems to go away without a push and shove or for big POP problems to solve themselves without a planned, strategic attack.

Your experience probably has already demonstrated that neither of these things usually happens; in truth, small problems grow into bigger problems and large ones can end up as a threat to officers' or civilians' lives.

Stay with what works, change what doesn't, and always be ready to think outside the usual boundaries to solve the POP problem facing your community and your division. The APTRA model should give you some different things to consider as you plan your next or ongoing POP project. If you need to, get as much advice as you can from POP project veterans, and measure that advice against your own instincts in determining what you think is right and what will work best.

Armed Robbers
Their Motives and Methods

The American Society for Industrial Security (ASIS) is a worldwide membership organization for security professionals. An article from the ASIS magazine *Security Management* raises some new and interesting issues related to convenience stores and the men who rob them.[1]

The Athena Research Corporation conducted a study using interviews with incarcerated c-store robbers. Not surprisingly, the research was funded by The Southland Corporation, the franchiser for the 7-11 chain of convenience stores.

The researchers interviewed 181 armed robbers in five state prisons in New Jersey, Texas, Illinois, California, and Louisiana.

The study indicates that for the majority of robbers, their *first* priority is to target stores near easy escape routes. Their *second* priority is to pick a store with easy access to cash. As one inmate put it, what *kept* him from robbing a store was "a bad escape route and a cashier who [safe] drops the cash too often."

The majority of robbers said that alarms, cameras, and the threat of long sentences didn't deter them, although these devices and punishments make it easier for us to catch them and lock them up later.

The proximity of the store played an interesting part in their choices. (Perhaps these guys were geography enthusiasts in school.) From a "Here's how we can catch them" perspective, one fact emerges in red and blue flashing lights: More than 40 percent of the robbers *lived less than two miles* from the convenience store they chose to hit.

With this in mind, we can continue to focus our perimeter activities— looking for cars or suspects matching the descriptions—within a few minutes' driving distance of the target store.

In terms of multiple offenses, more than one-third of the crooks had committed at least five convenience store robberies. The average number, before being caught, was 13. This should reaffirm our belief that c-store robberies are crimes for the recidivist, serial, or repeat robber, the one who chooses these places as his "crime of choice," over street rips or bank robberies. So if you know particular parolees in your service area have a history of c-store robberies, it's certainly likely they are up to no good at these places again.

The study raises a serious officer-safety issue as well. More than *60 percent* of the robbers said they robbed the stores with a partner. This accomplice worked either as a getaway driver/armed lookout in the parking lot or as an in-store armed lookout.

Most store clerks focus only on the man pointing the big gun at them and thus can give only one suspect description. This should give us more to think about if we confront an armed robber inside or near a convenience store, either on or off-duty; chances are good that he has at least one other player in his crew.

Whether it was crook bravado or the truth, the majority of the robbers said that the number of people inside the store—employees, witnesses—made no difference to them in terms of deterring their robberies. Most thought that with a gun and a partner, "they could take on/take down about 11 people."

The number or gender of the clerks or the presence of an unarmed security guard reportedly did little to deter these crooks either. And although they admitted that they were more deterred by an armed security guard or the possibility of an armed clerk, they felt their chances of survival or escape were still good, since they believed their opponents would not shoot or be able to hit them during the crime.

While "easy" cash was a requirement for the robbers, the amount they needed was not huge. Most described their need for money as "at least $200." In other words, they both expected to get this much and would be willing to rob the store if they thought they could get this much money. The study authors attribute this small cash amount to the cheap price and easy availability of crack cocaine. That is, crooks would take the risk of arrest or getting shot since the payoff provided at least enough money (however briefly) for drugs.

Most c-store policies instruct their employees not to resist the robber in any way. Other research reports have agreed by concluding that store clerks who resisted were almost 50 times more likely to be killed than those who "cooperated, gave up the money, did not make any sudden moves, [and] did not talk, stare [for better suspect descriptions], or try to be a hero."

This study concurs, as the robbers agreed that "most people get hurt when they resist, keep their hands out of sight, or make sudden moves." And, as we know from our own police contacts and arrest situations with these people, the other reported reason for injuries was that the robber was "nervous or high on drugs."

Criminologists talk about the crime fantasies or "scripts" crooks run through their heads in the days or weeks before they commit their crimes. Robbers often say the same things during the robbery because that's how they've practiced it inside their heads. Store employees can get hurt or shot when they "interrupt" these scripts by failing follow the instructions or moving in ways that deviate from the crook's original plan.

It's surprising to learn that so few of the c-store robbers cared about the presence of video surveillance cameras. They rationalized this belief by stating that "no one is watching the monitor at the time of the robbery" and that "they could always wear a disguise" if they thought cameras were in operation.

Further, the robbers agreed overwhelmingly that robbery is a tough crime to solve and said they rarely gave much thought to being caught or locked up for a long period of time.

Furthermore, the presence of police in the neighborhoods around the convenience store did little to stop these men. They believed that the police could not always be near these stores because of other service calls, and some admitted to planning their crimes around police shift changes.

In summary, this study draws some useful conclusions as to how to prevent convenience store robberies: keep the amount of available cash in the drawers down to an absolute minimum; put more barriers in the store to make it hard for the crook to get in and out quickly (displays, aisles, counters, turnstiles, double doors); install fences or gates to block off the rear of the store (a favorite pre-robbery hiding place or post-robbery escape route); install speed bumps and concrete planter boxes in parts of the parking lot to make it tougher on the getaway driver; and continue to use high-quality video camera systems to help us get a good look at the crooks when they case or rob the stores.

And as for the robbers' claims that they can wear masks and similar disguises to avoid being recognized on videotape, we know many of them favor the same shirt, jacket, hat, and sunglasses in each robbery. They get their media or police nicknames (e.g., "Red Ski Mask Bandit" or "Oakland Raiders Jacket Robber") from their idiotic desire to wear their "lucky" clothes time after time.

From a police perspective, this study gives us some new information while reminding us of what we already know about convenience store robbers: they are dangerous and here to stay.

Notes

1. Staff written, *Security Management* (October 1996).

The Art of Blending
Stop Dressing Like a Cop!

In my travels, I have the opportunity to attend a number of police-related training seminars. Many of them have to do with subjects I'm currently writing about or teaching, including domestic violence, stalking, and interviews and interrogations. At these programs, the audience is often populated with either brand-new patrol officers eager to learn or seasoned patrol officers eager to make rank or investigations.

And since many of these sessions are held at large hotels, the participants mill about the grounds just prior to the start of each program. As usual, it's easy to spot the cops. (Female officers can skip ahead if they want; I'm not describing your gender here.)

In the restaurants, a crew of steely-eyed Alpha males crowds around the table so that each member has a view of the door. Fanny-packs and mirrored sunglasses abound. Everyone has the same style of plastic sports watch attached to his wrist. Shoulder holsters filled with fat 9mm pistols bulge under dark-colored windbreakers or flannel shirt jackets. Pagers the size of fireplace bricks are attached to belts.

Wraparound, "Oakley-style" sunglasses, some mirrored, some tinted in "shooter's yellow," are attached to nylon cords around necks attached to heads with high-and-tight haircuts, flattops, and/or mustachioed faces. Levi pockets are filled with two wallets. The bolder officers wear cop-oriented T-shirts that say witty things like "I Kick Butt and Take Names," "Boyz on the Hood," or "West Valley Patrol—The Thickest Part of the Thin Blue Line."

So why is this rampant "sameism" such a part of the police culture? Why do we take the concept of the actual law enforcement "uniform" (blue, green,

15

tan, or otherwise) and transfer it over to the off-duty "uniform" so many officers like to wear?

Henry James said, "The greatest human need is the need for affiliation." As human beings, we all have the tendency to flock together by type. People need each other to survive and thrive. We find comfort in our daily, weekly, monthly, or yearly routines that bring us together—work, life, family, church, holidays, and so on.

As the old song so sweetly puts it, "People who need people are the luckiest people in the world." It's the true "loners" who end up with their photos in the newspapers, responsible for some heinous crime involving their parents and a collection of table saws.

Cops are famous for banding together, on and off duty, for the most familiar of reasons (and you can quote it along with me now): "Because no one else understands what we do."

And the built-in "us versus them" phenomenon that takes hold of even the newest rookie officer on Day One-Phase One is tied to this need for affiliation with the people who do this job now and way back when.

And so as males and cops we dress alike, cut our hair alike, talk alike, swear alike, and label crooks in the same ways that we all like to do. We're proud of our jobs and the role we play in society and in the street. Some of us adorn our cars with window stickers, bumper stickers, license plates, and license plate frames that tell the world, "I'm in law enforcement and proud to be!"

All this pride and need to affiliate with this profession and each other is admirable, commendable, and understandable. It also ain't safe.

Imagine for a moment that you are dispatched to a valid, in-progress burglary call at night. Would you race to the call, park right up front, whoop the siren a few times, put on your overheads, slam the car door, jingle your keys as you approached, whistle a little tune, shine your flashlight around and around, and then call for the guy to come out and give himself up?

Of course not. Why? Because you don't want to give your position away and lose your tactical advantage. Why? Because you don't want to be spotted and assaulted. Why? Because you want to stay safe as you approach and handle an unknown situation where the bad guy may know more about it than you.

Now put yourself back off-duty, wearing what you usually wear, acting as you usually act, and operating like you usually operate, with all of these visual clues that scream out, "I'm in law enforcement and proud to be!"

Although I shouldn't be, I'm always shocked when I'm in a bar or restaurant with a bunch of other off-duty cops and the waitress strikes up a conversation by saying, "You guys look like cops, or something . . ." These folks are good readers of people; they have to be if they want to make good tips. Service employees are constantly reading their customers to decide if a nice tip is in the offing. The guy with the $1,800 suit and the Rolex watch may turn out to be a stiff, but it's a better bet than the guy with the crusty gray T-shirt and the rope-for-a-belt pants.

Think of the tremendous tactical disadvantage you give yourself when you're off duty and you encounter someone who hates cops who suddenly realizes you're a cop. Remember, it might not be someone *you* arrested who will cause you harm when you least expect it; it could be someone another officer arrested, last night or last year, who wants to take a shot at you, literally or with a fist.

Before you push all this away as the rantings of a paranoid police pontificator, consider how easy it has become to find people or information about them today. We know organized crooks and gang members are targeting law enforcement by developing intel on them. Using the Internet or a pal who works at the Department of Motor Vehicles (DMV), your county courthouse, or a car with access to a credit checking phone line, a sophisticated crook who wanted to do you or a loved one some serious harm could probably track you down within a day.

This, of course, begs the argument that says, "Yes, but off-duty cops have their guns, and they can always defend themselves or their families if they have to." Think about the last time that you left your gun at home because you were "only going to the store, the movies, across town," or wherever. Think about how many times you may have sat in your car, in your bank, at a restaurant, or in a grocery store, lost in thought in Condition White and oblivious to the people around you. Lately, you can read too many robbery reports where an off-duty law enforcement officer was one of the powerless victims of a takeover crew.

The point to all this is simple: Be proud of who you are and what you do on duty and off. Wear your police uniform (or detective clothes) on duty and make the change to "average citizen" when you go off duty. Dress up or down when you need to fit in. Leave the obvious cop tools and calling cards off your body and car. Start focusing on how you can blend in with the situation and strive *not* to call attention to your private self in public situations.

Blue Power!

Police Fitness to Save Your Life and Career

A poster hanging in a police station locker room says it all. A photo shows a bulked-up inmate wearing a "Federal Penitentiary" T-shirt as he pumps iron in a prison gym. The caption below the shot reads: "EVERY DAY YOU DON'T WORK OUT, SOMEONE ELSE DOES."

Police fitness is not just for SWAT officers, academy instructors, or local department "jocks"; it's for everyone who puts on a badge and gun, regardless of whether they still go into the field or not. What is now called "survival fitness" is for today's working law enforcement officers who must face increasingly rigorous challenges from a growing number of criminal offenders.

Cops who are in shape can count on fewer injures, better stress control, superior job performance, improved morale, greater command and "force" presence, an enhanced professional appearance, and more confidence about their abilities to do the job safely and effectively over a longer span of their careers.

There is a neurobiological reason for being in shape. Police work is like few other professions in its effects on the body's adrenaline levels and muscle use. Going from the relative calm of the patrol car right into a hostile, hands-on battle puts a tremendous strain on the average law enforcement officer's heart, muscles, organs, and "fight or flight" systems. The cumulative effect of these stress "spikes" over the course of a career can be quite a collection of physical and psychological ailments.

We all know how difficult it is to juggle career, personal, and family obligations around a job that requires demanding shift work in all kinds of weather and locations. It's not too late to crank up your current level of fitness another healthy notch.

If it's been hard for you to develop the police fitness habit, see if these excuses ring familiar:

- "I'm not running up the street after some crook."
- "I've got too much gear on, and besides, some 19-year-old car thief wearing $100 running shoes has got a big edge on me from the start."
- "If I can't catch 'em with a car, then I don't go after 'em."
- "The only time I'll chase some dude on foot is if he shot a cop or something."
- "That hands-on, defensive tactics crap never works when you go to use it."
- "If some son-of-a-bitch tries to fight me, I'll just knock him on his ass. If that doesn't work, I'll screw my gun into his ear."
- "I don't have time to exercise. I work nights, and the hours are brutal."
- "My days off conflict with my wife's or husband's schedule, so that means I gotta stay home with the kids."
- "I'll get back to working out as soon as I change shifts."

If you've never said any of these out loud, then you've probably thought about them in your head. There are very few officers who haven't adopted any one of these—or something similar—to fit their own situations.

But remember that police work and physical fitness come together into an odd sort of paradox. This is probably one of the most physically demanding professions imaginable, save for oil well firefighter or underwater welder. Just the physical act of wheeling a squad car through the streets for eight or ten hours per day can be intensely draining. The constant routine of climbing out of the car, dealing with a stream of highly stressful problems, and then driving off to face another set of uncertainties is flat-out tough.

Even so-called intervals of "doing nothing" can cause you some physical discomfort: those long stakeouts, the tedious hours spent standing in courthouse hallways, or the last minutes of the night that you hope will disappear quickly as you wait out the end of a cold graveyard shift. Sometimes the stress and strain of just "being a cop" leaves us feeling drained and weary by the end of the workday. The mental "gear" we carry around can be just as heavy as the boots, belts, and bullets.

If your department has some recruiting posters hanging in the squad rooms or the locker areas, they probably depict the same things: one or two good-looking coppers—maybe male and female—steely-eyed, flat-bellied, and spit-shined to a high-buffed gloss. Where do they get these silver-screened street warriors? Usually, they come fresh from the academy!

And why shouldn't they? If you're trying to attract new recruits to the profession, why not show them how good they'll look? Putting a 10-year street cop up there—the one with the cracked leathers, the ripped and faded shoulder patches, and the spaghetti-sauce eyeballs doesn't do much to inspire the masses. But how many longtime street warriors do you know who don't carry the signs of every bad radio call on their faces? "Those recruiting poster babies," they will say with rightful indignation, "haven't been out there, doing what we do, day in and night out. This is a damned tough job!"

And so it is. The ones who can last, who can make it to the 20 to 30-plus years and a retired-badge pension, are those who know police work is a profession only for the durable. They fight the aftereffects of dealing with the worst society can conjure by protecting their most powerful street-survival asset—their bodies.

Modern police work takes brains. You have to think, act, react, and make thousands of choices during nearly every moment of your shift. And for the most part, we do a terrific job of thinking on our feet. We use caution, discretion, and control during extremely trying circumstances. (And even the most hardened ACLU lawyer must grudgingly admit that we now use deadly force in far fewer situations where it would be perfectly justified.)

But modern police work also takes brawn—not just large physical size or extraordinary strength, but muscles, stamina, and guts. Law enforcement is a hands-on thing, because while the mind can get us in, sometimes the body has to get us out. You can talk to some street creeps until the sun rises, but when push comes to push, you may just have to grab hold of their hands, arms, or legs and settle the situation in your favor.

When you were in the police academy, your instructors offered a balance of classwork for the mind and roadwork for the body. As painful as either might have been for you and your classmates, the efforts did make you well-rounded, aggressive new officers. With heads teeming with knowledge and bodies ready for adventure, you were all certain you could hit the streets running as part of the invincible blue line.

But as the years slipped by, the bellies started to thicken and the muscles began to sag. The breathing became labored and the whole system—mind and body—began to feel like it was slightly out of whack. What happened?

The Job crept up on you. The demands, the pressures, and the stresses of everyday police work can take their toll on even the most balanced person. Many of us entered the police academy in fair-to-average shape and left it in great physical condition. We fully intended to keep up that same level of high-quality fitness, but The Job had other plans for us. The Job gave some of us bad food, terrible hours, and mind-bending stress. The Job gave some of us

21

booze, cigarettes, and failed marriages. And The Job gave some of us pain, injury, early retirement, and even death.

Police fitness offers a multisided solution to the psychological and physical demands of The Job. It's about more than just looking sharp in a uniform. It's more than just feeling good about your body and improving your ability to catch that fleet-footed 19-year-old car thief. It's about getting in shape, staying in shape, and beating the negative effects of modern police work. It's a journey that starts with you.

Bullet Dynamics and the Myth of "Safe Cover"

Having had no formal or even informal training in physics, ballistics, or wound dynamics, I'll make this next statement brief and then I'll back it up with a story that demonstrates its wisdom. Cut this out and post it in your locker: *"Stucco or plaster walls, hollow-core wooden doors, or anything not made from steel, thick concrete, or heavy brick makes for lousy cover."*

What follows is a tale of the "Little Bullet that Could," which is subtitled, "How a 9mm Round Passed through Five Supposedly Solid Surfaces and Still Retained Its Shape."

Going along on a follow-up investigation with a detective from the San Diego Police Domestic Violence Unit, I had occasion to visit a home where a man stood not three feet from his wife, shot at her, and, just like in the movies, missed.

During a violent argument, said husband threatened his wife with his gun as she stood in a narrow hallway less than four feet wide. He fired at point-blank range at about waist-level. Call it fate, divine intervention, or maybe the wife in question had the moves of a bullfighter, but she was able to dodge the oncoming round.

Here's where this tale of attempted murder gets interesting. How do we trace the trajectory of lead? Let us count the ways:

- The bullet leaves the gun, immediately strikes the outside of a wooden bookcase located on the left side of this hallway, and then passes through it. (Hole Number One.)

- The bullet leaves the friendly confines of the bookcase, makes a hard right turn, and then strikes a plaster wall on the right side of the hallway. (Hole Number Two.)

- The bullet pierces the wall but does not go completely through to the other side. After holing the wall, it skids along the right hallway and just as it reaches the end, veers left, and punches a hole near the knob in a hollow-core wooden door standing slightly ajar. (Hole Number Three.)

- Once it passes through this wooden door, it makes a slight left turn and smacks into another wooden bookcase–waist-high and in the vicinity of the top shelf. (Hole Number Four.)

- Before it comes to its final resting place inside this second bookcase, it passes through the "NY" of a New York Yankees baseball cap sitting forlornly on the shelf. (Hole Number Five; and since I'm a lifelong Baltimore Orioles fan, this has a certain sense of baseball justice.)

- The round itself was of course misshapen, but not so fragmented that you couldn't recognize it as a bullet. (To get the idea, take the foil wrappers off a half-dozen Hershey's chocolate kisses and bunch them into a cylindrical ball.)

In hindsight, of course, if you squatted down and peered through each hole, starting from the first one at the top of the hallway, you could possibly trace this bullet's crazy path.

But since immediate hindsight is not a part of the on-scene evidence technician's kit and we cops certainly don't have any on hand, either, it took all three of us several long hours to discover this round using the usual trial-and-error method.

As I watched the evidence tech collect the bullet (and the Yankees hat), I felt a slight chill pass through me. Can you imagine what would have happened to the person standing on the other side of the hallway door, in between the bookcase?

Seeing that bullet pass through five distinct surfaces and continue along at the same relative height caused me to rethink my understanding of the differences between "cover" and "concealment."

Clearly, each of these solid surfaces offers much of the latter and little of the former. We all remember the rules of finding and using cover versus concealment. In the best case, perfect cover would stop bullets from bouncing against your body. In the best case, perfect concealment only shields you from the bad guy's line of fire sight. But one monkey wrench that always gets thrown into our search for this perfection is that we usually don't have the luxury of choosing our cover spots. And what we wish would offer good cover usually only offers adequate concealment.

What happens, all too often, is that we think if we can't *see* through it, a crook won't be able to *shoot* through it. As the five-hole bullet demonstrates, this is hardly the case. And it also explains why some officers still stand in front of windows with curtains, in the mistaken belief that linen, screen, and glass will stop lead. Or why some officers still stand directly behind hollow-core doors, screens, stucco walls, wooden garage doors, or near acres of drywall, hoping that hot, moving lead will not penetrate soft, standing surfaces.

In a hail of gunfire, one or more rounds shot in the direction of these bullet-porous surfaces will probably get through and may hit you. Granted, the bullet will have slowed considerably and may fragment into nothing or veer off before it reaches you, but who wants to bet his or her life on the faint hope that a two-by-four stud will be in the right place at the right time? (I can't find them when I want to hang pictures; who says a bullet will be any brighter than I am?)

While it's true that we can't always choose perfect cover, it makes good officer-safety sense to scan the setting, see what will make for adequate cover (good enough to save your life), and avoid what will make for mere concealment (not good enough to save your life).

To review, most of these surfaces or fixtures *won't* provide much, if any, safe cover: glass, plaster, stucco, drywall, aluminum (as found in backyard storage sheds), hollow-core front doors, garage doors, fences, or any wooden surface not latticed through and through with bullet-grabbing studs.

If used properly, most of these surfaces or fixtures *will* provide safe cover: cars (especially across the hood and engine block); concrete walls, pilings, abutments, curbs, stairs, or pillars; dirt (as you might find if you were crouching behind a large garden planter box); heavy brick walls, fences, or barricades; or any thickened steel surface.

Distance is often your best first choice for safe cover. As any SWAT officer can tell you, when dealing with a suspect armed with a high-powered rifle, two city blocks may not be far enough away.

And we know from seeing ricochet shots that bullets often hug the surface from where they came, i.e., a bullet fired onto smooth concrete may only rise two feet or less. However, for every ricochet bullet that does what it's *supposed* to do, there are 10 that go anywhere they please and blatantly disregard the laws of physics and motion. Keep this in mind as you pass through alleys, cross asphalt streets, or walk on concrete floors.

Don't think real crooks don't know about the differences between cover and concealment; some of them have been in more shootings by age 21 than a dozen cops have in their entire careers. Your safest bet is to make it a habit to put as many hard, thick, and sturdy objects between yourself and the potential for harm from hostile gunfire. You may not have the luxury of time or the best surface, but if you think fast, you can pick some spots that are better than others.

What you don't see *can* kill you. Even for the most basic radio call response or a field interview situation, give more than a moment's thought to the question of where you would move if a gun other than yours appeared on the scene.

To Chase or Not to Chase
The Rabbit Dilemma

If you're a fan of the comics page in the newspaper, you'll recall that the title character in the late Reg Park's old strip "Andy Capp" is a shiftless, lazy, boozing wife-beater. Andy is always pulling some kind of scam on his wife, his bartender, or the cops. In one small slice-of-life strip, Andy and his pal are fishing on the pier when they are surprised by a game warden who asks to see their fishing licenses.

Andy and his pal drop their fishing tackle, split up, and break into a hard run in opposite directions. The warden chooses to chase Andy, and when he catches him (and his breath), he starts to write him a summons. Andy pulls out a valid fishing license. "Why didn't you show me that in the first place?" asks the warden, huffing and puffing. "Because," says Andy, gasping too, "my partner doesn't have one!"

The hard lesson from all of this is that people who are either in trouble with the cops or *have been* in trouble with the cops, will, given the chance and the choice, run from the cops. And they will run for stupid reasons, which make no sense to anyone, starting with you and ending with them. So why chase them? It's a vexing question with no easy answer.

Time is on the side of those with patience. And as with many things in life, this holds true in law enforcement as well. When we rush, we make mistakes, and when we make mistakes, people get injured or killed, including our colleagues, our citizens, and the crooks we swore out an oath to arrest.

So let's reach deep into the barrel of controversy and swirl the waters by examining the reasons behind foot pursuits. Let's ask some difficult questions: Why do we engage in dangerous foot chases with people simply because they run away? Why do we chase people for infractions or even less, who run just because they don't like being messed with by the cops? Why do we charge after people when we're unsure if they've committed any crime?

When we lose sight of these people during the dash (as is not hard to do), we change the odds dramatically toward their escape and our pain. Doesn't losing a suspect around a corner or over a fence offer a good way to get ambushed, beaten, or shot?

If you haven't had anyone run away from you by now in your patrol career, you're either lucky or not looking hard enough. Many years ago, when I was a young and strapping officer, it took me until the 89th day of my 90-day field training program before I experienced the thrill of the chase. That's right; not until nearly the last day of my third and final phase did someone I stopped actually have the nerve, gall, or testosterone to disobey my lawful order to halt.

One minute I was asking two guys in a pickup truck to pull over from being double-parked on the wrong side of the street so I could give them a citation, and the next minute they were off in eleventy-billion directions, the passenger on foot and the driver in the car and then on foot.

Prior to that moment, I had never had to chase anyone anywhere. Everybody I talked to did what he or she was "supposed" to do when in contact with a cop, which is comply.

These two birds decided differently, and if it weren't for the wherewithal of my FTO, both of them would have gotten away cleanly. My partner grabbed the passenge before he could get up the block, while I stood there with my mouth hanging open, watching the driver speed off and then ditch his car and beat feet up the alley. It occurred to me to run after him only when he was far, far away.

It's easy to get complacent during the early stages of field investigation (FI) or a traffic stop because we are usually quite used to having people bend to our wills. Armed with big and shiny guns and big and shiny badges, we expect people to respect our authority and command presence and do what we say, when we say to do it.

Numerous times out of numerous times, when we say, "Stop!" or "Wait!" or "Stand over there!" or "Park over there and wait," most people do it. When they don't, our temptation is to drop everything and run after them, pell-mell, over fences, and up and down hills, and through maze-like apartment complexes. I'd like to suggest here and now that it's not always the best or brightest thing to do.

By now, those of you with a high sense of Police Moral Outrage will have torn this chapter from the book, crumpled the paper into a ball, or scratched off my name from the cover.

I'd like to offer two things in my defense: first, get over it, and second, pick your chases. I've been around long enough to go to at least one police funeral for a young copper who was shot in the head following a nighttime foot pursuit. During several discussions with veteran officers that have followed since this tragedy, the overwhelming consensus has been that he was killed for the statistical equivalent of an FI slip. This is not to denigrate the officer; it simply points out the inherent dangers when there are more of them than there are of you and you make the choice to run after them blindly in the dark.

Of course, there are those who will say that officers who work in so-called high crime areas chase people all the time. I'd argue this gives us all the more reason to chase with care. The criminals living in these "high crime" areas are often lifelong residents. Many times, we know who they are (having had to chase them before) or, better yet, where they live or with whom they hang. If you don't get them today, you'll get them tomorrow, or another officer will. It's not like they're going to run to the next state.

If they beat feet, get on the air and get help into the area. If that fails, go back to the station, do some computer work, and then go or send other officers to the suspect's last known address. Chickens always come home to roost.

Other officers are probably arguing, "Yes, but if we don't chase them every time, they'll think they can get away with anything and we won't go after them!" This argument can be made just as easily during vehicle pursuits. Why do we chase speeders who don't stop? Well, sometimes we don't. We call off vehicle pursuits anytime they become exceedingly dangerous to other innocent people or ourselves. Why can't you make the same judgment in that split-second before a foot pursuit becomes dangerous? Who says we have to let them win, but who says we have to let them beat us?

I'm not speaking out of school when I say that not every law enforcement officer has the physical strength or cardiovascular stamina to run after, catch, and subdue every young smartmouth in $130 Nikes and normal (not sagging-past-his-butt) pants. I have completed a full marathon, many half marathons, and even several triathlons, but I'm still as slow as a glacier in summer, even downhill with the wind at my back. I don't doubt my fortitude, just my ability to sprint after someone (for longer than five minutes straight) with 33 pounds of blue gear attached to my body.

For the officers who say, "What about true felony suspects? Are you suggesting we let them run away?" No, I'm suggesting you work even harder to catch these idiots, but you do it in a smart, tactical, and well-planned way, and most of all, with help.

Since we don't get into foot pursuits during every police encounter, what is it that makes some people stay and others bolt? Certainly if you have had prior contact with the suspect, and you know he's a rabbit, you're going to adjust your tactical approach to either box him in, surround him with cops, or catch him asleep somewhere.

If you must run, follow the rules of safety: If you lose sight of the suspect, break off the foot pursuit. If you run and talk in the radio, do it clearly and don't scream. Get immediate help, from the ground and in the air; don't wait until forever has gone by before summoning other officers, notifying air support, or setting up a perimeter.

As the ancient Chinese martial artists said, "Every battle is fought in the mind, before the fighting begins." In other words, know what you're going to do before you have to do it. Read the suspect's preflight body language. If he looks away, scans off in the distance, flexes some body parts, and pretends not to hear you, he's going.

If you're in midcontact and the suspect takes off, you should have already made your decision to either chase him on foot, by car, or in the air (by knowing if and where local helicopter is available), or just to let him go and catch him later.

If the suspect votes with his feet, take what he has given you: a name and date of birth (real or otherwise), his car, personal belongings, driver's license, and so on, and do your computer work. Pick your time, get enough support, and when the tactical advantage is on your side, grab him up.

Compassion for the Professional Victim

What do the following events have in common? A teenage gang member gets shot to death in a parking lot. A prostitute gets beaten and raped by one of her customers. A homeless man gets robbed at knifepoint, and what little money and possessions he has are taken from him. A woman who uses drugs, shoplifts, and hangs out with a bad crowd is battered by her live-in boyfriend.

In each of these cases, the common factor is that it's hard for police officers to feel much compassion or empathy for these victims. We have all been to these kinds of calls, and it's difficult to keep from saying, either aloud to your partner later in the car or inside your head, "Hey, too bad. You shouldn't have been in this situation in the first place. This never would have happened if you had your act together."

While lots of cops may come out of the police academy full of hope, idealism, and the desire to save the world, it doesn't take more than a few years before these same officers have had much of their compassion sanded clean off. This is caused in part by the utter despair they see, and it's coupled with the fact that they have to deal with people who could be correctly classified as professional "victims."

There are full-time misfits and victims roaming the streets everywhere. It's the guy who swears he was just on his way to the DMV office when you stopped him for an equipment violation and discovered that his registration has been unpaid for over one year. As he begs you not to tow his car, your response is probably the same as mine: "Sorry, pal. I pay my DMV fees. Why don't you?" (It always strikes me as odd that the people who tell me they have no money for DMV fees because they're flat broke always seem to have plenty of money for liquor and cigarettes.)

31

This is the person who tells you as you're both en route to jail, "But I have to start my new job tomorrow! I can't go to jail! How am I supposed to go to work now?" All of this suddenly becomes *your* fault; *you're* now the one who is impeding his only chance at a new life. *You're* now the reason he can't pull himself out of his current sinkhole.

And, as is common in the last domestic violence example from above, this is also the woman who lives in a filthy house with an even filthier boyfriend (who is also the erstwhile father of two of her three runny-nosed kids), who says, as she holds an ice bag to her broken nose, "But I *love* him! And besides, where am I supposed to go with all these kids, no money, and no job? And oh, by the way, do you have a cigarette?"

What these and other professional victims have in common is that they want *you* to take no less than full responsibility for *their* problems. As one veteran officer puts it after another long day of patrol, "These people expect you to arrive on the scene, listen to all the problems they've had for their entire life, and then give them a perfect solution that will fix everything immediately. If you don't, they get upset and accuse you of not doing your job. I get tired of telling people who are nearly as old as my parents to get their lives together."

It does feel a bit ludicrous for police officers to have to tell adults 15 years years their senior, "Stop smoking rock cocaine, shooting heroin, or snorting meth. Stop drinking at eight in the morning and hanging on the corner all day with your thug pals. Stop beating your wife. Gather your possessions, make a plan, get some money together, and move out with a friend, a relative, or to a battered women's shelter."

A case in point: A woman lived in mortal fear of her former boyfriend. He had sexually attacked her in the past, battered her in front of her kids, and then went on a stalking spree where he would park on her street every night and wait for her to come home. Her restraining order didn't keep him away, and he always seemed to be one step ahead of the arriving police officers. Finally, when the woman said she could take it no more, she told the police she was moving.

This sounded like a great idea. Get as far away from this abusive idiot as you can. Take your children out of harm's way. Make a fresh start.

Imagine their surprise when they discovered that she had moved out of her apartment and into a new one . . . about one block away. Some people just don't get the point.

So what's the moral to all of these sad tales of woe? There are really three lessons for all of us to learn:

1) **Try your hardest to be as compassionate as possible.**

You don't have to hug everyone you see or offer to let them move into your spare bedroom, but you do need to be empathetic to their problems. They probably don't want to be telling you their life difficulties any more than you want to hear them. But they did call you, or you did come across them in some way, and it's now up to you to offer whatever intelligent guidance you can.

2) **Treat every situation as if it were different, even though you may have seen this same kind of problem or this same type of professional victim before.**

As hard as it is, you need to check your past prejudices and expectations at the door and come into every new situation with as much of an open mind as you can muster.

3) **Help people break their patterns.**

Patterns, according to infomercial hypemaster Tony Robbins, are sets of behaviors (or ruts) that people get themselves into. The woman who can't leave her abusive husband needs to have her pattern changed (and so does her spouse, which is why we put him in jail when he hits her). Maybe it will take a lot of your efforts to help her change her life, e.g., driving her and her kids to a shelter, getting a legal aid attorney to talk with her about divorce proceedings, or helping her with an Emergency Protective Order (EPO) or Temporary Restraining Order (TRO).

The kid who lies dead in a pool of blood from a gang drive-by shooting is some mother's son. Your support may be what that mother needs right now as she deals with the death of her child. While *he* may have been a street hood, she might be a good person who struggled with him his whole life. She may have other normal, law-abiding kids and may have just lost the battle with this one.

Maybe she does need your shoulder to cry on as she stands at the crime scene. Maybe she does need information from you about what will happen to her child's body. And maybe she will want to know from you what can be done to protect her other children from this kind of harm as they grow up. And just maybe she has a good idea who did this to her kid and will tell you if you treat her with some kindness.

The point to all of this is simple: you can be compassionate and still do your job safely. You can be compassionate and still enforce the laws by locking people up when they need it. And you can be compassionate and still not lose your objectivity, toughness, or emotional balance.

The world and your city are full of professional victims. You cross paths with them every day, and, like it or not, they will need your help. Do as much as you can, within reason, to help them change their patterns.

CONTACT & COVER
Revisited
Remember Your Roles!

My first police book is still my favorite—*CONTACT & COVER: Two-Officer Suspect Control*. I coauthored this police officer survival text for Charles C. Thomas Publishers with now-retired San Diego Police Lieutenant John Morrison.

The book has become the operating guide for dozens of municipal, county, state, and federal law enforcement agencies and academies. For this, we are both grateful and proud. Then and still now, I have had the privilege of learning the many street safety principles attached to *CONTACT & COVER* from John Morrison, a man who knows police work on an instinctive, practical, and realistic level.

The widespread acceptance of the CONTACT & COVER principle should tell you one thing: it works.

There's no secret to why it works. It simply makes good sense, it allows you and your Cover Officer to take a more complete tactical advantage, and it's easy to implement and follow.

We know CONTACT & COVER is important to the safety and survival of you and your partner, but let's review a few concrete reasons why you need to use it:

- Sixty percent of police officer assaults happen in front of other officers.
- More officers are being killed with their own guns than ever before.
- There are more drugged, drunk, and mentally and emotionally disturbed people on the street than ever before.

- The suspects we encounter are armed more often than not.
- The number of high-risk arrest situations in front of potentially hostile crowds is also a constant threat.

If nothing else, this list should immediately make you stop and reconsider your own frequent or infrequent use of the CONTACT & COVER procedures. For this tactical approach to work effectively, all officers have to use it all of the time. It makes no sense for you to use it and for your partner or a responding Cover Officer to ignore it, or vice versa.

And yet, even with the success of CONTACT & COVER as a life-saving officer safety procedure, there is still much work to be done to make it more universal and concrete with new and even veteran officers. The main reason for this concern is not because CONTACT & COVER is difficult to follow or not applicable for nearly every field contact with actual or potential suspects, but because too many officers feel the need to "modify" the ironclad rules that make the method so effective.

This tendency for law enforcement people to add to or subtract from tactical procedures is all too common. We hear officers use such phrases as, "We did a 'modified hot stop' to make the arrest," or "I used a 'modified version' of the standard FBI handcuffing technique." To justify why they may have deviated from approved or time-tested field tactics, these officers often describe the suspect's actions as unique, out of the ordinary, or somehow so different that the "usual arrest methods" didn't or wouldn't work. And nearly as popular is the excuse of wanting to save time.

The old maxim "Speed Kills" applies in many ways to police work. Our willingness to sacrifice safety for our own sense of convenience, or to trade our awareness of the passage of time for our partner's desire to do a thorough job can mean the difference between a safe, successful encounter and one where one or more officers, suspects, witnesses, or victims gets killed.

At this point, it's time to blow the dust off the CONTACT & COVER guidebook and redefine the rules of engagement during any low-risk street or high-risk suspect encounter. Here's a review:

- CONTACT & COVER should be used during any situation where there is one or more unsecured potential or actual suspects in the immediate area.

- One officer takes the role of "Contact Officer" and is the on-scene leader of all law enforcement activities. The Contact Officer initiates the discussions and activities and conducts all of the business of the encounter with the suspect(s), witness(es), and victim(s).

- The other officer (and any subsequent arriving Cover Officers) takes on the role of "Cover Officer." This officer has two primary responsibilities: to observe suspects and protect the Contact Officer from a position of surveillance and control and to establish a strong sense of "force presence" while the Contact Officer conducts the business of the contact.

- Who is to be the Contact Officer and who is to be the Cover Officer should be verbally established prior to any meeting with the suspect(s). This can take place at the start of a shift, in the same car together, or, more typically, as the Cover Officer arrives to help an on-scene solo officer with a stop or radio call.

- The Contact Officer has a wide variety of important duties, each of which he or she is solely responsible for. The Contact Officer talks to the suspect; writes all of the suspect or incident information; performs all pat-downs and searches of people or vehicles; removes weapons, contraband, or evidence; writes all citations; and notifies the dispatcher of any relevant information. He or she is the primary field investigator and is responsible for the chain of custody.

- The Cover Officer observes all suspects and their associates, prevents escapes and the destruction of evidence, monitors the radio for any pertinent information the Contact Officer may have missed, and, most importantly, discourages any assaults on the Contact Officer. Because the Cover Officer is not distracted by the "business" of the contact, he or she can concentrate on the actions, movements, or conversations of the suspect(s).

- The Cover Officer must also be ready to use immediate hands-on or deadly force to prevent assaults, ambushes, gun takeaways, or any other extreme threat to the Contact Officer's life.

- The Contact Officer must know how, why, and when to disengage from the suspect to allow the Cover Officer to intervene or fire from a better tactical position.

- The officers can reverse the roles anytime it becomes necessary to reinforce the safety of the contact, for example, one officer knows the suspect better, has established rapport, or has additional field, narcotics, gang evaluation, or arrest expertise.

- The Contact and Cover Officers should communicate with one another by use of hand signals or police 10 and 11 code language not understood by the suspect(s).

- At no time should the Cover Officer directly engage in the information-gathering or enforcement activities that should be the primary responsibility of the Contact Officer.

- It's the frequent trampling of this last rule that causes many problems; too many Cover Officers get impatient and make their own decision to switch hats and become the "second Contact Officer." This often happens when there are two or more potential or actual suspects and the Cover Officer tries to "speed things along" by whipping out his or her field interview pad and firing some questions at the suspect who is not engaged with the Contact Officer.

Or the impatient Cover Officer breaks from his or her observation position and begins a pat-down search on an unsecured suspect or, worse yet, on the suspect's vehicle while the Contact Officer is busy over at the curb.

This can lead to the kinds of avoidable and unnecessary distractions armed or assaultive suspects like to see—one cop busy with one crook and another busy with the other. Disarmings, foot pursuits, fights, escapes, and similarly unpleasant things can occur when Cover Officers start seeing ticking stopwatches in their heads.

In their haste to "do something other than just stand here," get things moving, or "help" the Contact Officer gather suspect or witness information, recover evidence, test for field sobriety, or put handcuffs on people, Cover Officers often forget their role: observe and protect.

One of the many advantages of street policing is that time is your ally. As long as you can justify a legal detention or related investigation, you have the time you need to be thorough. It shouldn't be necessary for your Cover Officer to assist you unless the suspects are suddenly violent or he or she sees or hears something you missed, e.g., a suspect drops a drug bindle on the ground or the dispatcher relays some critical warrant information.

One veteran officer who uses CONTACT & COVER religiously puts it right in the faces of his Cover Officers when they lose sight of their duties.

Would you like me to search a car, talk on my radio, type on my Mobile Data Terminal, or start a field sobriety test with a suspect if you were being punched, stabbed, or shot at? No? Then why do you create that possibility during my field contacts by forgetting your role? Your job is to watch me work and protect me so that I can work safely.

For all its strengths as a tactical policing principle, CONTACT & COVER is only as effective as the officers who put it to good use. Whether you are the Contact Officer or the Cover Officer, stay focused on your primary role and responsibilities. Don't let your natural police instincts to take some kind of action interfere with your duty to keep yourself and your partner safe. If you and your partner officers will correctly use CONTACT & COVER as your operating plan, you can feel more secure and safe during even the most difficult field encounters.

Many officers who use the principles of CONTACT & COVER with great effectiveness have heard crooks tell them later, "Yeah, I'd have tried to jump you, but I knew that other cop was watching your back." Let's try to make this phrase the watchword for today's street hoods.

Use CONTACT & COVER with your beat and car partners whenever you've got one or more unsecured possible suspects near you both. It was designed with one simple goal: to help you survive.

Cops and Security Guards
An Old but Uneasy Alliance

If you think being a police officer doesn't get you too much positive feedback from the public or strokes from the media, think about your own response to the phrase "security guard." Unfortunately, through some fault of its own and thanks more to an ongoing image problem, the security guard profession must fight for every spec of credibility it gets.

The average security guard—who might well be a good person, possibly interested in a law enforcement career, or committed to doing a safe, legal, and professional job—is grouped together with the badge-heavy arm-breaker, the police "wannabe," the elderly sleeps-at-his-post type, or, in the worst case, the former jailbird.

In one of those sad-but-true phenomena, in the esteem of the public, most security guards rank just a bit higher than used car salesmen (and often get the pay and job security to match). For those associated with the security field, there is a well-known paradox known as the "vicious circle."

Here, two distinct elements chase each other: low pay and poorly qualified guards. As one goes, so does the other. The barely-above-minimum wages keep the better-qualified or career-minded workers from staying long in the profession; the uneven licensing procedures and the questionable hiring practices bring the wrong people into the profession.

This no-win circumstance is changing, albeit slowly. Looking at the crop of security guards most police officers come across over the course of their careers, it's hard to be overly confident in the future of the profession.

We still see undereducated, undertrained, underpaid, and overworked security guards who create problems as a result of their overreaction, underreaction, or their simple lack of knowledge as to their legal limits.

41

The security profession is built on the foundation that guards are to "observe and report" crimes or potential crimes to the police. In the purest sense, this is what the law governing their activities allows. A security guard who witnesses a misdemeanor or felony crime may make an arrest—just as any other citizen may.

The good ones have been schooled and tested as to their powers of arrest, rights, duties, and legal limits. The ones with criminal pasts, questionable backgrounds, or dragging knuckles, often work without supervision for unlicensed guard firms that may not know or care about this need for knowledge.

Guards who have been through state-mandated powers-of-arrest training and testing are issued a "guard card," which is usually a requirement for employment with a bona fide contract security company. The key phrase here is "bona fide," since, to continue with the used car sales theme, for every 10 licensed, reputable, bonded security firms, there is one company that is none of those things. This last guard operation is the kind that hires guards without the benefit of a background check, gives them chemical spray and batons and even guns without training, and puts them in difficult or even dangerous posts for way too many hours.

As you can guess, this mixture can lead to a wave of civil-liability problems. In one noted case in Los Angeles, California, a store security guard who had not been trained to use chemical spray blasted a whole face full into the chops of a combative shoplifting suspect. Once he handcuffed the thief, he took him to a holding area, began to write his report, and waited for the police to arrive.

All of us who *have* been trained to use these sprays know that after any dousing, we're required to wash the suspect's face in cold water, at least enough to remove the lingering effects of the spray. This did not happen here.

You can probably guess the rest. By the time the real cops arrived, the suspect had been cuffed to a chair without treatment long enough to be in absolute agony. After receiving serious chemical burns to his eyes and face, he successfully sued the store, the guard company, and the guard.

While this story is not indicative of the entire security profession, it does point to the fact that the level of training and good judgment exhibited by some guards is less than we would like.

Our contact with security guards usually comes about as the result of burglary alarm calls, where one or more of them might respond to the address or already be on post at the location; shoplifting calls in retail stores, with one or more suspects already under arrest; shopping mall calls, which can range from lost kids, loitering juveniles, or armed gangsters engaged in running shootouts; or bar, stadium, or sports arena calls involving various inebriates mixing with burly bouncers.

When dealing with security guards, consider the following: there are two types of security—in-house and contract.

In-house (or "proprietary") security guards typically are hired, supervised, and posted by the organization they are protecting. That is, if XYZ Company decides to staff its own guard force, it can hire them and put them to work on XYZ private property.

While this is more rare, it does happen inside some organizations that elect to manage and control all of their security operations. Large companies and hospitals may use their own guard services, retail chains may hire their own people to serve as store detectives, alarm companies may use their own people to respond to ringers, and smaller businesses may employ people specifically for in-house security services.

Most states *don't* require a guard card for these types of guards who work in a strictly in-house capacity, unless they carry a firearm and/or a baton while on duty.

Contract security is when an outside security firm bids to provide its own security guards for a company. Here, the security service does all of the hiring, supervising, and training; provides payroll, and so on; and accepts the responsibility to provide the guards, uniforms, benefits, and, in most cases, liability insurance to cover its guards' actions.

To work in a contract capacity, guards are required to have a guard card, as well as separate weapons permits if they carry exposed or concealed firearms or a baton while on duty. (In most states, pepper spray is now an over-the-counter purchase, and classroom training is no longer required to carry or use it.)

What makes this distinction important to the police officer is that it should help you to pinpoint where and for whom a guard works. This can be critical if the guard is in plainclothes, involved as a witness to an incident, or otherwise associated with any matters of civil or criminal liability.

For the purposes of your crime or arrest reports, you'll need to get as much information about the on-scene security guard as you can. This should include personal and company information, since there may be a chance either the guard or even the company will change addresses before you can get to court.

Under your state's civil and criminal codes (i.e., state civil code, business and professions, or penal codes), you have the right to demand to see a security guard's permits, licenses, and guard cards.

Since we know that some unscrupulous security companies hire people who can just barely pass the "warm body" test, training or other legal accreditation for little things like firearms, batons, defensive tactics, powers of arrest, CPR, and first-aid may be nonexistent. If you come onto a scene where an armed security officer is acting inappropriately or, worse, dangerously, you have the legal right to examine the guard's weapon and permits. If he's carrying a gun, he had better have the right type of exposed or concealed firearms permit issued by your state. We're talking about apples and oranges here; a guard's firearms exposed-carry permit and a CCW permit are two separate documents, which call for completely different qualifications.

Most of the security guards you'll meet are merely trying to earn a living. Some may be retired military personnel with time on their hands, others may be college students looking for extra income and a way to get paid to study, and still others may be people who want to get their foot into the law enforcement door.

The ones who are not recent parolees, garden-variety dunderheads, or badge-heavy "Rent-a-Cops" will probably be more than willing to go out of their way to provide you with information, serve as your backup in touchy suspect situations, act as an extra pair of eyes and ears, or offer access to resources you may be able to use, like a safe report-writing room or a telephone.

There is an automatic tendency for some officers to look down on these people, talk down to them, or otherwise treat them as if they were inferior. If this has been your attitude, adjust it. We know these people are not police officers, but some of them I know are braver than a few so-called street cops. Why? Because they work in some of our country's toughest neighborhoods, deal with many hostile or violent people, and see an untold number of crimes and crooks, all without much or any of the equipment (guns, vests, patrol cars) or communications (car radios and portables) that we often take for granted.

You should give good guards the same respect as you should give to good letter carriers who work for the U.S. Postal Service. Our mailmen and women go—unarmed and unprotected—into the worst ghettos of this country every day. There are streets and buildings in this nation where 10 cops armed to the teeth would feel uncomfortable, yet the letter carrier has to go there each day, and usually alone. As all crooks know, mail carriers often have letters and packages containing valuable merchandise, checks, money orders, and credit cards.

Many security guards have to work in these same environments. How would you like to work a guard post in a low-income housing project filled with dopers and gangsters, armed with a flashlight and orders to get to a pay phone two blocks away if there's trouble?

You can use the more professional security guards you meet as sources of good information. Some of the sharper guards on your beat are like walking POP files. By virtue of their working in one specific area all day and night, they know what's going on in their neighborhood or work area as well as or maybe even better than you do. The well-trained, motivated, and observation-oriented security guard can point out parolees, dope houses, problem kids and adults, gangsters, taggers, car prowlers, and any number of bad people up to no good.

If you need information, buy these security guards a cup of coffee and ask for help. They've probably got a whole notebook full of license plates, suspect descriptions, nicknames, dates, times, and addresses for you. They're just waiting for someone to ask them what they know.

The simple fact is that there are far more security guards on duty in this country than there are police officers. According to the Hallcrest Reports I and II (a two-decade national study of the trends in private security), the ratio of security guards to cops is three to one. This will not change, and the numbers gap between public law enforcement and private security will only get larger. Thanks to dwindling municipal budgets and rising crime, most businesses are calling on in-house or contract security personnel to help them keep order around their establishments.

This is not such a bad thing, just as long as the security profession continues to make a commitment to train and pay these people in a manner that will keep the good ones in the profession.

To be a good problem-oriented police officer, you need to be able to develop and use various resources to help you achieve your goals. Consider a more favorable working relationship with the qualified security guards you meet. Keep your professional distance, but be courteous to them. The life they save may be yours.

Creative Handcuffing
Unusual Ways to Restrain Unusual People

The newspaper photograph from May 20, 1998, haunts me. We see two veteran Tampa Police Department homicide detectives leading a murder suspect across a parking lot. One detective is about five feet in front of the suspect, with his back completely to him. The other detective is walking behind the suspect, carrying the suspect's rifle in his right (gun) hand and a zippered nylon rifle case in his left. A uniformed police officer is walking behind all three.

The suspect is dressed in shorts, a T-shirt, and running shoes. His hands are cuffed in *front* of his body, and he is *not* wearing leg irons or a body chain around his waist.

Moments after this press photo was taken, the suspect was loaded into an unmarked police vehicle driven by the two detectives. At some point during this ride, the suspect, Hank Carr, 30, managed to slip out of one or both handcuffs, grab the driver-detective's gun from his holster, and shoot and kill both detectives in the car.

When the car came to a stop, he recovered his own rifle from the trunk and used it to carjack the driver of an approaching pickup truck. In the ensuing chase, the suspect used his rifle to kill a responding Florida State Trooper, age 23.

Carr finally barricaded himself in a gas station and held police at bay until he ultimately shot himself prior to a SWAT team entry.

This case involved three dead law enforcement officers, a hostage from the gas station, and the arrival of about 170 police, sheriffs, and state troopers who responded to the various crime scenes.

According to reports, Carr was taken into custody for questioning in the suspicious shooting death of his stepson. Carr claimed the 4-year-old boy was dragging Carr's rifle behind him, and when Carr and the boy's mother yelled at him to stop, the gun "went off," and shot the boy fatally in the head.

Researching Carr's record later, Tampa Police found that he had arrests for burglary, grand larceny, cocaine possession, and "resisting an officer with violence."

In hindsight, Mr. Carr was not a nice man, by any measure. And while the Tampa detectives may not have known much about his long criminal past, his immediate criminal activities were well known. That is, he was a suspect in the shooting death of a toddler. And for this crime he was handcuffed in the front? For this crime he was allowed to walk in between two armed detectives? For this crime, he was allowed to ride in a police vehicle with his hands in his lap?

I have never, ever understood the practice of some police agencies in this country, which allow their officers to handcuff suspects in the front. We see this on the television news quite a bit—the cops or court bailiffs taking some hapless murderer from one location to the other, his hands cuffed in front all the while.

In the past, we have even seen these suspects (or convicts) raise their hands up to their heads to wave at someone nearby or gesture to the cameras. If they can move about with this much freedom, what else could they do with their hands, arms, elbows, fingers, or fists?

This particular TV scenario is so common that we can forget there are bad dudes—killers, rapists, robbers, bombers, and such—on the other end of those bracelets. It's only after a significant tragedy like the one in Tampa that we remember why it's so dumb and so incredibly unsafe to handcuff any suspect's hands in front.

Most law enforcement officers don't engage in this dangerous practice. They handcuff everyone in the rear, from the teenage shoplifting suspect waiting for his parents at the police station to the mentally disturbed elderly woman heading to a treatment center to homeless drunks to triple murderers.

The policy and the street rule is, if you're going to sit in the back of *my* police car, you're going to wear handcuffs, and you're going to wear them the way God intended you to—with your hands behind your back.

Let's change tracks here and think about the possible (and probable) reasons that you may *not* be able to follow this ironclad rule. While it may be against your department policy to use front-side handcuffing, there are certainly situations where you may have no choice to but to switch from "usual" handcuffing to "creative" handcuffing.

As an example, some officers can tell stories of having to arrest suspects who were in wheelchairs. These people have committed crimes ranging from attempted murder to bank robbery to spousal abuse. I recall arresting a woman we found snorting meth in the passenger seat of her boyfriend's car. Imagine my surprise when I said, "Step out of the car," and she said she couldn't, and pointed to her wheelchair in the backseat.

Did I handcuff her hands in back before my partner and I carried her to the backseat of our police car? Not just yes, but hell yes! Was I embarrassed about doing it? Absolutely. But is it not possible that people in wheelchairs may be more ambulatory than they appear? Who among us has not seen the "disabled" homeless guy with the big metal crutches running pell-mell after a bus? (These are the same charity cases that squirt ketchup on to their bandages to look more pitiful.)

It may seem harsh or unnecessary to handcuff wheelchair-bound suspects to their chairs while inside a police station, hospital, or mental health facility, but keep in mind that some of these people have tremendous upper-body strength, and in some cases, tremendous rage about their current situation.

In another wheelchair case, the man I arrested for hitting his girlfriend with a baseball bat had been shot and paralyzed years before by his brother after attacking him while high on PCP. To say this disabled suspect was anti-police was to understate his hatred of cops. He didn't want to go to jail, and the fight was on. The atrophied muscles in his legs were well compensated by his huge arms, shoulders, and chest. It took many of us to get him into handcuffs.

People with other disabilities can offer us officer safety challenges as well. In another case years ago, my partner and I took custody of a notorious drug smuggler-gun runner from U.S. Customs. He had a long record on both sides of the border and was known as armed and often violent. While his right hand was normal, he was missing most of his left hand and fingers. And his left hand was wrapped in a flexible bandage wrap all the way down to his forearm.

The Customs agents told us he was known for carrying a small pistol inside his wrapped hand. While that was one problem to face, the other was that it was not possible to handcuff him in the usual way because of his missing fingers and deformed left wrist. After removing his bandage wrap (no gun inside this time) I handcuffed his right hand to his rear center belt loop, wrapped my nylon cord cuff around his left forearm, attached the hook to the handcuff, and rode in the backseat with him to jail.

We already know how to use two sets of linked handcuffs to contain the hands and arms of fat (sorry, overweight) suspects or those who have spent too much time at the prison gym or the local fitness center. But what about using two sets of linked cuffs for the suspect who complains of a "bad shoulder," recent joint surgery, or some other ailment that precludes him or her from complying with the usual "hands in back, wrists touching" request?

And just as amputee suspects require creative handcuff and nylon cord cuff use, what about suspects with casts on their wrists? This offers a significant officer-safety issue, because not only can you *not* get a cuff around most casts, thereby giving the suspect a free hand, those casts can be a heavy and hard weapon against the side of your head.

Cuff the suspect's free hand as safely as you can, use your cord cuff safely, humanely, and creatively, and get another officer to ride in the back with the suspect until you can get him safely to jail.

Assuming you've been issued one, if you haven't used your nylon cord cuff on a prisoner in a while, it's time to take it out of your pocket or from your gear belt and dust if off. When used properly with your handcuffs (read that as legally and within your current department policies), you can prevent flexible or limber suspects or from slipping their cuffs to the front, or contain special-needs prisoners in ways that will allow you to process them with more confidence.

As always, check your cuffed prisoners frequently for too-tight or too-loose cuffs, keep your hands and fingers from getting in between the chains, double lock them ASAP, watch for suspicious movements en route to the station or at the holding areas in the jail, and be ready to cuff creatively when the usual ways won't work.

Criminal Profiling
Past Behaviors, Future Crimes

I've become increasingly more intrigued with the art and science of criminal behavior. With me, it's not just the "Who done it?" of police investigations, but what you might call the "Why done it?"

What is it about certain people that leads them to pick up a gun and put a bullet into a stranger or, even more disturbing, a supposed loved one? What makes a man rape and then apologize to his victim during the act? What causes a teenager to stray down a violent or thieving path that takes him from a juvenile facility to a county jail, and then to a state or federal prison, especially when every person he knew thought he was "such a nice young man"?

To this end, I've attended a number of graduate school level courses and police investigations training seminars on everything from rape and homicide profiling to stalking and domestic violence suspect typologies. Each one has added a few more mosaic tiles to the total picture of what makes a criminal, and yet each has raised even more questions.

And more to the point, each new exposure to intensely violent or disturbing crimes and the people who commit them has left me wondering if our society is not slipping a bit closer toward the edge of the abyss each day. As every police officer will attest (especially those who work daily in the aftermath of violent crimes), it's hard to look at yet another homicide or sexual assault of a woman or child and not think the whole world is bad save for cops, their families, and their kindly grandmothers.

At this point, I feel the need to use some highly technical psychiatric terminology. To wit: the "nut factor" in this country is getting higher, stronger, and more prevalent. We've seen more bombings lately; more utterly senseless violence, including drive-bys that kill young children; more family murders involving multiple victims found dead in one heartbreaking incident; more mass murders at the workplace; and more crimes of every type that certainly cause even the most rosy optimist among us to shake his or her head and wonder what the world is coming to.

In these instances, some perspective helps. If you were a doctor, nearly 100 percent of the patients you saw would have something wrong with them. If you were an auto mechanic, almost every car that pulled into your shop would need a repair. As such, many busy doctors tend to see people as basically sick, and auto mechanics tend to see every car as one that needs fixing.

Cops are no different. Exposed daily to the worst this nation has to offer, the cop finds it's easy to continue to perpetuate the usual "us versus them, all people are jerks" stereotypes. And yet it is this exact and magnetic connection between police officers and the people we so often put through that human car wash known as the criminal justice system that makes them more subject to our capture nets.

And even more to the point, it is this frequent (and revolving door) contact that tells us when and where to look for these people, especially if they have moved into the rarefied air of the serious criminal. Up at these high altitudes, we don't find those folks with uncleared misdemeanor warrants for littering in the park, the occasional drug taker, joyrider, or only-when-desperate car prowler.

On this small precipice, we find the serial rapist, the gangbanging shooter with multiple drive-bys and several murders to his credit, the 100-case burglar or auto thief, the stalker armed to the teeth, the serial pedophile, and the psychopathic killer.

What these crooks share is a history of crime, criminal acts, and associations with criminals who talk about and do similar things. Are we surprised that while in jails and prisons convenience store and bank robbers congregate together to talk about their weapons and escape routes? Should we be shocked to know that jailed pedophiles, serial rapists, and other sex offenders swap fantasies, stories, and techniques for enhancing their activities while not getting caught? What do lifelong gang members talk about with each other in jail? Who, how, where, and why they're going to "bang" their archrivals if and when they finally get out.

As an example, two rapists serving time together in the California Men's Colony at San Luis Obispo discovered they had a mutual interest in bondage, torture, and rape. They whiled away their hours discussing these very things and what they could do together once they were paroled. Using a soundproofed van, they traveled throughout southern California kidnapping, raping, torturing, and murdering one young woman after another until they were caught.

Did these men suddenly get interested in rape while in prison? No, since we know now they were already serving time for rapes when they met. It's certainly more likely that they acquired their taste for blood and violence as part of their incredibly abnormal development into adulthood.

It takes quite a twisted psyche to approach these high levels of sadistic violence, especially as they relate to sex. It should come as no further surprise to learn that rapists often start out by committing what we now euphemistically call "sexual nuisance crimes," e.g., window peeping, indecent exposure, or performing or having sex acts performed on themselves in public places. It builds from there to the breaking and entering of empty homes, to hot prowl burglaries of occupied homes, and to rape, kidnapping, or murder.

Profiles of criminals with dangerous, violent, and even murderous acts to their name suggest a less-than-wonderful childhood. Psychologists, criminologists, and sociologists like to point to the presence of the "Big 5" in adolescence as potential warning signs for adult violence. These include chronic acts of lying, fire setting, or theft; being unusually preoccupied by violent fantasies or daydreams; and numerous acts of cruelty to animals. (Other behavioral experts prefer to call this the "Homicide Triad," as it refers to animal cruelty, arson, and bedwetting.)

Now this is not to say that you should turn yourself in if you ever played with matches, stole some penny candy, or terrorized some frogs. But studies of serial murderers, rapists who murder, and others who have a capacity for tremendous violence suggest that we need to look at the past as a primary indicator for the future.

With this knowledge in mind, when you stop a suspect trespassing through a quiet (read that as non-drug-infested) apartment complex, do you still write only "burglary" in the "Crime Potential" box on your field interview slips? Is it not possible that this person is actually gearing up for more than just a daylight burglary?

Most haphazard burglars—juveniles, dopers, and opportunists—don't case their targets at night, when the occupants and their neighbors are home to see them and call the police. They show up during the day, when the law-abiding of us are already at work or in school.

The chronic window peepers, experienced hot prowlers, exposure enthusiasts, obsessed stalkers, and the bona fide rapists select multiple targets for their crimes. It's not unusual for these people to have six to ten victims under their special brand of "surveillance." As one rapist put it, "When one target went bad [improved her security, moved in with her boyfriend, etc.], I just switched to the next one and waited for my chance."

If this is the case, why not try running the names of your late-night prowlers and peepers in your computer system to see where else they have been stopped by the police? If they are on foot and in their own neighborhood (another profile characteristic, where suspects have attacked neighbor/victims even in their own apartment buildings), chances are good they are casing not houses, but women.

We've all received calls to check on the "guy sitting in the park watching the little kids play" or the "stranger waiting in his car in front of the elementary school that none of the other parents recognize." Even if you weren't a cop, if you have kids, you know your own protection instincts about these kinds of people are already well honed. And as cops, we know that out instincts for what "fits" on the street and what does not are already in place as well.

The guy in the park may be in fact eating his lunch and listening to his radio when you stop to talk to him. If so, no harm, no foul, and he's on his way. But chances are good that if someone called about it, it's out of the ordinary. Sex offenders don't usually commit one act then quit for life; the term "repeat offender" was invented for them.

Studies suggest that not only do sex offenders have a 75-percent or higher recidivism rate, but they are rarely "rehabilitated" to the degree where they totally lose the urge to attack a woman or child, or both, ever again. (The most brazen ones willingly admit to their prison psychiatrists or counselors that they will strike again if paroled, and yet this message seems to fall on deaf ears when they are eligible for release.)

With the park or school kid-watcher, don't just fill out the FI slip and move along—dig a little. Take a gamble and ask, "Have you ever been arrested for a crime involving a child or a woman? Are you a sex offender registrant? If so, when did you last register?" (Those that are will know and look at the ground in embarrassment or anger as they admit to it; those that aren't won't know what you're talking about.)

If these answers are in the affirmative, don't just write an FI slip, write a book about the encounter. If it's a consensual stop, they can always refuse to answer, just as you can discover perfectly legal ways to make it a court-defensible detention.

Keep up to date on both your series crime cases and investigative supplementals. If there is a predator in your area—not just the usual robbers, burglars, and hypes—start looking for his tracks. Frequent the alleys he roams and, in between radio calls, sit in the shadows and watch and wait for him to case a street, parking lot, health spa at closing time, or the back way onto a school campus or into an apartment complex.

Look for a man sitting alone in the passenger side of his car (e.g., "Oh, hello officer—I've just been sitting here alone for the last three hours waiting for 'a friend.'"). Look for the presence of windowless vans or those with smoked windows that seem to appear regularly near potential target areas. At the least, it might be a 72-hour notice tag or someone sleeping in the vehicle, at the worst, an attacker who wants privacy.

If you work in a high-prostitution area, start talking to these women about who is out and about and who gives them the creeps. If you can build any rapport at all, they may identify the one or two subjects who make their danger signal intuition kick into high gear.

Part of this job demands that you turn over a few rocks to look for the real crooks who dwell between the cracks. Start putting yourself in their quarry. Be willing to do some computer work, talk to your detectives, and keep looking for the ordinary that is actually out of the ordinary.

Deadly Distractions
Using Mobile Data Terminals (MDTs) Safely

Since many progressive law enforcement agencies have moved ever so swiftly into the Information Age, computers in patrol cars have gone from being a novelty to an everyday fact of working life. (If your department has not yet made the leap into on-screen policing, save this section for when they do.)

Never before in our history as a law enforcement community have we been able to do so much. Now it's license plate information at our fingertips; instant radio call dispatching; updated field, warrant, or crime case information; and car-to-car communication, all at the touch of a few computer keys.

But has all of this technology arrived without a price? More than one street cop has raised serious officer safety questions and concerns about the Mobile Data Terminals (MDTs.)

The complaints I've heard from other officers stem not from the effectiveness of these devices, but from the officer safety aspects of their use. We can all agree that the MDT makes our jobs much easier, but many cops have asked, "It may make our jobs easier, but does that always make our jobs safer?"

There's no doubt that having instantaneous data right on the screen in front of you helps your decision-making processes. And you can now do in seconds what used to take long minutes or even an hour (e.g., request a tow truck, run people for warrants, verify driver's license information, etc.).

You can now do things from the comfort of your car such as get crime case numbers, fill out your journal, check the activity of your beat partners, or see what cases are holding in your area. Nearly all of us will agree that these modern conveniences make the data collection part of police work a snap. But there are some officers who complain privately and otherwise that the MDT, for all its power, can cause cops to become too *reliant* on it.

"Get your head up off the screen and pay attention to what you see on the streets," complains one veteran officer.

"Stop spending so much time with your head bent over the keyboard when suspects are roaming around your car during a traffic stop," says another.

"Stop typing messages to your friends and getting into car accidents," goes the weary lament of the supervisor who must investigate yet another patrol car crash.

"And don't send inappropriate messages to each other," warns the communications supervisor, recalling the MDT car-to-car messaging problems identified immediately after the Rodney King car stop incident ended in Los Angeles.

"Make sure you tell the dispatcher that you have arrived on the scene," says a concerned Cover Officer. "Pushing the button on your computer doesn't tell me anything. I won't know if you're there until you say it out loud."

This last one is a hard habit to break, especially if you rotate from working a two-officer unit and then back to riding alone on a regular basis. In a two-officer car, it's not always necessary to tell the world you've arrived. The dispatcher knows it as soon as you hit the button, and he or she will keep track of you. But if you roll up to a priority call alone, jump out of your chariot, and get into a scrap, no one will hear of it, least of all your cover unit, unless you make some noise with your portable radio.

The other difficulty about MDTs and going from a two-officer car to solo patrol involves traffic stops. In some cities, depending on the crime rate, time of day or night, and activity level, the percentage of two-officer units that, without fail, tell the dispatcher where and when they make a traffic stop is probably fairly low. There's no hard data to prove this, but experience suggests that unless they're stopping a carload of clearly identifiable bad guys, most two-officer units just make the stop and rely on each other for CONTACT & COVER protection.

In these cases, the "Stops" button on the MDT can get cobwebs on it. Whereas a single officer will almost always take the time to type in the license plate and location of his or her traffic stop, partnered units tend to wing it. And this can lead to another bad assumption: that the little red "Emergency" button on the MDT box will act as a homing device should you have to press it. As good as the MDTs are, they are not geographically oriented to global positioning satellites.

If you hit that button in a real emergency, it can only tell the rest of the world where it *thinks* you are. And that information is based on what you last told it. No input from you, no beeline charge from the rest of the cavalry. If you don't tell the machine where you happen to be when the stewpot gets kicked over, you can't expect to get a pinpointed response from your helpmates.

A veteran SWAT officer said that it pains him to see officers parked alone in unsafe locations, heads down, fingers on the keys, instead of parked tactically, heads up, and alert for approaching people or cars.

It's easy to get entranced by the golden screen of the MDT, especially when you're waiting for information to come back to you. How many times have you sat in your police car alone, waiting for driver's license status information to come back, and spent all your time looking at the screen instead of at the suspect and his vehicle? And how many times can you honestly admit that while in an MDT-induced haze, people (crooks, traffic violators, and regular citizens) walked right up to your car window and surprised you?

To encapsulate the top six officer-safety issues described by other concerned officers about MDT use, it would be these:

- *When you're responding alone to a hot call, tell the dispatcher—and at the same time your cover unit—when you reach the scene.*
  This alerts the cover unit as to how and when he or she needs to get there to provide support.

- *Keep your head up and your wits about you when using the MDT.*
  Look up frequently and keep your eyes on suspects if you have to type alone. If you have to extract a lot of information from the MDT and need to spend more than a normal amount of time typing, copying, or writing, get a cover unit to stand by.

- *If you have a partner, don't type and drive.*
  To paraphrase Mothers Against Drunk Driving (MADD), "Partners don't let partners type and steer at the same time." This makes for some interesting in-car wrestling matches that can wear out the swivel on the MDT rack, but it's important that the driver-officer just drives and passenger-officer just types. Failure to do this can cause crashes that become difficult to explain to cranky traffic investigators.

- *Don't type any message that you wouldn't be fully prepared to stand up in court and explain to God and country.*
  If you'd be embarrassed to repeat it in front of a judge, don't type it. Those messages are stored on computer backup tape; they don't vanish just because you or the receiver hit the clear button.

- *Don't forget to be a cop.*

Some officers have grown so reliant on the MDT to "guide" them (running license plates, displaying radio call details so they don't have to write anything, etc.), that when the system crashes or goes down for maintenance, they drive around aimlessly. Police work is still about making car and ped stops and talking to people who look like crooks. Don't let the machine run your life.

- *Finally, use the MDT as it was designed—as a tool for officers to make police work easier.*

But don't sacrifice convenience for safety. Whenever you're looking at the keyboard, you're not watching the streets. Balance yourself so you can do both.

Domestic Violence Calls
The Safe and Effective Patrol Response

In the old days, a married couple or a boyfriend and his girlfriend would get in a loud argument or even a fight, and a pair of world-weary cops would show up, separate the parties, give the usual "go forth and sin no more" speech, and drive off in a cloud of dust.

If the cops were lucky, that would be the end of the problem, at least until they finished their shift and it became a radio call for another pair of next-watch officers.

If they weren't so blessed, they would find themselves returning to the same house over and over every few hours until somebody—usually the male—went to jail.

If things really went downhill, the cops would return to the house for the umpteenth time and find one of the combatants dead on the kitchen floor.

Oh, how times have changed. With the same couple fighting, the only thing that stays the same is the fact that the cops are probably still world-weary. Today, domestic violence, or even the threat of it, brings a hard and swift police response rarely seen in the old days.

Thanks to copious amounts of victim-initiated lawsuits applied like hot irons to the feet of police agencies and even individual officers, the way we respond to domestic violence has changed forever.

Now we arrive on the scene, separate the parties, listen to the stories, evaluate the injuries, and, more often than ever before, handcuff the batterer and take his butt to jail.

The days of "no autopsy-no arrest" are long behind us. Today, officers must document all domestic violence-related threats, assaults, and injuries.

Further, what used to be a judgment call is now a penal code mandate. Visible injuries? Married, living together, or the parents of a child? If the cops ask and the answer is "yes" to both, the puncher, slapper, or kicker is going to jail in matching silver bracelets.

Most penal codes across the nation now order police officers to write thorough reports for all domestic violence (DV) incidents. Since domestic violence calls now require so many reports, the beginning and often the end of any domestic violence problem begins with the responding patrol officer. He or she must document each event so that later, the detectives can evaluate the case and step in with solutions when they can.

To break the cycle of violence, the criminal justice system now can offer victims and even suspects a range of alternatives, including mandatory individual counseling; family counseling; legal, medical, and psychological services; and, when necessary, temporary restraining orders, emergency protective orders, jail time, and strict probation requirements.

But before detectives and prosecutors can help the victims of domestic violence, they'll need to see the reports. The responding officer must capture all of the sights, sounds, impressions, and feelings of each incident. Using crime case reports, first-response patrol officers can help the second-responders decide how to help solve this growing national problem.

With that in mind, here are a few tips and suggestions for patrol officers to consider as they respond to DV radio calls.

- *Arrest, arrest, arrest!*

If the elements for felony DV are apparent, make an arrest. Better to have your district attorney or city attorney's office drop or change the charges than to leave the suspect with the victim in a highly volatile environment. If you see the injuries and the relationship is established between the parties, don't wait; make the felony arrest.

- *Be a cop.*

Do some digging. Don't just fill in the report boxes and leave. Many of the suspects in DV cases will have several misdemeanor warrants, and many of them have active felony warrants. Dig deep and run checks on these suspects. If you can make a warrant arrest, do it. Not only does it remove the main antagonist from the crime scene, but it may also take a felon off the streets. If the suspect makes threats, won't leave, will probably continue to escalate the problem, has a DV warrant and is on DV probation, make the arrest. He's already demonstrated that he has a real problem with anger management at a minimum and domestic violence at the extreme. If the victim won't authorize a citizen's arrest for a misdemeanor case and the suspect is drunk, high on dope, or a warrant collector, remove him from the area through these non-DV but creative means. The old one that starts with, "Hey Buddy! Come out here to the sidewalk so we can talk," can also lead you to an easy drunk in public or under the influence arrest if it will help to get the suspect out of the house.

- *Stop interviewing your partner!*
This is a common error and one of those classic police "timesavers" that can come back later to haunt the responding officers. Instead of talking to both parties prior to writing their reports, some officers talk to just one, usually whoever cooperates the most. Then, back in the safety and quiet of their patrol cars, they ask their partners, "Okay, what did he or she say?" By only documenting the paraphrased version given to you by your partner (complete with his or her "spin" on the situation), you do a disservice to the case. Further, no officer likes to be embarrassed in court when the suspect's defense attorney says, "Now, Officer, you didn't *really, truly, actually* speak to my client, did you? So your report must be an inaccurate fabrication of what really happened?"

- *Respect the dignity of same-sex relationships.*
DV calls involving homosexual or lesbian couples can be difficult for some officers to handle. Whether you agree or disagree with either life-style is immaterial; stay focused on providing service, and do your job professionally. Further, the participants in these cases can be just as violent or volatile, if not even worse, than in opposite-sex relationships.

- *Use extreme discretion when considering an arrest for a female suspect.*
Regardless of what it looks like when you get there, the female in the incident is probably not the actual (primary-aggressor) suspect. She may have actually fought back this time, and if you do some digging, you'll probably discover a number of reported and unreported DV cases. Females who fight back often do so only after months or years of abuse. Unless the circumstances truly dictate arresting the woman at the scene, avoid it. Look hard at the history of the relationship first. Tonight's violence is probably the tip of the iceberg. To the highly distraught victim, the arriving police officer can change in an instant from the "rescuer" to the "harasser." Suddenly that mean cop is trying remove the "breadwinner, who I love, from this house!" Here, the suspect changes suddenly from the "harasser" to the new "victim," who now needs to be "rescued" from the cops.

- *Look at the female's wounds carefully.*

Some DV injuries are not always immediately visible. They may be hidden by hair or clothing. If you expect to make an arrest, you must do a thorough job of documenting and photographing the injuries to all parties, not just the victim. Put on rubber gloves and feel the victim's head for bumps and broken skin. Ask discreetly but directly about injuries covered by clothes. Get a female officer to help you search if necessary (e.g., for wounds to the victim's breasts or genitals). Decide whether the female's wounds match the male's fists or feet. Women who say they "fell down the stairs" don't usually have bruises on their backs and heads. Look for protection or self-defense wounds on her hands, arms, and shoulders. If the male points to a nasty bite mark on the top of his forearm and says, "She bit me, and for no reason!" it's probably because she was being choked and resisted him in lieu of passing out or dying. Examine defensive wounds, like her bite marks on the suspect's forearms during his choking assault. Just like child abuse cases, see if the story matches the injuries.

- *Avoid mutual combat arrests.*

Nationally, the male is the victim in DV cases only about 5 percent of the time. So 95 times out of 100, the one able to inflict the most damage or restrain the victim (i.e., the male) is going to be the primary aggressor (unless it's a clear-cut ambush or retaliation assault by the female after an argument has ended). This should tell you something immediately: No matter what *he* says, assume that *she* is the victim. "In the field," says Sgt. Anne O'Dell (Ret.), founder of the San Diego Police Domestic Violence Unit, "a good cop assumes certain people fit the profile of a gang member and assumes certain people fit the profile of a dope user. Make the same assumptions about DV suspects and DV victims."

- *Look harder for Temporary Restraining Order violators.*

In these cases where a woman calls to report a TRO violation, some officers get lazy and just drive up, document the incident, and drive off. Go out and scout around for these suspects. They are probably around the corner, on foot, in their cars down the street, or in the neighborhood. If you just show up, write a report, and leave, they may return and start up all over again. If you find them lurking nearby, run records checks, confirm the TRO, and make the arrests for the violations.

- *Impound all firearms.*

Take all guns and similar obvious deadly weapons (crossbows, swords, etc.) out of the house. Leaving a loaded gun in a chronic DV household is like parking a Corvette in front of a halfway house with the keys in it. You're just asking for trouble.

- *Make sure you fully explain the citizen's arrest or police arrest process to the victim.*

In many misdemeanor cases where there is not enough evidence to arrest, you must explain to the victim that she has the right to ask you to make an arrest on her behalf. If the victim declines, document this in your report and make sure you write that you offered it as an option.

- *Never leave the victim's phone number box blank.*

In some cases, the victim will want to leave her home to stay with relatives, neighbors, or friends. In every case, if there is no home phone number, get a message phone number for a relative or a friend, a pager number, a work number, or an emergency contact phone number for the victim's parents, relatives, or employers. It's very hard to follow up with the victim if there are no phone numbers at all. Do the best you can and get a message number at least.

- *Remember all of the little details in your report.*

Who called the police? Neighbors? A child in the house? The victim? The suspect? This information can be very important to the investigating detective. What does the room look like? How many times have the cops been called to the address? What is the background of each party in the dispute? If you use a Computer-Assisted Dispatch (CAD) system, remember to put your Incident Number in the report. This helps the prosecutors get the phone and dispatch tapes if necessary. These 911 tapes can be quite illuminating and can help the judge and jury understand the intensity of the crime as it was occurring, especially if the victim or suspect tries to recant or minimize the incident in testimony.

- *Be ready to give your victim(s) information about counseling, legal services, or battered women's shelters.*

They might need this information later, even if they don't want it now. Make sure you have answered all their questions before you leave.

- *Learn to read between the lines.*

In many DV cases, the reporting officer will describe the physical and emotional states of both the suspect and the victim. Invariably, the description is the same: "He was calm and cooperative, and she was emotional, crying, and angry." Of course he's "calm and cooperative"! He's just vented all of his stress on her, and she had to bear the brunt of it! The other reason he's usually so helpful with the cops is that he's afraid they're going to take him to jail. He's trying very hard to give you the impression he's got everything under control and that his wife or girlfriend is the one who is overreacting. Experts in these matters point to the DV cycle (developed by Dr. Lenore Walker), as a repetitive pattern of periods of tension, violence, and remorse. The police arrive on the scene after the violence has taken place and when the suspect may feel the most remorse or fear for his freedom. Just because he's Mr. Cooperative when you arrive, don't be fooled or misled into believing he's not the bad guy in the situation.

- *Create an environment of safety for the female DV victim.*
  You're there to help her. Make sure she feels like you're doing that. Don't act macho, roll your eyes, or act like she's wasting your time. Offer empathy and make her feel like she's done the right thing by calling you. Don't make her feel worse or side with the suspect just because she may be crying or hysterical. Saying, "Why don't you just leave him?" is an easy and wrong question that usually has a complicated answer.

- *Strive to take clear photos.*
  Most police on-scene Polaroid photos are worthless. They're either too far away, too close, or out of focus. If you have a Polaroid, practice with it until you can take clear, complete, and focused photos. Use enough film to properly document the case. If you have access to a 35 mm camera, use it. Write good notes on the back of the photos, including the date and time, the location of the injury on the body, the time the photos were taken, the victim's name, and the case number. Good photos can really help make a case; bad photos can really hurt one.

- *Write more than just a "good" report.*
  "The right response by patrol officers can do more than just stop the current violence," says Sgt. Anne O'Dell, a leader in the cause for increasing help for battered victims. "If we can intercede while the problem is still in its earliest stages, we can often stop a murder later on." Since most states, counties, and cities require so many police reports, the beginning and often the end of any DV problem begins with the responding patrol officer. He or she must document each event so that the follow-up officers or detectives can evaluate the case and step in with solutions when they can.

To break the cycle of violence, patrol officers, detectives, prosecutors, judges, and probation officers can offer victims and even suspects a range of alternatives, including mandatory individual counseling; family counseling; legal, medical, and psychological services; and, when necessary, temporary restraining orders, emergency protective orders, jail time, and strict probation requirements.

But before they can help the victims of domestic violence, they'll need to see the reports. The responding officer must capture all of the sights, sounds, impressions, and feelings of each incident on paper.

Chances are good that if you work primarily night and weekend patrol shifts, your daily journals are already chock-full of DV radio calls and reports. These calls and the subsequent paperwork can be tedious, no question. But the role you play in these high-stress (and high-risk) encounters is a critical one.

Do your police work thoroughly, make arrests when you can, give the victim the benefit of the doubt, and try to see things from the victim's point of view. Nobody wants to be beaten up, least of all by someone they're supposedly in love with. Do your best to help break the cycle of domestic violence.

Every Day Is
MOTHERS Day
Dealing with Meth Freaks and Tweakers

Ugh! Why is it that everyone we run across has been or is under the influence of some mind-bending chemical? Thanks to this country's seemingly insatiable urge for street drugs, and thanks to all the amateur chemists in our cities and rural towns and in cookeries south of the U.S.-Mexican border, we have more meth in this country than we know how to destroy.

Into this tremendous mess comes the hardworking police officer, bent on keeping the streets safe for normal people who don't steal $200 worth of stuff each day or have strange, ether-like chemical odors emanating from their garages, bathrooms, or rattletrap motor homes.

What you see in terms of dope probably depends more on your state or town's geography than any other factor. No doubt you've driven up to your share of methamphetamine enthusiasts, busily tightening the head gasket bolts on their primer-gray El Caminos at zero dark hundred hours.

It's still possible to hear sad stories about two- and three-year "veteran" police officers who have yet to make an unassisted meth arrest, even though they have bumped into scores of tweakers on calls and stops.

My police training philosophy has always been simple: If you don't know how to do something, ask someone who does. If you feel uncomfortable or unsure about how to recognize the symptoms of meth use and abuse, or how to conduct the controlled lighting exam, or even how to complete your agency's narcotic arrest forms, get with someone you know and trust and have him or her show you. Then go out and find a live body—usually a guy wearing a "Defy Authority" or a faded black Metallica/Slayer/Slaughter T-shirt—and practice your newly learned observation, arrest, and report-writing skills on him.

One such meth expert is San Diego Police Sergeant Fred Wilson. Fred is not only a longtime SDPD member, but he spent some years fighting crime for the Honolulu Police Department. Digging through my notes of one of his lectures about meth users, I recalled his use of the acronym MOTHERS to help street cops remember what to look for and what to write when contacting and busting these people. Keep this handy phrase in mind as you stalk your streets for methheads.

M = Mouth. Frequent meth users will show signs of a dry "cotton" mouth. You may see a slimy, white coating on their lips, on the edges of their mouths, and on their tongues. They may lick their lips frequently and try to wipe this milky coating off their mouths.

O = Odor. These people usually stink. Personal hygiene is not a priority when you've been up tweaking in the same clothes for several days. As one old dope cop puts it, "Imagine if you went to work in the morning, sweated all day, went home, stayed up all night, went to work again all day, came home, stayed up all night, and never showered once. That's what meth freaks smell like."

Since the drug causes some people to sweat constantly, you'll be able to spot their matted hair, grimy clothes, and oily faces. Besides the body odor, some users will give off a strong chemical smell as the drug excretes through their pores.

T = Twitching. Could you stand still if your pulse rate was shooting to the moon and every nerve in your body felt like it was firing off at the same time? Neither can meth users. They can't seem to stand still for a second. They shift from foot to foot, move their hands, adjust their clothes, and generally fidget like children in church.

H = Head. You have to have head problems just to take street drugs, so you know meth users will have a number of kinks in the ol' coconut. The drug can intensify the senses. Look for signs that your suspect gets startled by ambient or background noises. As one officer says, "These people get jumpy when a jet plane flies over them."

E = Eyes. An easy and dead giveaway here. If your suspect looks like he or she has dinner plates for pupils, better get out the cuffs. Some meth and coke users have pupils so large that they are actually right off the pupilometer scale card. If you see pupils blown into the 6.0 to 7.0 mm range, even with your penlight shining nearby, you have found someone under the influence of a stimulant. However, don't always use the pupil size as your only indicator of meth use. As a narcotics detective points out, "Chronic, longtime meth users who have tweaked for 5 to 10 years may not have 'blown' pupils. Because their eye muscles are small and easily damaged after too much abuse they may not open and close normally anymore. So you could have a classic meth user with all the other symptoms but still with pin-dot pupils." Remember to compare the suspect's pupil size with that of another witness officer for your report.

R = Rapid pulse. Another deadbang ringer. If you stop someone on the street and take his or her pulse rate, it normally shouldn't be over 80 to 90 beats per minute. (Even taking normal nervousness and fear of the police into account.) Meth users will have pulse rates in the high 100s (120 to 170). It's not unusual to find a tweaker with a pulse of 160 even after he or she has been sitting in your police car for more than an hour at your station or at jail. Take the pulse rate several times during the arrest process, and make a note of each one in your report.

S = Speech. Shut up already. Talk, talk, talk, talk, talk. Meth users certainly won't win any awards for silence. Their speech is rapid, talkative, occasionally paranoid, distracted, and disconnected. Now that you know what to look for, you know what to do next: Seek these dopers and ye shall find.

Fatal Contact
Avoiding AIDS, HIV, TB, and Other Killers

I've written about police work since 1986. If you had told me back then that within a few years, a disease would appear with the potential to sweep the globe and threaten our existence, I wouldn't have believed you. And yet, AIDS is heavily upon us. There is no place you can go in this nation or in this world and not hear about how this disease affects people. Some of us know those who have the final stages of this disease and are just waiting to die, others of us know those who have already died from it, and still others of us wonder who the next victim will be.

For all of the stricken celebrities like Arthur Ashe and Magic Johnson, there are thousands of other people who suffer and die in anonymity. Worse yet, there are potentially many millions of people who may carry the HIV virus and don't even know it yet. As police officers, we come across both groups: those who have HIV or full-blown AIDS and know it and those who have HIV and don't.

To avoid having my house or office picketed by militant fanatics who may misconstrue any of what follows, I make this general statement: This chapter does not have anything to say about homosexuals, high-risk sexual behavior, needle users, civil rights, pharmaceutical companies, or medical funding. It's only about protecting cops from a deadly virus that may lurk figuratively in the shadows of the streets they patrol.

We have all had encounters with people who cause the chilling phrase, "Uh-oh" to creep into our minds: the victim of a bloody car accident; the gunshot victim who calls out to us for help; the coughing, retching, needle-using drug addict who leans against our patrol car and waits to be handcuffed; the mentally ill person who bleeds from self-inflicted wounds and begs to be taken

73

to a mental hospital. Such encounters often force us to stop and think, at least momentarily, "Might this person have HIV or AIDS? Am I at putting myself (or my family) at risk by being in close contact with him or her?"

Since we don't have X-ray vision, and people who have HIV or AIDS don't wear neon signs announcing the fact, it's hard not to worry when blood is spilling about. As cops, we encounter the worst drug users imaginable, and since we know needles transport the virus, our alarm is well justified.

AIDS is a final disease. You can't take a few pills and go sleep it off. The officer who reaches blindly under a car seat and gets stuck by an exposed hype kit certainly wishes he could turn back the hands of time and replay that eerie event with more care for his personal safety. The officer who gets bit by an enraged suspect (a not uncommon event) certainly wishes she would have been more careful. And the officers who give two-person mouth-to-mouth resuscitation to a bleeding victim wonder privately whether they made the correct decision, knowing full well that without this breath of life the victim would have certainly died. But still the fear lingers on.

Even the dead body, drained of life and lying in a pool of blood at a crime or accident scene, is not without its risks. According to a report by the Funeral Directors Services Association of Greater Chicago, based on a study conducted by doctors at St. Luke's Medical Center, the HIV/AIDS virus can dwell in the dead. Looking at blood and tissue samples from 41 dead patients confirmed to have the AIDS virus, the researchers were able to detect HIV in the blood of the dead bodies even *21 hours* after death. The funeral directors group called for its members to hold bodies of known AIDS patients for at least 24 hours before processing them for burial. "Refrigeration of the bodies," says the report, *does not* appear to affect survival of the HIV virus."

This is disturbing news, to say the least. While medial researchers have proven that the AIDS virus is relatively fragile when exposed to open air, the fact that it could remain alive for at least 21 hours after the body's blood system has failed should give you good reason to be just as cautious around homicide and death scenes as you are with live, injured people.

Moreover, all this concern about AIDS and HIV should not cause you to lose sight of other evil viruses that dwell inside people you may contact. You can be exposed Hepatitis A, B, or C, tuberculosis (TB), and even the common cold, just as easily as people who might carry the HIV virus.

Since it's still not possible to atone for our mistakes after we make them, it certainly makes sense to take a few—pardon the expression—healthy precautions to avoid exposure to any virus (HIV, AIDS-related illness, Hepatitis C, TB, etc.) that may be out there. If you aren't already practicing "safe cop" behavior, think about changing your ways and taking the following precautions:

- *Always wear your rubber gloves.*

Get a fresh box and put it in your gear bag. Carry several pairs on your person at all times. Many officers carry their gloves inside their vest panel. This keeps them accessible for you (or another officer who has forgotten) in a pinch. Better to have them on you rather than put away, keeping the trunk of the car safe.

- *Double up.*

In any situation where you will have to put your hands on obviously bloody areas; put on *two* pairs of gloves first. Some rubber gloves are notoriously thin and cheap; they aren't all like the kinds surgeons wear while operating. Further, in the heat of the moment, while you're struggling quickly to put them on, it's possible to tear them in places you don't see. Two pairs can give you more peace of mind.

- *Use a plastic mouth-to-mouth resuscitator.*

If you were given one of these guards in your first-aid or CPR class, keep it handy. If not, buy one and get trained by a qualified medical professional or first-aid instructor as to how to use it safely and effectively. Keep this life-saving device out of the bottom of your gear bag and get familiar with it from time to time. Reread the instructions and make sure you can use it during a medical crisis.

- *Keep your hands spotlessly clean.*

Buy and use an alcohol foam cleaning scrub; use plenty of soap after pat-downs and (rubber gloved) body searches; and keep your nails short and clean (sorry ladies). Follow the old patrol cop's maxim, "Wash your hands *before* you go to the bathroom. You know where your private parts have been; you don't know where your hands have been."

- *Cover any open cuts with bandages.*

Don't get obsessed and end up looking like a mummy, just make sure you cover obviously open wounds on your hands and other exposed areas.

- *Keep your distance from people with heavy coughs, scabby wounds, or other signs of severe sickness.*

You don't have to wear a haz-mat suit, but it makes good medical sense to keep away from people with hard, hacking, phlegm-filled coughs, oozing wounds, and the like. I remember writing an FI on a guy in a bar near the beach, who kept wiping his face with a bloody cloth. "Oh, it's nothing," he said, when I asked why he looked sick, "I just have scabies." Nice to know someone has a mange-like skin disease when you're standing four feet away.

- *Take the usual precautions at injury scenes.*

Put on your gloves as soon as you get out of the car, just like the fire fighters and the paramedics do. The car accident victim who went through the windshield is just like the gutshot gangbanger—an injured person with exposed, bloody wounds. Put your gloves on and don't touch anything unless absolutely necessary to do your job. I recall giving myself that queasy feeling one night while leaning in to read the odometer of a car I was impounding at a major accident scene. I placed my hand on a gray sheepskin seat cover littered with windshield glass. I'm not sure if the glass was bloody, and it didn't pierce the skin of my hand, but I felt lousy about making such a mistake.

- *Search slowly first, carefully always.*

Don't dive right into your prisoner's pockets without a little chat first: "Do you have any needles on you? Are you carrying any sharp objects? Is there anything at all that might cut me? Are you sick right now?" While you may not always get the whole truth, you can save everyone much grief by firmly asking for the bad stuff up front.

- *Let there be light.*

Go slowly, wear gloves, and don't root hastily around dark pockets, purses, backpacks, or wallets. Use your penlight or flashlight to look inside things, like pockets. Run your hands around suspected areas (waistbands, socks, etc.) only after you're sure nothing sharp is lingering nearby. This goes doubly for car searches. Look first—with flashlights even in daylight—under car seats, inside glove compartments and trunks, and in between seats.

- *Use common sense.*

The HIV virus that causes AIDS and the hepatitis trios are not airborne beasts. They don't linger like a cloud of smoke in the atmosphere. You cannot get infected with the HIV virus or hepatitis unless it is introduced internally into your body. Taking normal precautions against exposure to blood and other bodily fluids that aren't your own is the best way to avoid these biological killers.

You don't have to come to work dressed like the Cop in the Plastic Bubble, nor should you poke your bare hands willy-nilly into or around anything sharp or bloody. Do your job with professionalism and concern for others, but be careful what and whom you touch and how and why you touch them.

Fighting for
Your Own Tickets
Traffic Court Survival Strategies

Follow our hidden cameras as we witness the following odd event: The scene is traffic court. The time is early morning. The room is filled with cops, defendants, defense attorneys, the prosecutor, the bailiff, the court clerk, and the judge.

As we lean in closer to hear the proceedings, an officer is carefully explaining why he wrote the defendant a speeding ticket for driving 53 miles per hour (mph) in a 30-mph zone. Everyone in the room listens as the officer carefully fills in the picture for the day in question: late in the evening, busy street, well-known for accidents and high-speed drivers. The officer takes the time to list all of the significant details about his radar gun and its operation. He discusses his training with the device and his experience both with the radar gun in general and on that particular stretch of road.

He paints a clear picture of the defendant's actions in her vehicle. He discusses the stop itself, what was said, what was written, and after a few other clarifications requested by the prosecutor, rests his case.

The defense attorney rises and brings up a number of side issues that have little to do with the fact that the defendant was exceeding the posted speed limit by 23 miles per hour. Things like the location of parked cars, bicyclists, or pedestrians fill the air. The defense attorney engages the officer in a long discussion about the speed survey for the street in question. He also asks the officer many questions about the identity of the driver.

The officer answers each question skillfully, using his training, job knowledge, experience in court, and expertise as a traffic officer.

Finally, the defendant enters the fray. Under oath, she admits to all present that she was probably driving "about 42 miles per hour" on the night in question.

To the other officers and interested observers in the courtroom, this seems to be a rather startling admission; after all, the posted speed limit for this street is a mere 30 miles per hour, and clearly, the defendant has just testified to driving at a speed 12 miles over the posted limit.

Many of the officers in the courtroom nod knowingly at one another and fold their arms across their chests in a gesture that says, "Yep. She's guilty on this one."

After more legal wranglings and much back-and-forth chat about various fine points of law, the judge prepares to render a verdict. By now, the officers, especially those who have just come from the graveyard shift, are weary of all the talk but feel certain justice will triumph once again.

However, to the utter surprise of all in the room, save for the judge, the defendant, and the defense attorney, the judge finds some sliver of reasonable doubt in the entire episode and finds the defendant not guilty.

The officers in the room are, to say the least, quite taken aback by this ruling. Many police jaws hang agape at the news. The defense attorney and the defendant pack their collective papers and—after thanking the judge, of course— rise to leave.

The court clerk calls the next officer's case, and the officer rises to place his diagram on the board nearby, we see his face tighten in concentration. The next courtroom drama begins to play as we fade out.

Unfortunately for all concerned, with the exception of the suddenly not-guilty party and her paid and pleased lawyer, the details of this small legal drama are true.

Can you do everything right and still lose a perfectly good ticket? Sadly, yes. The officer in this episode did everything by the book. Short of standing on his head with an American flag in one hand and a current vehicle code in the other, I don't know what he could have done to be more correct in his testimony.

Yet in light of this distressing event, what can we do? If the other side can hire defense attorneys (paying $150 to fight a $150 ticket), we can certainly put as much effort into fighting for our own tickets as the defendant.

Get ready to switch hats, fellow officers, because we all just joined the City Attorney's Ticket Fighting Team.

So in our valiant attempt to keep the streets safe from chronic speeders, hit-and-run smashers, and red light runners, we may have lost sight of what it takes to actually win a ticket case in certain courtrooms.

To wit, some suggestions from some battle-scarred traffic court experts:

- *Pull your copy of the cite and review it carefully.*
Read your field notes, look at the description of the violator and his or her car, note the weather conditions, the time of day, the direction. In sum, look at everything on both sides of the ticket and, short of memorizing the thing, be

able to speak knowledgeably and confidently about it when asked by either side. (A little Marine Corps ditty might help here: "This is my ticket. There are many like it, but this one is mine.").

- *Go back to the scene of the ticket and look at the intangibles.*
Most officers know to go back and look at the street where they wrote the ticket. They look at the signs, the curves, and the location of cars—parked or moving—nearby. But start giving your ticket locations a more practiced scan. Put yourself back into the day or night in question and ask, "In the six or so weeks or months since I wrote this puppy, what has changed here?" Are there more or fewer bushes? New road signs? Barriers? Missing trees? New signal lights? New pavement? Crosswalks? Street lights?

Many traffic defendants think if they bring a few grainy Polaroids to court and describe the events (e.g., "There were bushes there in front of the stop sign," and so on), the judge will get confused and make that long leap of faith into that unpleasant land known as Reasonable Doubt. Since this is certainly possible, be ready to say something like, "Your Honor, I drive by that spot 247 times per day, and I know the bushes have never obstructed the view of the stop sign."

- *Put every necessary piece of information into your field and courtroom diagrams.*
If you feel it's important, put it in there. Besides "Not to Scale," "North," and the streets and addresses, put in all of the little stuff that makes the judge think you're an upstanding, thoughtful, fully prepared officer. Circles, arrows, speed charts, calculations, dots, dashes, lines, road sign positions, lane markers, street widths and lengths, braking distances, whatever. If it adds to your argument, put it on the diagram. Better to have too much than to be put on the spot when some smart-mouth defense attorney asks you if the road is made of chip seal tar or asphaltic concrete.

- *If possible, meet and greet the city attorney beforehand.*
These poor people are chronically overworked and underpaid. Give them the benefit of the doubt and offer as much help as you can. They don't want to see righteous tickets fly out the window any more than you do. But since they have less of a personal stake in your own actual, real, hard-copy ticket, they may not be as prepared to go to the judge with all of those extras that can mean a conviction.

Further, some of the city attorney folks are new to the job, both as lawyers and as traffic court experts. Friends who have worked for the city attorney's office tell me they made court appearances before the ink was even dry on their business cards. As much as they might want to win, some of them just don't have the time in grade to ask you all of the right questions to beat the defense attorneys, who, on good days, might crank out arguments against five tickets before lunch.

- *If the city attorney fails to ask you a particularly important question, take a second to pause during the proceedings and suggest it to him or her.*

Just as when you were new to this job and you appreciated every small piece of helpful advice to get you through the day, so do these folks. A simply whispered, "Ask me about my training in skid measurements," can get you both back on track so that important information doesn't bypass the judge.

- *Don't let the city attorney wrap things up until you've had your whole say.*

Make sure everything that needs to be covered gets covered. If you feel some of the infamous reasonable-doubt issues may rear their ugly heads, dig into them some more. Don't be in a big hurry to wrap up and take a seat. Go over all of the facts as you know them so you don't have to slap your thigh in the car on your way home and say, "Dang! I should've said something about the flames coming out of the back of his tailpipe as he raced past me!"

- *When in doubt, don't leave it out.*

A traffic officer who impressed me with his on-the-ball courtroom demeanor had the good sense to tell the judge that he remembered the defendant telling him he was eating a taco at the time of the offense. The officer made a point to use said alleged taco as his own point of reference for this defendant. Based on the smoking taco, the judge seemed convinced the officer remembered the defendant, his speed, and the other fine points in the case. Chalk up a "Guilty!" for our side.

The point is, if you remember something significant about the event, say it. "Your Honor, on the night in question, the defendant had five house cats in the car with him. After my stop, he told me the cats had distracted him and he was forced to speed through two red lights and a flashing railroad crossing gate."

If you go into any bookstore in town, you can usually find two or three books (some written by ex-cops, sad to say) about "How to Fight Your Ticket." Just because they can read them, doesn't mean we can't find a way to fight back ourselves. In the never-ending battle for truth, justice, and road safety, don't think your latest "slam dunk" speeding ticket is going to go down so easily.

Work hard—in fact, work harder than the defendant and his or her defense lawyer—to fight for your own tickets. You wrote them. Be willing to go the extra 5,280 feet to win them.

Ground Fighting

If you've never had to use physical force to arrest a suspect, please skip this chapter. If, during your entire police career, all of your suspects have gone along with the program, calmly placed their hands behind their backs, and waited for you to apply the handcuffs, feel free to read something else in this book.

I feel fairly confident that you're still with me at this point because we've all had at least one crook look right at us and say, "I'm not going with you. No way, no how."

This foreshadowing statement usually comes before a string of terrible curses and insults, followed by a gut-busting fight for control of your balance, handgun, and knee or elbow tissues.

We live and work in cities and towns filled with "Yes-Maybe-No" people. The "Yes" folks will let you arrest them, either because they're afraid of what you might do if they don't or because they feel guilty, remorseful, or embarrassed about what they did.

The "Maybe" folks will probably go along for the same two reasons as the "Yes" folks, providing you catch them on a good day when they aren't too liquored up, high on drugs, or feeling especially resentful about the role of the American law officer in modern society. "Maybe" folks might need a little prod in the form of a firm hand on their wrist or a stern command, but for the most part, if you demonstrate tactical superiority (that is, more friends in uniforms, bigger muscles, tougher facial expressions, good positioning, and so on), you can usually get them safely and quickly into cuffs.

"No" folks could care less about you or your problems. It doesn't concern them that you're wearing your "Monday" uniform, that you're only five minutes away from your normal dinner time, or that you don't really feel like touching angry idiots covered with blood, vomit, ear wax, or other slippery bodily excretions. They would just as soon kick your butt as spit in your face, and sometimes they plan to do both.

"No" people will not put their hands behind their backs. "No" people don't care to help you relearn any of those swell handholds you practiced in the academy; the ones that put docile suspects into all of those user-friendly, easy-cuffing, 15-moving-parts positions. And "No" people will go out of their way to make sure that you are just as injured or as angry as they are by the time the whole arrest process is finished.

When they know the application of handcuffs is imminent, "No" people like to tighten up their arms, curl into a standing fetal position, and wait for you to start the ol' "Asphalt Tug-of-War" with them. If you're stronger or have immediate help from your cover officer, you can probably twist their mitts into the reverse-prayer position after a few long seconds or minutes of shoving, hard breathing, and well-placed yells of encouragement.

But if this "No" person outweighs or out-muscles you by a country mile or you're working alone, you'll probably become an unwitting participant in "WrestleMania 13."

Experience and a critical eye tell us that a high percentage of street fights end up with one or both parties on the deck, scrabbling at each other like crabs in a pot. Under no circumstances (unless you're an Olympic-caliber grappler) will you want to go to the ground with some urban guerrilla bent on supplying you with major amounts of harm and grief. The ground is an unforgiving place, and should you happen to linger there for even longer than 10 seconds, you could receive a body-thumping even General Custer would shake his head at.

Human beings are meant to walk around vertically. We are out of our element on the ground, and, as a rule, unlike animals, we have very little experience fighting from this vulnerable position. And yet, it happens.

But as bad as the ground is for you, it's a terrific place to not-so-gently put your attacker. If you can get him off his feet while you keep yours, the encounter changes dramatically in your favor. It's just easier to handcuff someone when you're on top of him or her rather than the other way around.

If you both happen to end up on the ground, here are some tips that may help you escape and regain control:

- *As fast as you can spin on your side or butt, get your feet up next to the suspect's head.*
  With your steel-toed shoes up by his melon, it's much easier to kick at him and it's much harder for him to disarm you.

- *Use your leg muscles.*
Your legs are the largest and most powerful ones in your body. Use them to kick and kick and kick until you've stopped his attacks.

- *If you can't kick at him, at least get to your feet as quickly as possible.*
If you can't get all the way to your feet, try to get into a three-point stance, forming a tripod with one foot up, one knee down, and your hand out front for balance. You may be able to catch him with a hard punch, kick, or healthy shove back down as he tries to get on his feet after you.

- *If the suspect gets up before you do, sit up into a "lever" position.*
Get on your butt, with your palms flat on the ground to support your weight, put one or both legs in the air, and use your hands and feet to spin like a child's top. By pivoting around, you can follow the suspect's movements and fight him or her off until you can get up safely.

- *If you're trapped on the ground, don't just lie there.*
Keep moving! Spin, slide, twist, scream, and yell, but don't come to a complete stop. It's much harder to hit a moving target or remove that moving target's duty weapon.

- *If you can get to your feet before him, push him back over each time he tries to get up.*
Use this opportunity to gather your energy and catch your breath. Shove him back down each time he comes up into a three-point or four-point stance. He'll soon learn how draining it is to pull himself up to a complete standing position time after time.

- *Once you've turned the tables and kept him on the ground, don't be in such a hurry to handcuff.*
Gather your energy level, get your breathing back to normal, and make sure he's totally out of gas. Go into an approved handcuffing technique for prone suspects only when you have the tactical advantage again. Better yet, wait for adequate cover to arrive so you can give your full attention to getting him properly secured. (Needless to say, your gun pointed at his body can help to keep him from attacking you again.) Trying to put hands on after a rolling ground brawl may just start things up again.

- *If you're the cover officer and your contact officer ends up on the ground fighting with a suspect, don't just jump right into the fray.*

Stand by and carefully evaluate the problem until it becomes clear how and when you'll need to help.

- *If you do intervene to help the contact officer, think about your best force option for the situation.*

As difficult as it is to stay clear, in most cases, you can protect yourself and your partner far better if you take the "helicopter view" from above for a moment or two. If the suspect is clearly unarmed, you may want to use a hands-on technique or your well-aimed baton to get control. In other situations, verbal commands given at the point of a gun may be necessary. Keep in mind you may have to shoot the suspect if he starts to disarm or actually succeeds in disarming your partner on the ground. Your survival instincts and good training will help with this decision.

As unpleasant as it sounds, any time you pull out cuffs with the intention of putting two wrist bones inside, you run the risk of fighting tooth and nail with their owner. The longer the fight lasts, the more chances you have to break Newton's Law of Gravity, so that one or both of you ends up on the ground.

Cuff tactically, keep your balance, and, most importantly, know when to break free from touching the suspect while you're still in a vertical position of safety. Holding on for dear life as you ride the suspect to the hard deck is a good way to leave pieces of your uniform or body where they don't belong.

Gut Check Time
Officer Safety for the 2000s

We've always had more problems with "No" people—the ones who won't go to jail without a fight, who won't yield during long and dangerous pursuits, and who bring guns to solve their problems. The old police cliché about the "war on the streets" seems to be truer than ever before. We're running across more people who are willing to use drugs, guns, knives, and fists to get their way, either against other citizens or against us.

Police work is a profession of options and choices. The more you have, the better things seem to turn out. With this in mind, review the following list of what I call "gut checks," or things to examine about yourself and the way you do business out there. These ideas may help you to make more safe and correct decisions in the field:

- *Get adequate cover before you go in.*
Many of our confrontations involve numerous bad guys. Have your "safety sensor" tuned to the highest degree and decide immediately what you can handle alone, with a partner, with another cover unit, or with several cover units.

- *Expect to have to use deadly force when responding to high-risk calls.*
New studies suggest that nearly 95 percent of all police shootings happen within *eight minutes* of the arrival of the first officer. If it's going to go to guns, it's probably going to go there in a hurry. Be prepared when you arrive on scene at a call with one or more armed or out-of-control suspects for the distinct possibility that you may have to respond quickly and accurately with deadly force.

- *Develop your upper-body strength, cardiovascular endurance, and muscle flexibility.*

Each of these, working together, can prolong your career and save your life in the field. If you're lacking in any of the three, work on it. Watch what you eat—too much sugar, too much caffeine, or too much fatty food can turn your blood sugar levels into a roller coaster ride. Pace yourself and focus your activities to match your energy and enthusiasm throughout the shift, especially during those long graveyard hours.

- *Know both Contact and Cover Officer roles and use them.*

Pay attention to how you control space, distance, and movement. On any contact with potential or unsecured suspect or suspects, immediately get to the position of advantage and put them at the position of disadvantage. Use the sun, shadows, police car lights, curbs, and so on to help you.

- *Get everyone's hands out of pockets and in plain sight.*

Use approved pat-down methods, not the so-called modified pat-down (where the officer stands directly in front of the suspect), which often ends up with a punched cop or a fleeing crook.

- *Read the behavioral signs of a pending fight.*

Clenched fists, talking aggressively or through the teeth, focusing on a body target, and "squaring off" movements are all things you should watch for and prevent.

- *Few people just "hang out" all day and night because they have nothing better to do.*

Most people who "hang out" day and night are casing, preparing to make a dope deal, or waiting for crime opportunities, either alone or with other crooks. Keep everybody moving and on his or her toes about where you might be and when you might show up to interrupt their plans.

- *The eyes tell us everything.*

As the "window to the soul," they signal if the suspect is high or drunk, what type of chemicals may be in his or her bloodstream, and what he or she may plan to do next, e.g., flee, fight, lie, or snitch on someone.

- *Follow approved tactical procedures when putting on the bracelets.*

Get them out and on quickly, but don't forget about them once they're in place. The average 12-page rap sheet crook has been in cuffs a number of times and usually ignores the discomfort. Your solid-citizen drunk driver has not felt metal on his wrists before and will be the first to complain (or sue) if the handcuffs are too tight or incorrectly applied. Balance your need to handcuff quickly and tactically with your need to be humane.

- *Look at key rings, lighters, belts, and watchbands for anything that looks like a weapon.*

As always, search carefully for needles and knives, especially in and around car seats, glove boxes, and pants pockets.

- *Replace old pepper spray, torn rain gear, worn boots, and cracked or broken holsters (check the thumb break wear and tear carefully).*

Fix anything that needs repair; replace anything that might become a safety hazard.

- *Train to shoot more at closer distances.*

Since most police shootings happen at close range, common sense tells us we should. Go to your range and meet with the training instructors. If they have time, they'll create a training program for you. Practice immobilization fire training, head shots, and the correct way to use your sights during distant and close-up encounters.

- *Expect a knife attack. Expect to find a knife during a pat-down.*

I saw a TV documentary about "hobos" illegally riding railroad freight cars. Several interviews with railroad police officers and other "hobos" (the narrator's phrase) uncovered the fact that most if not all of these "happy-go-lucky travelers" carry knives. More and more, the knife is the weapon of choice for street people who cannot get access to a gun. It's small and concealable, noiseless to use, and requires very little accuracy or training to induce fatal results.

- *Most humans fight forward.*

As a rule, this means they usually move forward and backward rather than laterally during a confrontation. Use this knowledge to your advantage and keep moving to the side should a fight arise. Use your hands to "parry" or push your opponent's fists and forearms away from you. As a martial artist, I know from painful experience that the best way to be on the receiving end of a punch is to be in its way when it gets there. Move your head and body out of range and you can avoid a punch to the face.

- *Find "new" body targets.*

  Around the local watering hole, some cops will admit that during a knock-down drag-out fight in the streets, the best place to hit the suspect is in the private parts. It's no secret that one well-placed strike to the groin can even bring down a bull elephant. But keep in mind that the cost of one damaged testicle is now about $100,000. Courts have held that cops who kick or baton-strike to the groin and cause ruptures to suspects can be held liable for excessive force.

Current defensive training teaches that the best way to defend yourself with any kicking movement is to use your knee to strike the suspect's abdomen. This can knock the wind out of him and help you get him safely to the ground. Another good knee-strike target is the major nerve site that runs up and down the side of the suspect's outer thigh. As kickboxers attest, a well-placed and hard strike to the center of the outer thigh can bring the crook down in a hurry. Be careful where you aim, and use only enough force to end the fight and get control.

Know that you and your colleagues do a good job of policing your city. Whenever he heard other cops complaining about the public we serve, a veteran patrol partner of mine used to put it this way, "They just don't know, do they? A single ride-along would do more to educate the public about this job than anything else."

Be proud of your profession and proud of your department. Take advantage of new training techniques, new safety equipment, and the skills and knowledge of officer safety experts on your department and around the country.

Work hard, work smart, and don't let bad news get you down. People who don't understand why we did something have never, ever been placed in a life-or-death situation. Be careful, because you *do* know what it's like out there.

Handle with Care
Elderly Calls

While we like to think we spend most of our time fighting crime, parts of our patrol shift get taken up by service calls that aren't always of a criminal nature.

The standard "Check the Welfare" call offers a prime example. This service request often involves an elderly person who has fallen out of bed, slipped in the bathroom, or, worse yet, has not been seen by worried friends or neighbors. You could arrive to find a normal scene that doesn't require any of your aide or a full-blown death case.

New statistics tell us that the "graying" of America continues at an ever-increasing pace. By the year 2010, 14 percent of our population will be made up of people 65 or older, and this will rise to 22 percent by 2030. We are an older society, with the average age of a citizen standing at around 34.

But while our society as a whole grows older from a statistical standpoint, our police patrol officers don't. Younger officers typically fill police patrol ranks. The old "graybeards"—having done their time in patrol—have usually moved on to supervisory, administrative, or investigative positions. Is it unusual for a 23-year-old officer to answer a call involving a 73-year-old woman who has fallen in the bathroom? No. Nor is it unusual for a 25-year-old officer to go to a call involving an 85-year-old man and his bedridden wife. The point is that these age gaps are inevitable and can cause perception problems on both sides. The "generation gap" can lead to communication problems, embarrassment, and feelings that neither side understands the other.

Police service calls affecting the elderly usually fall into three categories: auto accidents, crime cases (including the growing problem of elder abuse), and health-related matters.

89

While it's not fair to stereotype elderly drivers, many of them do have problems relating to eyesight, hearing, reaction time, and distance calculations. My grandfather—God rest his soul—was a wonderful 80-year-old man and a tremendous inspiration to be around. But for the last five years of his life he was not the best driver in the world. He had a terrible habit of waiting until oncoming cars were directly in his field of view before he turned right at a signal light. This often lead to the inevitable horn honking, finger-shaking, and swerving from the other driver.

The man started driving cars in 1927, so I hardly felt qualified to comment on his abilities, but the safety issue became a factor in his driving. My grandmother spent most of her time giving him directions and pointing out potential hazards, which made driving all the more stressful for her, too.

We've all seen or written several hit-and-run property damage reports involving elderly drivers who truly had no idea that they had hit another car. I recall one elderly woman who sideswiped the entire length of her car against a parked vehicle while she backed out at a supermarket. She said she never heard the crunching of metal or felt the impact. She was so hard of hearing that I had to scream my questions at her. A road hazard? Sure, but no officer likes to be the "bad guy" and ask the DMV for a recertification exam, although it offers one way to ensure her safety and those around her.

We've also seen officers on traffic stops fly off the handle and berate elderly drivers for their hazardous violations. It's easy to understand their frustration, but you have to see things from the elderly people's point of view as well. Driving a car is something they've probably done for most of their adult lives. A license offers them mobility, freedom, and a large dose of independence. It lets them do what they want, when they want, without having to rely on their friends, family, or our public transit system. (It always pains me to see an elderly woman standing next to a group of unsavory characters as they all wait for a bus. You can see her tightly clutching her groceries and her purse as she waits in fear.)

When we talk with elderly drivers about being on the road today, some common themes come up: "Everybody goes so fast! Everyone is in such a hurry! People are always tailgating me and cutting me off!"

These are valid complaints. Elderly drivers tend to be more cautious and will drive at the speed limit or just below it. This only serves to irritate the "only going with the flow of traffic" guy who is always 15 minutes late to everything.

Further, elderly drivers can have eyesight, hearing, or memory problems that force them to drive slowly and carefully. They don't want to miss their exits or turn the wrong way, so they take their time. So many people drive erratically and quickly these days that the elderly driver, moving at the speed limit, can really stick out.

If an elderly driver deserves a hazardous movement citation, write it. But if his or her driving behavior can be corrected with a traffic warning or a verbal warning, then do that instead.

One of the nicest letters ever sent to me (via my chief) was from an elderly lady whom I stopped for driving with her high beams. I wrote her a warning and gave her some suggestions about driving at night. She took the time to write the chief about what I had done for her.

Keep in mind that an elderly person can get quite embarrassed during a traffic stop. Here's some "kid," young enough to be his grandson or granddaughter, lecturing him about how to drive. And his anger or embarrassment is not always directed at the officer, it's just that this traffic stop force him to face the fact that he's getting older and his reactions, eyesight, and driving judgment may be slipping.

Crime cases offer another opportunity to meet elderly people. A home burglary or an auto theft case can be devastating to an elderly person. Many of these folks are longtime city natives who can remember when the bad part of town was good and when they could leave their houses and cars unlocked with no problems. A theft, street robbery, or other crime case can leave many elderly people feeling anxious about the future and upset about how "times have changed" around their neighborhood, and not for the better.

In many cases, they look to the police—whom they almost always respect and admire—for help, support, and, most importantly, reassurance. Take their crime case report, and tell them you are there to help them and try to solve their problems.

Even more disturbing than seeing elderly people victimized by strangers is the growing crime of elder abuse. Police agencies across this country are forming units of specifically trained officers and detectives to target those who abuse the elderly. These criminals may be caregivers, medical providers, and even the relatives of the victims. They will abuse, assault, mistreat, ignore, and steal from the elderly, using a million rationalizations and justifications.

Lastly, health issues are a major concern for many elderly people. For all the times you go to that "chronic" check-the-welfare call, imagine how embarrassing it is for the elderly person who was forced to call you. Do you think these folks enjoy having police officers come into their homes to help them out of the bathroom or back into bed? They're certainly grateful for the assistance, but they would much rather take care of themselves.

Certain parts of your community may have more elderly people living nearby than others. Officers working the graveyard shift may go to several assist-the-elderly calls per night. In many of these cases, paramedics will also respond. As much as we like these ambulance angels, it's hard not to notice they get a bit jaded (just like cops) when working with the elderly.

I remember going to an assist call on a cold graveyard night. An elderly man on a respirator had fallen out of bed, and his wife was unable to help him. We arrived with paramedics and did what we could. One of the paramedics began "interviewing" the man and his wife about his medical problems.

When he began shouting questions at him the man calmly said, "Look here, young man, I'm old but that doesn't mean I'm deaf, too! You don't have to yell at me!"

Sometimes we equate old age with deafness, just like we have a tendency to scream in English at a foreign speaker who doesn't understand us. If an elderly person can't hear you, they'll let you know. Many times they'll ask you to give them their nearby hearing aid, and things will go smoothly after it's in place.

Imagine how you would feel if you were in your eighties and two young-looking police officers and a pair of young-looking paramedics came into your bedroom and began firing confusing questions at you. It's no wonder these folks regret having to call for help only to suffer the embarrassment of having a bunch of well-meaning strangers tramp around their house.

It must be frightening, embarrassing, and a bit humiliating all at once, because their need to make that call may tell them that they can't care for their basic human needs anymore. Many times a kind word from you or a hand squeeze can offer the reassurance they're asking for.

Always remember that many elderly people have been conditioned since childhood to respect the law and see the police as "crime-fighting public servants." Realize that elderly people have certain perceptions of you in uniform just as you have certain perceptions of them. Be polite and remember to treat them with as much dignity and respect as the situation allows.

Home from the War

A partner of mine relayed the following, which reveals not so much about him, but rather about the police profession: "I can't believe how much I curse on this job! I never talk that way at home, but it seems like when I'm in a patrol car, I can't stop using profanity. My partner is the same way. We curse a blue streak on the job and yet, at home, we never talk like that. It's like we're completely different people when we're in a police car."

He went on to talk about how his wife knows when he's getting ready to go to work: "She says she can actually see the change in my face. When I'm getting my gear together or preparing my uniform, she notices how serious I get."

Another officer told me that sometimes he feels like he's getting ready to go into battle. He puts his "game face" on and girds himself for the coming 10 hours, even before he gets to the station.

I've heard another officer say that his religious beliefs stipulate that he avoid caffeine, cigarettes, and profanity. At home, he is the model of compliance to these rules, and yet, at work he drinks Pepsi by the bucketful, smokes throughout his shift, and swears more times than he cares to admit.

So what is with these apparent Dr. Jekyll-and-Mr. Hyde police officers? What causes them to shift from loving, caring family members with wives, husbands, kids, and other people who love them into hard-driving, aggressive, street cops? In two words: The Job. This profession changes people, profoundly and for life.

The Rodney King riots, which successfully shut down the second largest city in the United States, have demonstrated aptly that police work is one tough kitty of a profession. While the loudmouthed critics, politicos, and other so-called community leaders/experts were safe in their homes, cops from one end of California to the other were working double shifts and dealing with urban guerrillas, all of it in mostly unfamiliar and hostile areas and most of it under uncertain or hesitant leadership.

Another case in point. During one of our CONTACT & COVER seminars, John Morrison and I met a woman at lunch who made an off-hand comment about a dream she'd had the previous night. She went on to describe a series of events where she had the drop on some crook, but when it came time to arrest him and a gun battle began, her weapon wouldn't fire. No matter how many times she tried, her gun just would not operate. The bad guy kept coming and she kept pulling the trigger, all to no avail.

In a hesitant voice, she asked around the table if this was "normal." She even made a self-deprecating remark to the effect of "I must be going crazy!" Both John and I (and the other cops at the table) were quick to tell her that this type of police dream—one where you or your equipment fails to get the job done—is quite common among cops. Whether they will admit it freely or not, many officers have similar dreams, if not frequently, at least often enough to make them question their abilities.

During certain periods of your life when you may feel especially apprehensive, angry, or preoccupied, these dreams can appear frequently, almost as if they were trying to send you some sort of weird subliminal message. While they may seem real and frightening, you shouldn't try to read anything significant into these episodes. They are just dreams, no matter how vivid or terrifying they may be. They do not reflect your competencies as a police officer or your safety habits. What they may tell you is that you are under more stress than normal or you have certain job-related problems you need to work out.

The fact of the matter is that police officers are not very good at "reentry" into the civilian world. It's hard for anyone in a high-stress, high-risk job to turn off the adrenaline "afterburners" and come home back down to earth as if his or her body did not go through some significant physiological changes.

As professionals, those in police work in the United States have not come to the simple conclusion that we are failing to prepare our officers to become normal human beings after wearing a badge and gun for an entire work shift. As a veteran officer wryly suggests, "We have a preshift lineups, where cops get to talk about their jobs, what they did the shift before, and why they did it. They can tell stories, share jokes, and create a common professional bond among each other. Why don't we have a postshift lineup? Cops need to be able to vent their emotions, tell a few war stories, and reaffirm the fact that they successfully completed another demanding shift. SWAT teams always have an after-action meeting; so do military assault teams. Talking about what you did is a normal part of reentry and the stress-reduction process."

In Japan, for example, police officers have access to outdoor "quiet areas" within their stations. Some of these no-talk zones are designed around beautiful gardens, small fish ponds, waterfalls, sculptures, and trees. Officers can sit in these secluded areas and just reflect on what has happened to them over their patrol shift. They can look at things that are visually pleasing, feel the sun and cool breeze, and generally reenter the "regular" world at their own pace.

If you're having problems unwinding from a demanding shift, try changing your environment from the negative to the positive. Spend time telling your fellow officers some of the things you did that day. Listen to their stories, too, and give them encouragement for doing a safe job. Before you go home to eat, sleep, and interact with other people, try riding an exercise bike, going for a run, hitting a heavy bag, or lifting some weights to vent your pent-up energies or frustrations.

Create an unwinding ritual for when you get home. Some people make it a habit to greet their family and then immediately head off to a spare bedroom, den, or patio area to read the newspaper for 15 or 20 minutes (avoiding the antipolice articles and crime news, of course). Others like to shower or change clothes or take a short nap immediately after arriving home. They wake up refreshed and ready to enjoy the rest of their off hours.

These at-home rituals serve two purposes: they give you private time to relax and readjust to the demands of home life, and they protect your family and loved ones from any residual anger or frustration you may have carried home from the station.

Here's a short prescription to keep you on a healthy, positive track:

- *Learn to relax!*
  The art of relaxation is a life-saving skill. The better you feel, the longer your life will last. Go to the bookstore and get a good stress management book, or a stress-fighting cassette tape or CD. If you don't have one, buy a small cassette or CD player and a good set of headphones. Choose a convenient time to listen to your relaxation tape(s)—preferably at least once per day, e.g., after work or before bed.

- *Take a break!*
  Use a few quick working breaks to recharge your batteries and renew your energy level. Find a safe spot where you can walk around and stretch your legs, eat a small piece of fruit or a muffin, and just try not to think about crooks or police work for a few minutes.

- *Eat right!*

Even if you have to eat in your car or on post, make sure you put something wholesome into your stomach to keep you going. If you're watching your weight, try to eat a small, well-balanced portion of food. Give up the "feel good" foods, like sweet rolls, soda, candy, and donuts. Eat more protein, more fruits and vegetables, fewer sugars, and less fat.

- *Get enough sleep!*

Getting by on four or five hours of sleep each night will affect your concentration level, your officer safety, your motivation, your enthusiasm, and your resistance to illness. Use your relaxation tapes or CDs if you have trouble falling into a deep sleep. Try to go to bed at the same hour and avoid "catching up" on days off.

- *Take vacations!*

If you're entitled to a day off, take it. Every three or four months, take an extra day off and give yourself a relaxing four-day vacation. Stay at home and catch up on your house projects, favorite hobbies, sports, workouts, or pleasure reading. Go to the beach, mountains, or a nice park, and refresh your energy level. Leave your work worries back on the street and give yourself permission to create your own healthy and positive "attitude adjustment."

- *Be positive! Think positive! Talk positive!*

Your self-image is often influenced by the information you take in. Associate with positive, reaffirming people and you'll start to feel more positive yourself. Hang around with the "doom and gloom" types, and you'll end up thinking, talking, and acting like they do. Try to avoid negative people (especially as work or love partners), negative newspaper or magazine articles, and, most importantly, negative news programs and television shows. What you say about yourself gives clues to other people about how you feel about yourself. Don't put yourself down in front of others or to yourself. Speak positively about your skills and accomplishments, and you'll improve your self-image.

- *Get a stronger grip on your frustrations!*

When we're really frustrated by some event, we often say, "I can't believe it," or "I can't believe this happened to me." The definition of frustration is "expectation mixed with disappointment." Instead of harping on what happened or being unwilling to accept reality, say to yourself, "I believe it, it happened. Now I'm going to fix the problem."

- *Debrief with your squad mates!*
Spend a few minutes telling your fellow officers about your work shift. Mention something exciting or amusing that you saw or did.

Allow enough time to vent negative, hostile, or aggressive feelings before you head home or to your family. And remember to give yourself a mental pat on the back for finishing another safe tour of duty before you reenter the regular world once again.

How to Read a
Crook Like a Book

Standing in the hallway at court, you see a male street person parked on a nearby bench, rocking back and forth and talking quietly to himself. He appears to be looking down at the floor, and his arms are folded tightly across his chest. He's rocking steadily, and while you can't quite make out what he's saying, it sounds like he's having a two-way conversation with himself. Every few minutes, he looks up from his one-way dialogue and quickly scans the surrounding area for trouble. His eyes bolt open wide when he sees you in full uniform looking back at him. He rises and comes toward you . . .

You roll up to a disturbance call with a cover unit on your heels. Climbing out of your car, you approach three people standing on the lawn in front of a house. Two of the participants are male and one is a female, and the female stands off to the side crying and talking incoherently. One of the males starts griping to you about the problem. Apparently, each man claims the woman is his girlfriend and wants the other guy to leave. Out of the corner of your eye, you see your partner talking to the other man. As he tells his story to your Cover Officer, you see him look at the other boyfriend and start to take several deep breaths, loudly exhaling each time. After three or four of these bellows breaths, he starts to clench and unclench his hands, all the while looking hard at the other suitor. Then he shifts his head and neck muscles from side to side as if he were trying to loosen up . . .

You stop a teenager walking through an alley late one night. You climb out of your car and call him over. After a brief chat, you pull out your field interview pad and start filling in the blanks. Through your conversation, you discover your juvenile is on probation for auto theft. As you talk to him, you notice he's wearing *really* nice running shoes. He starts to shift from foot to foot, flexing his ankle muscles, going up and down on his toes a few times, and wiping his sweaty hands on his thighs. . .

With your 20-20 hindsight vision safely stored away, take a guess as to what might happen in each of these common street scenarios. A quick review: Scene #1—suspect has wrapped his arms tightly around himself and is carrying on a deep conversation with said parties unknown. Scene #2—Suspect is taking in large quantities of O_2 and flexing his fists. He's also trying to loosen that small tension-based kink in his neck. Scene #3—Suspect is flexing his leg muscles and drying his nerve-wracked hands on his pants.

If you guessed, 1) "Punch me," 2) "Punch the other guy, and 3) Head for the hills," give yourself a gold star. People act just like animals. They move around like animals, think like animals, and, in some cases, eat and even look like animals. If you know how to read the signs of impending danger, you can take the necessary steps to avoid an ambush, attack, disarm, or fatal injury.

Remember how the Saturday morning cartoons always showed an angry bull pawing at the ground and snuffling his steamy breath before he charged after someone? This is known as a "preattack stance." The human movements described in each of the three scenarios above also illustrate preattack positions. When wild animals are put into potentially dangerous or life-threatening situations, they react by gearing themselves up to fight or scampering off in the opposite direction of their foes.

Humans are no different. If you see someone shifting his position to a more bladed, sideways stance, flexing his hands and fingers, or staring at some area on your body where a punch might do some damage, look out!

Your failing to read body language in time can give a crook that extra-second "action versus reaction" jump on you. Having had my face and head punched repeatedly in martial arts training, I know from painful experience that you cannot possibly react faster than someone else can act. This means by the time the punch is a mere one foot away from your chops, it's probably too late.

In the first scenario in the courthouse, you're certainly dealing with a mentally ill person. This "holding it in" posture gives a good indication that the person has paranoid or delusional feelings and may be trying to talk himself into a violent confrontation with real or imaginary enemies.

In the two boyfriends-one girlfriend confrontation, the suspect has lost interest in what the officer is saying to him, choosing to gird himself for a sucker punch aimed at the other boyfriend's noggin. His "target acquisition" stare, the warm-up breaths, and the flexing of hands and neck are all just ways of telling you, "I'm preparing myself for a fight. I'm getting my lungs and fighting tools tuned up and ready to go."

In the third scenario, your suspect is selectively warming up his leg muscles and associated lower bones, joints, and tendons for the 5,000-Meter Across-the-Alley sprint. In flexing calf, ankle, and leg muscles and wiping his sweaty palms on his pants, he's telling you, "I don't plan to be here much longer."

So what should you do when you spot these kinds of body language signals in the field? Immediately start by talking with your suspects about their nonverbal behaviors. Tell them that you've notice these movements and you already know what they're planning to do.

If you're dealing with potentially dangerous and emotionally disturbed people, start talking to them. Maintain a safe distance, but make sure they realize you're speaking to them and you think they may need some help. Don't ignore the signs. They may be trying to give you a warning—just like a dog growls, a cat hisses, and a snake coils up and rattles.

If you see someone clenching up, moving into a slight boxer's stance, and getting ready to fight, immediately break his chain of thought by saying, "Hey! Calm down! I can see you're upset, but just back off!"

If someone looks like he or she is preparing for a track meet, move in and block the escape route. Have him change positions to close the distance between you and place some physical barriers (cars, walls, etc.) between him and his freedom.

Many times, when you call people on their nonverbal behavior, you can catch them off guard. It can take the wind out of their sails and show that you've already spotted their danger signs and will take action if they continue to move.

Militias in Our Midst
One Deputy's Story

My wife, Leslie, comes from a family of tough, civil service-minded folks. Her father, Mike, spent over three decades with the San Diego Police Department, rising from patrolman to assistant chief. Her grandfather was the fire chief in Tucson, Arizona, for many years. And she has uncles and other relatives on both sides of the family who work or have worked as cops. This story is about one of them.

The old saying, "It's not the size of the dog in the fight, it's the size of the fight in the dog," certainly applies to Deputy Bob Parcell. Bob is not a huge man, but he packs a lot of deputy into what God gave him.

To put it simply, the guy has been places and done things. In the small Montana town of Condon, just outside of Missoula in the northwest part of the state, he is the law. Working for the Missoula County Sheriff's Department, Bob Parcell is the resident deputy in Condon. He is also the search-and-rescue team, the lake and river patrol officer, the tracker, the K9 handler, and the scuba evidence recovery diver. He makes his own hours, working patrol at different days and times. His closest cover unit is about 30 minutes away in the next town.

If you're thinking that his job would take a wide variety of experience, rest assured he has it. He has been a smoke jumper (yes, those people that parachute out of perfectly good airplanes into raging forest fires) and a Marine officer and is now a colonel in the Marine Reserve, with combat experience.

To say that Bob Parcell is not too popular with the local hoods in town would be an understatement. They hate him with a purple passion, plain and simple. He is widely despised by the town dirtbags because he is a stickler for

103

the law and a hard-nosed cop. The townies like to get drunk, race their trucks, and shoot their guns, in no particular order. Bob sees to it that they don't kill themselves or anyone else with their harebrained antics.

And all is not peace and sunshine in his neck of the woods. A group of people exists who don't like following laws and make no bones about their hatred of the government. These scary folks—known as "Constitutionalists"—choose not to pay taxes, register their assault weapons, vote, or have valid driver's licenses or similar governmental attachments. Their politics lean toward the redneck racist side, and it's probably an accurate guess to say they align themselves with nearby white supremacists across the Idaho border. These are people who don't cotton to cops.

In late June 1992, Bob Parcell was called to investigate an assault-with-a-knife complaint in nearby Lake County. He arrived at the scene and talked to the participants until his partner and another deputy arrived. They arrested the assault suspect and learned that they still needed to talk to a potential witness/suspect—the driver of the car the suspect had been riding in earlier. They were told by a deputy who knew him that this person was not a problem case, was very religious, and would tell the truth if contacted.

Bob and his cover units went to this person's house and were told he was not home. The Lake County deputy with the prisoner headed north, and Bob and his partner—in separate patrol cars—headed south. As Bob went down the highway, he saw the vehicle in question pass him going north.

He made a quick U-turn and called on his radio to tell the Lake County deputy he would be making a stop on the car. As soon as Bob hit his overhead lights, the car pulled quickly to the side of the road and the passenger door flew open. A bearded man jumped out of the car and ran east into the darkness of a wooded area.

Bob called for the man to stop and tried to use his flashlight to locate him. It was very dark, windy, cold, and, to make matters worse, raining. As Bob moved quickly into the woods—about 20 feet from the road—he heard a popping sound, which he immediately recognized as gunfire. He pulled his .41 magnum S&W revolver and returned fire, aiming at the suspect's muzzle flashes appearing in the darkness.

Bob knew he was in a bad spot because the glare of the car headlights had silhouetted him for the suspect. He felt a hard thump in the upper left portion of his chest. As he moved to cover he felt another thump in his right hip.

After the suspect fled, Bob made his way back to his car and put out a cover call, telling the dispatcher he was hit. Then, grabbing his shotgun from his car, he "persuaded" the driver of the suspect's car to lie on the ground so he could handcuff him.

The Lake County deputy arrived just then, and Bob exchanged his shotgun for an AR-15 rifle to cover the woods until his own partner arrived. When Bob's patrol partner reached the scene, he asked him to look him over for bullet wounds. His partner lifted up Bob's deputy star and pointed to a hole right under it. The suspect's .41 magnum round had hit Bob directly under his badge and bent it, with the bullet partially entering his chest after being stopped by his body armor.

Bob opened his shirt, reached under his vest, and came out with a handful of blood. With an ambulance en route, Bob sat in his patrol car, had some photos taken of the wound, and recorded a statement about the incident. After a short ambulance ride and a quick helicopter flight, he arrived at the Kalispell Regional Hospital.

Doctors located a round hole in Bob's upper chest 2 to 3 inches deep and 2 1/2 inches in diameter. They closed the wound with stitches, but since it was in such a tough spot, the stitches kept tearing out. He spent two days in the hospital and then changed his own dressing twice a day for the next 10 weeks until the wound finally healed. (The suspect's other round hit Bob in his gun holster and did no physical damage.).

When the suspect, a right-wing fundamentalist Christian who considers himself a "Soldier for Christ," was arrested many months later (another long story as to the delay), he was armed and dangerous and mentally unstable.

One month after the shooting, Bob flew to Michigan to receive a new bulletproof vest from the Second Chance Company. He is their 550th official "save." As a family, we are grateful that Bob is still with us.

This incident contains three important tactical messages:

> *Your physical condition, especially as it relates to your cardiovascular fitness, is paramount to your survival in any high-stress situation.* If you are severely injured, a high level of aerobic conditioning may save your life. A strong heart will beat longer and harder than a weak one. Bob Parcell's story should be all you need to read to motivate yourself to get into and stay in better shape.

> *Adrenaline will keep you alive and help you continue to fight back.* Even though he had been shot twice, Bob was able to keep his mind on police work. He returned fire from a position of cover and then returned to the suspect's vehicle to arrest the driver—by himself. Only after the scene was secure—one in custody, cover units on site, and a broadcast

of the missing suspect out—did Bob stop to evaluate his own wounds.

A gunshot (or any serious wound) is no indication of your imminent death. Many officers (and suspects, unfortunately) have been hit with many bullets and still continued to return fire and, ultimately, survive. Medical studies suggest that if you don't die in the first five or so minutes, you'll survive your wounds—if, and only if, you don't give up the will to live. You can make arrests, protect your partners, and care for other civilians even if you've been hit. As hard as it is to think about, you must not let the presence of your blood stop you from surviving and thriving.

Never, ever give up! Sheer willpower, good cardiovascular conditioning, and the determination to stay alive saved Bob Parcell. He's sort of a hero in our family—a tough, no-nonsense guy with a nose for police work and a will to survive.

Night Work
Darkness Is Your Friend

We're here to contemplate the mysteries of night police work. Since the warming rays of the sun hit us about 12 hours per day, chances are good that if you drive a patrol car year round, some or all of your work life will be spent blinking into the inky depths of nothingness.

Working graveyards or the last hours of second watch means you'll probably spend most of your patrol car time adjusting your eyes from various stages of light to various stages of darkness. How well you do this can affect how safely and efficiently you do your job.

Contrary to what you see in all of those poorly made Hollywood horror movies, the dark is not always so bad. True, some evil types do lurk in the safety of the shadows, but what works for them can work for cops too. They use it to hide; we can use it to hide. They use it to cover their movements; we can use it to cover our movements. And they use it to flee; we can use it to catch them.

The biggest problem surrounding night patrol is that it's not always conducted in the dark. Cops spend their entire shifts going from brightly lit rooms, cars, and streets back into gloomy, dim, or pitch-black locales. In the space of 10 minutes, you can go from a dark police car to a brightly lit convenience store and back again; from a well-lit station house to a dimly lit alley. This constant back-and-forth is tough on your pupils and makes it hard to keep and maintain proper "night vision."

Since we can't always control when, where, and how we encounter light or its absence, we have to make adjustments based on our own physical make-up, genetics, and the environment we encounter. Police work at night demands a tactical look at light, darkness, and the use of either to *your*—not the suspect's—advantage.

If you're blessed with perfect 20-20 peepers, it's certainly much easier for you to see things close up, far away, during daylight, and in the gloom of night. Some of you below-age-30 types can see a weevil sitting on a piece of cotton at 80 paces. Others of us need expensive glasses or contact lenses to read the license plates of the cars directly ahead.

If your parents had sharp eyes, chances are you do to. Strong eyeball genes and plenty of healthy food as a kid probably gave you good night vision and sharp visual acuity at a variety of distances. As one veteran police officer with combat experience has pointed out, "In Vietnam, we could practically walk right up to the enemy at night. Their night vision was very poor because of their dietary deficiencies. Not enough veggies and other eye-healthy foods gave them terrible eyesight at night."

Blindingly bright police flashlights, retina-burning highway flares, and even your patrol car lights, takedown spotlights, and amber or red and blue flashers can seriously affect your night vision. The old trick of shining your lights at an approaching beat partner can put him or her out of commission (eyeball-wise) for the next 10 to 20 minutes. It takes that long for your eyes to adjust to the shock of bright lights and the slow return of gloom.

But just as these things can blind you if you let them, you can also use them to disorient your suspect, keep him off balance, and protect your position.

As an example, light coming from behind you may "silhouette" you to the suspect, but it can also serve to temporarily blind him or tamper with his night vision. While it's certainly true that you should avoid the backlit position whenever possible, if you don't linger in this area too long, you may avoid the consequences. Even if you do get caught in this zone, keep in mind that the suspect has to look hard into bright lights to find you. The time it takes for him to readjust his vision is all the time you need to move to a completely different location.

The trick is to think tactically and make the best of the lighting situation you have. Use the shadows to protect your position and venture out into the available light only when necessary. A SWAT officer puts the "silhouette" idea this way, "Many officers, having the fear of being silhouetted drilled into them by zealous instructors, will go to great lengths to avoid being back-lighted by vehicle headlights. The same officer will then place himself against an off-white wall while checking an alarm call, and never even have it mentally register that he has presented a perfect target."

Good eyesight or not (like when someone has to hold a newspaper up in the other room because you forgot your reading glasses), it is possible to help your eyes see more at night. Here are some suggestions to get you through the night:

- *Get plenty of rest.*
  Try for both sleeping rest and the rest you can give your eyes just by closing them from time to time.

- *Get regular vision checkups.*
  Keep your prescription current and tell your eyecare doctor that you work nights and want the best night vision you can have. He or she may prescribe glasses for you to wear only at night.

- *Avoid glare and eyestrain when you can.*
  Protect your eyes from glare-filled TV sets, computer screens, and other daytime bright lights. Give your eyes a break from reading by looking across the room every few pages.

- *Wear good-quality sunglasses.*
  Buy a good pair with optically correct lenses, because even the minor distortion found in cheap glasses can do more harm to your eyes than good. Invest some money in a pair that will filter out 100 percent of the ultraviolet rays that bombard your eyes. And know that extremely dark sunglasses may be more dangerous than no glasses at all, because the darkening effect will cause your pupils to dilate and allow damaging UV rays to hit the retina.

- *Minimize the use of your flashlight.*
  In all but a few cases, you should be able to use the available "urban glow" around you to see properly. With so much light coming from street lamps, the moon, car headlights, building lights, etc., it doesn't make sense to use your flashlight unless no light exists. Use good judgment, however; don't fall over something just because you don't want to use your flashlight. But on many traffic stops or radio calls, you can rely on the many sources of surrounding light on brightly lit streets to see.

- *Disorient suspects, especially in groups, by "accidentally" sweeping their eyes with your flashlight.*
  We're not out to blind anyone, of course, or scorch their corneas, but if bright lights temporarily ruin your night vision, you can do the same to suspects by making a few passes across their eyeballs as you write your cites or FI slips.

109

- *Avoid the normal human instinct to head for the light when out on foot.*
  Stay in the shadows whenever you can. Walking in the "cones" of light offered by street lamps just makes you a better target. Stay near fences, walls, and buildings where the light is lower.

- *Remember that good crooks almost never use flashlights.*
  Professional burglars don't always rely on flashlights to see; neither should cops. If you have the chance, stand outside your car for a few minutes and let your eyes adjust to the available light before you handle the call. If you have to use your flashlight, keep it in your nongun hand and as far away from your body as is comfortable. No sense giving the bad guys a shiny target to aim for.

- *Instead of picking out the details of specific shapes and forms in the darkness, be alert for movement first.*
  Don't try to focus on specific particulars, colors, or objects. In low light these things are hard to spot. Just be alert for any sense of movement. You'll be able to guess accurately what is moving by looking at the outline of the object. Since there are few six-foot-tall squirrels, you'll know what is human and what is not.

- *Spend just as much time listening for movement as looking for it.*
  Stand still, keep those keys quiet, and just listen for a few minutes. Studies of foot pursuits tell us that the crook hiding in the weeds may know the cops will not spend a significant amount of time looking in one specific area, but rather, making a quick scan and then moving on. In night searches, take up a good, safe observation position and sit for minute, watching, waiting, and listening for movement. You may just hear your hood come crashing out of the bushes the minute he thinks the coast is clear.

- *Don't look directly at approaching car headlights.*
  It's hard to avoid this habit, but even a brief glimpse at a bright passing car's headhights can throw your night vision out of whack. Passing thousands of cars over a long shift can force your eyes to constantly adjust. Shift your attention to the side of the windshield area instead or look just above the top of an approaching car.

- *Choose areas to walk through that have less light rather than more.*
  Get comfortable with the shadows and with the smallest amount of light you can operate in safely. Noisy gun belt attachments and shiny metal gear make for an inviting bullet-stopper. Don't expose your position just because

you want to feel more secure in the light. Darkness will save you more times than light. They can't hit what they can't find.

- *Monitor your use of light inside your car.*
  Try to use the smallest amount of interior light, especially when you write reports. The combination of the paper glare and the bright lights that seem so popular in police cars can ruin your night vision for a long time. Use outside lighting to help you see inside the car and avoid the collection of too-bright interior dome lights.

- *Close one eye as you go to a scene where good night vision is important.*
  This sounds dopey, but it really works. You can trick your pupils into cooperating and speed your night vision along. The next time you have to walk from a brightly lit area into a dark one—e.g., from the street into a bar—keep your "strong" eye closed and squint slightly as you approach. You'll make the adjustment into "night vision" much faster.

- *Use all of the natural and manmade sources of light whenever possible.*
  Put away that flashlight and start relying more on what's around you: the moon, the light reflected from low clouds onto the street, streetlights, window light, building lights, car lights, passing headlights, other officers' lights and flashlights, and so on.

- *Don't take your need for visibility for granted, ever.*
  Light-poor and low-visibility blues put you at greater risk of being hit by cars. During after-dark traffic stops, especially on the freeway, your blue uniform just about disappears from a distance. This is no startling realization. Every cop out at night knows that blue is less visible than nearly every other color. The problem comes when this realization slips out of your mind for that brief split-second it takes you to walk too close to a traffic lane or fail to put a solid barrier between you and an approaching drunk driver.
  For every nighttime tactical advantage we acquire on radio call and hot crime approaches (the ability to snoop around without being spotted), we lose visibility when we may need it most, e.g., on extended traffic posts, while measuring skids or collecting evidence in the street, during freeway stops where there's no guardrail to stand behind, on alley FI stops, while crossing streets or parking lots, and so on. While we all know that too many people drive around in daylight deep in Condition White or under some type of chemical impairment, at night the numbers of these potential cop-injurers (or worse) grows exponentially.

The point to all this is simple and singular: Don't ever take your visibility, or the lack of it, for granted. Never make the assumption that the cars passing your position or nearing it will see you without help.

- *Heighten your visibility.*
The ways to make yourself more visible are limited only by your imagination, good officer safety sense, and the tactical demands of the situation. This could include steps like waggling your lit flashlight at approaching traffic behind you as you approach a car, contacting all drivers from the passenger-side window, illuminating your fixed traffic position with a pile of flares, or, my favorite idea, buying one of those DayGlo orange and yellow fishnet vests that says "POLICE" across it and putting it on every time you will be in one place at night where people need to see you first and fast.

Be tactically creative but be visible. Use the light around you—from streetlights, headlights, flashlights, and building lights—or the barriers around you—curbs, metal or concrete guardrails or medians, your or other cars, or any other fixed, heavy car blocker that will help keep one and one-half tons of metal off any portion of your body.

When you are in uniform and out at night, you are a target, more from steel cars than steel bullets. Get and stay visible. Don't assume any driver, who may be spilling a beer, lighting a cigarette, looking at a map, or dozing off, will see any part of the blue you.

As one night watch officer says, "Night vision is a tool, just like your handcuffs, your flashlight, and your handgun. The only difference is it's built-in. The fact that it's there all the time leads to taking it for granted, abusing it, and failing to maintain it appreciatively. Treat it well—maximize it—and it will pay better dividends than your insurance policy."

Working at night demands extra vigilance. The "playing field" is not the same at zero-dark-thirty as it is at oh-bright thirty. Protect your eyes, treasure your night vision, and use your knowledge of light and its absence to stay one or two jumps ahead of the enemy.

Officer Safety Starts at Home

In the field, we're careful to lock our patrol cars to keep prying eyes and hands off our personal and police belongings. Any officer with more than six months in the field has "lost" at least one pair of sunglasses, a baton, a ticket book, a jacket, or a lunch box cooler from his or her police car. Notwithstanding those items that disappear as a result of our own carelessness, or because other officers have "borrowed" them and failed to put them back, there is the usual possibility that a party or parties unknown have made off with some police stuff just for the sport of it.

From a public and police safety perspective, losing sunglasses to a crook is one thing; losing a shotgun, a backup gun, or police-related keys is quite another. Depending on where you work, it's easy to get into the habit of leaving your patrol car unlocked for "just a minute" while you go off and do police work or buy a cup of coffee. Since we know out of sight is out of mind, it only takes a fraction of a minute for a smart crook to steal your briefcase or, if he has real nerve, to pop open your trunk and really go to town. This is especially true in parts of our city where we are less than popular or during crowd situations where many police cars are left unattended while we jump into a fray.

And while we would not think of storing our gun, gun belt, or vest in the backseat of our patrol car, at home we make certain assumptions that it's safe to leave these tools of the trade either in plain sight or in a convenient closet. As an example of a disturbing trend, a North Carolina police officer's home was burglarized, and the thief or thieves took his body armor, duty gun, handcuffs, pepper spray, station/police car keys, and uniform shirts. A sheriff's deputy in Florida suffered a similar burglary when a 13-year-old crook stole

113

his vest from his home. He sold it to another teen at his school, and it was swapped or sold several times before an adult recovered it and returned it to the deputy. The point of these cases is short and blunt: store your police gear at your station in a locked locker. If you must bring it home, don't just toss it in your bedroom closet.

It's not difficult for your neighbors to discover one way or another that you work in law enforcement. The more this information makes the rounds between homes or apartments near yours, the better chance it will reach the ears of a current or future burglar. Even the dumbest thief can do the math and assume that a police officer will have at least one to two guns at home and be gone during some 8- to 12-hour period of any 24-hour day. And if the officer has a marked take-home car—as may be common with some agencies in your county or state—it's easy to guess when he or she is home or at work. When the cat's away, here come the mice with their pry tools and pillowcases. At a minimum, a burglar hitting a cop's residence might retrieve a back-up gun, ammunition, uniform shirts, station keys, or personal information or proprietary police data that could cause some significant damage later. In the worst case, the crook who gets your duty gun, belt, vest, uniforms, and badge has just turned himself into an excellent carjacker.

Most patrol officers leave their gear safely stored in station lockers, but what about those times when they change divisions or assignments, take their equipment home for polishing or cleaning, or change to a detective assignment and leave vests/uniforms in their closets? Old habits are hard to break. If you've always come home and put your gun on top of the refrigerator (with no kids in the house, of course), then it's tough to hide it in a place where you might forget it in a rush to get to work. Too bad, but it's not safe. If you must keep police gear at home, start putting all your valuable equipment (gun, uniforms, vest, and actual or flat badges, etc.) into safe, well-hidden, protected places. For their guns, badges, and pepper spray, some officers use a closet with a solid-core door and a dead bolt, an above-ground floor safe in their closets, a standing gun safe, or, in the best case, a rifle safe, which offers plenty of vertical room. Barring the use of a safe, find a place that the average crook with time on his hands wouldn't find without a hard, disruptive search of the other-than-usual places.

Don't forget that just because your uniforms are in the care of your favorite local dry cleaning shop, they are not safe from theft. As the Rodney King riots proved, real crooks know that a brick bounced off the shop window will give them a selection of uniforms from nearly every city, county, or state law enforcement agency. Keep your uniforms locked up at work, not hanging for days at the cleaners. Not to be paranoid, but the longer they are off your back or out of your control, the better chance they have of being stolen or permanently "misplaced." Officers or deputies who hang clean uniforms in their personal cars or toss dirty ones onto the backseat for cleaning and then leave their cars alone are only asking for a window smash.

It may seem like a hassle to put a double-throw dead bolt on one of your closets, but if you keep police equipment at home, it's time to give more thought to protecting it from those opportunistic types who either know or will soon discover what it is you do for a living.

On Stage at the Guerrilla Theater

The scene is a high school. Two creepy-looking characters loiter in the parking lot with drugs and the sale, purchase, and consumption of same on their minds. A lone male figure approaches them. He is dressed in a long army-green trench coat that nearly touches his knees. He is wearing black combat boots, dark blue pants, and dark sunglasses. The coat is wrapped tightly around him, and his hands are in his pockets.

He approaches said dope aficionados, and a conversation ensues about how he is looking for some recreational medicinal products if they are in the market to sell him some. Being true-spirited entrepreneurs, the sellers agree and certain usable quantities of narcotics appear in the sunlight. Suddenly, the buyer whips off his green coat to reveal a full police uniform, including gun belt, badge, dark blue shirt, and vest. He swiftly removes two pairs of handcuffs and within seconds, two forlorn-looking dopers are being marched back to his marked police car, parked just around the corner.

As the scene closes, shouts of, "That's not fair!" and "Aw, man! This is bogus!" fill the air. Fade out.

True story? Yes. Legal? Perfectly. Good police work? Of course. This episode should demonstrate two things to you: there is lots of room for creativity in policing, and you don't always have to follow the "Patrol Theory Rule Book."

It offers an example of a smart-thinking, hard-working patrol copper who saw a drug problem on a high school campus on his beat and decided to do something about it. Just as it's legal (and devious) to say, "Pizza delivery!" when you're trying to get some crooks to open their doors, you can go "under-

117

cover," as this officer demonstrated, without changing a stitch of your normal uniform. And speaking of rules, take your example from street hoods; they don't follow the rules too often, so, in our attempt to get our hands on them, why should we?

Smart veteran cops have often said that all of street policing is like urban guerrilla theater. The bad guys act out their parts, and we act out ours. The only difference is that they have a lot more latitude to do what they want, dress how they want, and invent their own script as they go along.

If I was in charge of the police academy (a frightening thought, I'll admit) I would put more emphasis on the creative side of role playing. Most new cops are trained to stay within the lines and not deviate from proven policies or procedures, and they don't know how or when to bend the envelope when it comes to creative ways to get people into cuffs. It's only after they get out on the streets that they realize the world is *not* an orderly place. People don't always act the way we expect them to or, worse, the way we want them to.

The traffic offender who pulls to the left side of the road, gets out of his car into the middle of traffic and starts back to your driver's window has just thrown your traffic stops rule book into the dirt.

And to continue that thought, when was the last time you had a highly abusive motorist threaten to fight you as you tried to write him a ticket? Depending on where you work, it may happen often or never. The point is, we can fall into a routine where we *assume* people will do what we tell them or what we expect. When they take us out of our respective comfort zone (i.e., stop car, contact driver, write ticket, have driver sign ticket, leave), then we can get too rattled to think quickly, thereby giving them an immediate tactical advantage.

Here's a good cop story that demonstrates the psychological principle known as "thought stopping." As a veteran officer approached a car on a traffic stop, a large and obviously enraged driver jumped out of his car, ran up to him and screamed, "I'm gonna kick your ass!"

In a split second, the cop countered with, "Hey! It's a good thing I'm into that!" The guy looked at him blankly for long enough for Greg to step back, get some help, and handle him safely and swiftly. That's a good example of changing someone's pattern; that is, altering his or her preprogrammed behavior with some new data. The irate driver was all set for a fight. When the officer responded with a statement that implied he got pleasure out of fighting, the guy was thrown for a loop. He didn't know how to respond, and often, that gives us enough time to counterattack.

I'm reminded of scenes from two Hollywood movies, which illustrate the power of role-playing, acting, and changing people's patterns. One is the 1981

Paul Newman-Ken Wahl NYPD film *Fort Apache, The Bronx*, and the other is the 1972 Joe Wambaugh film *The New Centurions*, with Stacy Keach and George C. Scott.

In the first movie, Paul Newman and his partner are in uniform when they come across a crazy man armed with a knife. While Ken Wahl keeps the guy at bay with his firearm, Newman, who plays a wily old veteran officer, decides to out-crazy the crazy man. He turns his police hat around sideways, sticks his tongue out, and starts dancing around like a lunatic. You can see the feeble thought processes going on inside the suspect's head: "Hey! *I'm* the one who's supposed to be nuts! What's going on here? Why is this cop acting crazier than I am?"

The guy was so thrown off by what he was seeing (in effect, having his pattern changed by Newman) that he gave up. After a gentle smothering by blue-shirted bodies, he went off to jail, still confused as to who was saner, him or Paul.

While I'm clearly not advocating this as a textbook way to handle knife-wielding suspects, it makes a point: Crooks expect the cops to act a certain way or respond to *their* actions in certain ways. When we don't, they get terribly confused, which can give us the psychological and physical upper hand.

In the Wambaugh film, Stacy Keach and his patrol partner (George C. Scott) have stopped an angry (and large) Roger E. Mosley (who later played helicopter pilot T.C. in the *Magnum P.I.* TV series). Informed by Keach that he was under arrest for several traffic warrants, Mosley said, "I'm not going." Keach calmly (and that's the key) walked back to his patrol car, and in a loud voice, told his dispatcher that he needed an ambulance at his location. Surprised, Mosley looks around and said, "What do you need an ambulance for? There's nobody hurt around here."

Keach smiled and said, "There will be if you don't get into the back of my police car." Mosley looked hard at Keach and Scott, realized he was all done for the day, and headed for the car. As they drove to jail, George C. Scott said, "You'd better cancel that ambulance." To which Keach replied, "What ambulance? I never called for an ambulance."

By this time, Roger Mosely knew he'd been bluffed (and bluffed well). He smiled and said, "Man! This is the first time I've ever laughed on the way to jail!"

Where is the old "phantom ambulance" ruse written in the patrol rule book? I've looked; it ain't there. But just as every season the ol' hidden baseball trick works to pick off at least one unsuspecting runner at first base, this one will work for some unsuspecting suspect.

Law enforcement is one of the few professions left where the employees have lots and lots of latitude to do their tasks in ways that will solve their problems. We get to make all kinds of choices in the field: arrest, don't arrest, cite, don't cite, fight, or don't fight. Why not think of some ways to do these things that call for a little acting ability?

LEARN TO ROLE PLAY BASED ON THE SITUATION

Sometimes you need to act like John Wayne (or Jane Wayne); sometimes you may need to act like Mr. or Ms. Friendly. Dealing with children frequently calls for you to play roles; that is, innocent, lost kids get one face from you, murderous 14-year-old stickup artists get another. If you have to tell some lies to defuse dangerous situations, try it. You might need to wholeheartedly agree with an enraged wife-beater, right up until the moment when the last handcuff click locks his wrists into place. Start talking and see what part you need to play to solve the problem. It could be tough cop or nice one, crazy cop or sane one.

TRY BEING A LITTLE CRAZY

And speaking of crazy, we talk to plenty of people whom life did not equip for the struggle. Emotionally disturbed persons (EDPs, to coin the latest politically correct phrase) have their own agendas, their own ideas about what's right or wrong, and their own thoughts on their place in the world. Sometimes you need to interrupt their disturbed thought patterns with a story of your own; sometimes you may need to start talking about complete and utter nonsense just to get them distracted enough to handcuff safely, and sometimes you may need to have them believe *they're* totally sane and *you're* totally crazy.

Some officers have become quite skilled at playing the role of the "street psychiatrist." They can talk to EDPs about their medicines, their treatments, what hospitals they have been to, and so on, in an effort to make the EDP feel as if the officer understands what the EDP has gone through in his or her life. Some officers will sit or squat right down next to a disturbed person (with good cover and officer safety in mind, of course), so as to present a more non-threatening, understanding posture. Anything you can do to safely dissolve their anger or lower their emotions is good for everybody concerned.

BE CREATIVE BUT SAFE

Like the uniformed officer in the trench coat, think about the ways you could blend in with the crowd and approach different scenes in safe tactical ways. Who says you can't wear your police windbreaker inside-out, so the patches don't show, so you can walk right up to dark-alley suspects at night? I've heard and seen episodes where officers borrowed citizens' bikes to ride up on crooks, and I know cops who used the pager and telephone booth numbers of dope salesmen to set up their own buy-bust deals with them. These officers have used some ingenuity and lots of creativity to get good results.

You can play different parts, act out different roles, bend the reality envelope, and still stay within the boundaries of good officer safety and tactics. Keep the limits of good cover and concealment in mind, as well as the need to practice CONTACT & COVER whenever necessary. Balance your creativity and the need for peace or aggression with the availability of close cover units. There's smart bravery and dumb bravery, real courage and tombstone courage. If there are 23 of them and two of you and every cover unit is 46 miles away across town, it's important to know when discretion is the better part of valor. It's always easier to go out on a limb and try a little role-playing if you have extra friends in the room or on the way.

NEVER LET THEM SEE YOU SWEAT

The more tense it gets, the cooler you should get, at least on the outside. You can be shaking like a leaf inside—that's perfectly normal in scary situations—but you have to learn to present yourself in a way that looks like this is just another day in the park for you. I'm reminded of a call where I covered another officer for a fight at a recreation center basketball game. We arrived to find the players ready to square off with the rec center manager, a guy with a large mouth and a small everything else. As we tried to sort it out, the crowd grew to include many police-unfriendly types who mistakenly believed we sided with the rec center guy. My partner got everyone separated into two sides of the parking lot, while I sent the rec center manager back inside. As I returned to the crowd, I heard my partner say, as he pointed to the departing rec center manager, "What's with Mr. Hitler over there?" Instantly, the group cracked up and even the most antipolice guys smiled. My partner defused a potentially violent situation by thinking outside the box.

Police writer James P. Weiss says that fear is natural and in some cases healthy, because it can serve as the foundation for action, courage, and self-protection. However, he says, "the fears and self-doubts must be turned to self-assurance and a mind-set for positive action. Such training is a step-by-step hardening process."[1] We have all been in situations where we were shaking in our boots, maybe a little, maybe a lot. Good officers know how to manage, control, and then overcome those fears.

Two-legged street lizards, like all true animals in nature, can see and even smell fear in the cops they encounter. You need to harden your personal self and make them think you are positively fearless. This takes practice and a strong sense of self-confidence that says, "I'm a well-trained, well-armed professional law enforcement officer. I will survive any situation I encounter."

Use body language to send off signals that say, "I'm experienced, ready to do battle, in control, and don't know the meaning of the word 'fear.'" People who do brave things, especially in combat or other violent situations, often exhibit a sense of unswerving determination. It's as almost as if they feel unstoppable. They will not be denied the opportunity to persevere and win. Body language, or how you hold your physical self, plays a big part in this. You must be able to radiate an air that tells crooks you are brimming with confidence, authority, and command presence. They're sizing us up all the time; the officers who do well in the streets are filled with so much command presence (and it often has nothing to do with physical size, although it certainly helps) that the bad guys think to themselves, "Uh oh, better not mess with this cop."

TALK, TALK, TALK, TALK, TALK

I know few successful police officers who do not have the gift of gab. Even if they are not normally talkative by nature, working in law enforcement has taught them how to talk—to all kinds of people in all kinds of situations. They can work their way out of rooms full of angry gang members just as easily as they can work their way into rooms of reluctant victims, hostile witnesses, or disturbed suspects. And as you'll notice from your Use of Force Policy/Continuum, your skillful use of words can serve as one of your most powerful weapons. It's always easier to talk first and fight or shoot later.

* * * * *

While you don't need to go out and invest in tubes of greasepaint, fake wigs, or other tools of the acting trade, start thinking about the roles you play now in the streets and the roles you *could* play to make your job easier and safer.

Notes

1.   Weiss, James P., "Fear: Perspectives for the Police," *Law and Order* (September 1994).

Patrol Car Seat Belts
A Real Officer Safety Issue

Do you ride around in your personal car without wearing your seat belt? "Of course not," you say quickly, "That would be dangerous!" So why do you ride around in your police car unbelted? Those of you who do this know who you are.

Why the double standard? Is there any difference between your personal car and your police car? Well, maybe yes, but mostly no. Before I begin any literary finger-pointing, I should preface my remarks with that old biblical standby, "Let he who is without sin cast the first stone."

I'll be the first to admit that the patrol car seat belt habit was a hard one for me to acquire. Over the years, I seemed to go through phases where I would buckle up in a police unit religiously, then other times where I just flat out didn't do it. I suppose it was a lot like flossing your teeth—some days you did, and some days you didn't. The excuses for both are similar: "I can't be bothered with that right now. I'll do it next time." But when the dentist peers inside your mouth and takes a mini pick ax to your pearlies, you tend to get the flossing fever right quick. Nothing like the sound of high-speed drilling to make you a convert.

And so it goes—at least for me—with police car seat belts. Weeks and months would go by without incident, and then I would get involved in a particularly hairy pursuit or hear about a nasty police car crash—complete with 8-by-10 glossies mounted on the lineup room door—and become a seat belt convert once again. I also suppose that the arrival of my daughter has also hastened my desire to belt up. No man wants Mommy to have to say, "And this is a picture of Daddy before he put his head through the windshield."

If you took a random poll of cops across the land, I'm sure the litany of anti-seat belt excuses would be the same: "Oh yeah, of course I wear it in my personal car, but I don't like feeling confined in a police car. I may have to get out right away, and that extra time I spend unbuckling my belt could cost me my life in an ambush." Or, "I hate the way the police car belt gets tied up with my equipment. It always seems to get wrapped around my holster, or my radio, or underneath my ammo magazines. Worse yet, when I have the dang thing on and I forget about it, every time I go to bail out of the car I practically tear my legs off." Or, "I don't like the way the belts are designed. No matter how I wear them, they always seem to rub my neck, strangle my chest, or pinch my waist. I don't want to be bothered by them."

Are these valid excuses? To a small extent, yes. Police equipment around your waist and car seat belts don't, in fact, go together well. But can you balance some initial discomfort with a lifetime of pain and suffering?

Some officers still say, "I only put my belt on if I'm in a pursuit or on the freeway." But why force yourself to focus on one more distraction during a highly stressful episode? Isn't it easier to train yourself to wear your seat belt any time you're in a police unit? The old "can't bail out, I'm stuck to my equipment" controversy remains, but you'll just have to do your best to minimize it.

If you can make comfort adjustments in the seat belt system in whatever patrol car model you drive, do it. Don't sacrifice safety for comfort, stylishness (who cares about wrinkled uniforms?), or misplaced machismo (e.g., "I don't get in car accidents, other people do.") As to the latter, well, those people who do get in accidents may find your car first, out of the thousands on the road to hit.

Still, no matter what the facts say, what your department policy says, or what your personal experience says, some officers still feel wearing a seat belt is a matter of personal choice. Many still say, "I feel like I couldn't get out of the car in a hurry if I had to. I don't feel safe." But to be safe in the police car and to be safe in the police car during a crash is not always the same. A 13-year study conducted by the International Association of Chiefs of Police (IACP) looked at the deaths of Maryland law enforcement officers from 1976 to 1989. The results revealed that 506 officers were killed in traffic accidents, which was one-quarter of total police deaths in the state, second only to deaths by gunshot. According to other IACP studies, city and county law enforcement officers are more than 10 times more likely to be involved in a car crash than someone from the general public. And more than 25 percent of all police crashes result in an average of 23 lost work days due to injuries.

In an article in *9-1-1 Magazine* on this subject, Brookhaven, Pennsylvania, Police Chief John Eller drove the seat belt safety point home: "Many law enforcement officers have numerous reasons why they feel they don't have to wear a seat belt, such as, 'I don't drive fast on routine patrol.'" Even if this were true, and we all know it's not, Eller cautions that speed is not the issue. "A crash at 30 miles per hour is like falling off a three-story building."

In response to the other popular excuse of, "It takes too long to buckle and unbuckle my belt," Chief Eller asks, "Is three seconds worth the time and effort to save your life?"

So here's what we already know about seat belts, car crashes, injuries, and deaths:

- Drivers wearing seat belts have better control of their cars because they can hang onto the steering wheel during severe movements or changes in direction.
- An unbelted driver involved in a crash at speeds as slow as 12 miles per hour can still be killed.
- You are 25 times more likely to be killed if you're not wearing a seat belt and get ejected from your car.
- The old maxim, "If I wear my belt I'll be trapped in the car if it catches on fire or goes into the water" is a fairy tale. Car fires or submersion in water occur in less than 1 percent of all accidents. And if you're unbelted and knocked unconscious, you couldn't get out of the car if it was on fire or in the water anyway.
- Lame ideas like "In a crash, I'll just hold on tightly to the steering wheel" offer little protection either. Acceleration-of-mass studies demonstrate that the force of an auto accident can generate well over 1,000 pounds of force against your arms and torso. So unless you can bench press half a ton, buckle up.
- Transportation studies show that seat belts can reduce the type or severity of car-crash injuries by 50 percent.

Frankly, some officers you know would not be on the planet today if they had not been wearing seat belts during their own police car crashes. And what about your agency? What is the policy on seat belts? I'm guessing it reads that you will wear them, no ifs, ands, or buts. Lots of officers allude to long-standing rumors in their cities and counties that suggest their agencies won't pay for their medical bills if they're involved in an unbelted on-duty car accident. This fear can lead to any number of lies that get told to a Traffic Investigations Unit officer or detective (e.g., "Of course I was wearing my seat belt! How could you say such a thing?") Here, the outraged officer is holding an ice pack to the bump on his head that neatly matches the cracked windshield found on the inside of his patrol car. In many agencies, you're entitled to medical bill coverage, but you may not be entitled to long-term disability coverage if you cannot work after the crash.

I suppose some of the seat belt apathy on police departments comes from both early training and peer pressure. If you hearken back to your phase training days, how many of you can honestly say you saw your training officer buckle up on your first ride? We learn by example and by exposure to others. Chances are probably good that if you saw other officers not bothering to snap on a seat belt you didn't bother with one either.

So why not set an example for other officers you ride with? Who cares if seat belts don't look macho? It's your life. The only difference between a police unit and a regular passenger car in a crash is the paint job. Just because we have lights and sirens doesn't mean we have some kind of crash-free immunity from harm every time we get behind the wheel.

With your bullet-proof vest, driver's side airbag, and a seat belt used in conjunction, you may be able to walk away from a horrific car crash in one piece.

The choice is yours. Look hard at the facts, then buckle up.

Phantom Crimes
False Victimization Syndrome

The scene is a familiar one. You arrive at a minor-injury accident to find the usual pairing of crumpled cars and disgruntled motorists. You take the requisite information from both parties and transfer it to your traffic accident forms.

Once you've inquired as to the possible medical needs of the injured, paced or measured off the initial contact points, and documented the damage with a few pen marks on the report (that is, colored in the rear bumper panel on the crashee's car and colored in the front bumper panel on the crasher's car), it's time to leave the scene to find a quiet spot to finish your paperwork before the end of shift.

Now let us fast-forward six to eight months. You receive a call from Party Two, or his or her personal injury attorney or insurance agency investigator. This person provides copious details about how the car actually has a bent frame, a bent axle, or was so badly scarred in the crash that it is virtually or actually undriveable.

Further, the driver's "complaint of neck pain" at the time of the crash has now become an excruciatingly painful upper, middle, and low-back injury that has made it impossible to work, eat with silverware, or walk completely upright.

The aforementioned party or parties on the telephone begin to quiz you as to why you didn't "accurately document" said vehicle damage and said traumatic injuries.

* * * * *

New case, different day. Now let us suppose that you are called to take a daylight burglary report at a home where the owner tells you he "just went to the store for a minute" and left his garage door open and his inside house door unlocked. When he returned to his unprotected property, he found his new quad-runner, weeks-old mountain bike, video camera and matching VCR, grandfather's Rolex, prized hunting shotgun (the one with the inlaid silver stock), and commercial-grade espresso-making machine missing.

Your witness check of the area reveals that most of his neighbors were either not home, or those that answered your knock did not see or hear anything amiss.

In other words, no one saw a flatbed truck, a moving van, or a team of burglars driving a fleet of U-Hauls pull up to the guy's house. Upon inspection of the home and grounds, you see no signs of forced entry, footprints, stray cigarettes, pry marks, or fingerprints. As you complete your report at the scene, you ask the homeowner if any other property is missing, only to hear him say, "Well, I haven't checked on my collection of rare stamps or coins from ancient Greece. Can I have an extra of my property loss report form so I can inventory the contents?"

Heading back to your patrol car, you think about the narrative for your report and wonder what you will write. A month later, you receive a call from the property owner's insurance adjuster, questioning the validity of your report. Your response begins with the words, "Uh, tell me which case this was again, please?"

* * * * *

Late one evening, you respond to a call of a disturbance at a popular bar. You arrive to find a sea of people, loud electric guitar sounds, and an angry woman standing near the entrance. She tells you that a certain male patron— being held not too gingerly by the boulder-biceped bouncers—put his hands on her body in a highly inappropriate manner. This incident took place in the parking lot of the establishment, in an area near both her car and the suspect's camper-shell-covered truck.

You speak with her at some length, asking her about any injuries, bruises, bite marks, torn clothing, and so on. She admits no injuries, but says that he put his hands on her chest and hips in a very offensive and suggestive way. She wants him arrested for sexual battery, as she thinks he reached under her clothing at least once.

For his part, the suspect admits he did touch the victim in ways she described, but it was with her complete and total consent. He never made "skin to skin" contact with her in any fashion and since both parties had "a bit too much to drink," perhaps the whole thing has been taken out of context. You speak with the outside doormen, the parking lot security guard, and some patrons whose cars are parked nearby. They all agree they saw this man and woman standing together near their cars, but didn't see anything out of the ordinary until the police arrived. Based on her information, you place the suspect under citizen's arrest for sexual battery and take him from the scene.

Eighteen months later, you receive a subpoena from the victim's attorney to testify at a deposition hearing for her pending civil trial. It seems that on the night in question, she was actually raped by the suspect in the bed of his truck, and she is now suing the bar owners, the security firm working the doors and the parking lot, and the suspect for injuries and pain caused by his attack.

Pulling your report, you see no signs that any such sexual assault ever occurred. Over the telephone, the victim's attorney explains that she has repressed the memories of the incident and, due to its violence and severity, is now suffering from Post-Traumatic Stress Disorder. At deposition, attorneys for both sides will want to know why you didn't offer to take the victim to a hospital for a sexual assault exam.

* * * * *

The good news is that each of these after-the-fact incidents comes from the deep recesses of my overly vivid imagination. The bad news is that each is based upon similar incidents that have confronted police officers in the field. The first scenario involving the traffic accident is ripe for questionable conduct among all parties concerned. It's far from uncommon for people involved in rear-ender accidents to try to get the other party's insurance company to fix every dent, scratch, or scrape on the car, whether it was related to the accident or not. Perhaps you have spoken to people who point out *two* nearby sets of fresh damage to their cars from separate crashes weeks, months, or years apart, and who say they plan to get the other side's insurance company to pay for both repairs. While you don't have to make a scratch-by-scratch inventory in your report, make sure you pinpoint what you perceive to be the damage caused by the current crash and note older damage accordingly. Most officers develop this habit while filling out the impound reports on towed cars. It only takes one complaint from a driver who says that the tow truck driver tore off his front bumper while moving the car to make officers more vigilant when documenting existing damage before the car is taken away. Don't just color in the vehicle diagram; add a few descriptive sentences such as, "Car is currently missing its Mercedes-Benz hood ornament," and so on.

The burglary with the high-dollar losses presents myriad problems. On the one hand, it might be perfectly possible and absolutely true that these items were swiped in the burglary in question. But to discount the possibility of an insurance scam is to ignore certain facts. Are the elements of the crime of burglary evident in the case? Is there any bona fide physical evidence to corroborate the victim's story? And does the evidence at hand match the victim's version? For instance, do you find broken window glass *outside* the home, indicating the "burglar" broke it from inside the home?

Are there any independent witnesses who can corroborate first, the existence of any or all of the goods allegedly stolen, and second, that the crime might have or have not taken place? Statements from neighbors like, "I never saw Jim with any quad runner" or "he sold that mountain bike at his yard sale last summer," or "his garage door has been closed and locked all day," should raise appropriate doubts in your mind.

Careful questioning of the burglary victim on your part can help him or her "suddenly remember" that the stolen bike was in fact sold last summer, and that the Rolex is safely stored away at the bank.

In cases like these, where you just aren't sure, go ahead and take the report, but attach an interoffice memo to your area station detective, and use that format to express your doubts. And in cases where the loss doesn't seem to match the circumstances or the victim, consider calling a detective to the scene for his or her evaluation.

Lastly, the rape accusation presents an even tougher problem because it brings the emotionality of a sex crime to a scene where the actions of both parties can cause much doubt later in time. In these "he said-she said" cases, the responding officers must make careful, critical observations—in their minds, on notebook pages, and later on the final report—of the victim and suspect's demeanor, overall physical appearance, emotional state, relative sobriety, English-language skills, mutual history with each other (if any), and desired level of cooperation.

In these kinds of cases, which mix the real possibility of an actual sexual assault with the other real possibility of a plaintiff's lawsuit, officers must take great care to capture the visual portrait of the setting (lighting, weather conditions, surfaces, vehicles, locked or unlocked doors, etc.), the victim, the suspect, and the totality of the alleged crime scene.

For a case similar to the sexual battery scenario, your report should include your evaluation of the victim and suspect's demeanor, for example, "She appeared calm, lucid, and sober," or "She was crying hysterically, talking about how she couldn't tell anyone what just happened," or "He admitted to drinking five beers in a two-hour period." The victim or suspect's appearance might show torn clothing, undergarments, blood stains, scratches, bites, or bruises, disheveled hair or makeup, or you might not see any of these telltale signs of a struggle.

The setting is important as well: What is on the ground around them? Clothing? Beer bottles? A condom packet? Muddy footprints? A purse with its contents spilled out?

Always ask (and note in your report that you asked) the victim if she has covered injuries, no matter how slight; clothes torn from the inside; hidden bumps, cuts, or bruises; or any need of medical attention, up to and including paramedics' response or a trip to an emergency room for a full examination.

Make sure you speak to the victim and suspect (if still on-scene) away from other people, so that each can make statements to you in privacy. Ask the victim if there is anything she needs or wants to tell you about what happened and note her answers in your report. And in the mirror image of this, extract as much information as possible from the (admonished) suspect. His full statements in your report will either support or attack his story and will help to repaint the picture that was this crime scene months or even years later.

All of the above does not mean to suggest every car accident victim stretches the truth, fakes injuries, or wants to scam an insurance agency. Nor does it imply that every burglary victim is out to file a false claim for nonexistent stolen property. And it is not meant to demean the real and horrifying sexual assaults of victims who do indeed suppress their stories out of shame, stress, embarrassment, humiliation, or fear of further retaliation. These real events happen to people every day. However, we also should know that for some people with situational ethics and a strong need for cash, the "truth" often comes in various shapes and sizes.

Ask probing questions to determine what, if any, crime took place, make careful and legible field notes, date and keep your notebooks in a safe and dry place, and always keep this thought in the back of your mind: "Someday, I may see this situation and these people again, and I will need to recreate what is going on in front of me right now."

Playing the Numbers Game
Social Security as ID

Police work dwells in a world of numbers. We find them everywhere—on street signs and houses; in our penal and vehicle codes; in our reports, citations, and field interviews; and in our heads. And don't forget our wallets; besides credit cards and all the other flotsam and jetsam we carry around with us, one equally important set of numbers appears in the form of our Social Security number (SSN).

If our eyes are the windows to our souls, then our Social Security numbers are the gateways to every other part of our lives. Want a new car loan? Break out your number. Want a new credit card? Offer up your number. Need to check the balance of your checking account using your bank's automated telephone system? Better know your number by heart.

In short, most things related to money or other personal assets—either getting some or keeping what's yours, you'll need to have and know your Social Security number. Not surprisingly, the access power related to these nine little digits is not lost on our criminal population. Many skilled crooks who use keypads or keyboards instead of guns say, "Give me a person's Social Security number and I can take over his or her whole life."

Much of the fraud, embezzlement, misrepresentation, and theft of financial information that occurs starts when a crook steals a number from some unsuspecting person who either gives it up willingly, prints it on publicly read documents or mail, or otherwise makes it too easy by failing to recognize the SSN as being as valuable as a diamond.

And since we use the SSN as an identifier, it's a common denominator on many police forms, is included on our reports and FI slips, and is in our county and national criminal record computer systems. Even the dumb crooks know their SSN follows them around on a variety of documents that flow through the criminal justice system. And because there are nine numbers, it's easy for one or more of them to get transposed, dropped, or otherwise misplaced so that the real SSN suddenly loses its value as an information-gathering tool.

The best crooks can tie cops in knots, using different but similar versions of SSNs each time they're stopped or arrested by different officers. Mix this with different first, middle, and last names, convoluted birthdates, and bad addresses, and we can easily start the "name game" off on a bad foot.

One thing we know about criminals who have managed to fool us in the past is that while they may be able to feed us a line about names and numbers, they can't fake their fingerprints. So while their words may lie, their lines, loops, and whorls (fingerprint jargon) cannot. Any version of the name game with an arrested suspect should start you on the short path from the back of the police car right over to the fingerprint rolling pad and then into your state's or the national system.

But while you wait for the prints to come back to turn John Doe into a show contributor on "America's Most Wanted," why not have some fun with the numbers he gives you? Being a little smarter than the average bear requires you to know certain carved-in-stone facts about our Social Security system. With a few simple parameters in mind, you can quiz Mr. SmoothTongue until he trips himself up.

Start by recalling that the nine SS numbers are issued to fit a somewhat geographic orientation. Since most people get their SSN near either the time or place of their birth or near the time or city of their first paying jobs, the number given relates to the state of issuance. Therefore, to look at an easy example, if a suspect says he was born in California and received his SSN there, and yet gives you a number not in the California range (545-573 or 602-626), you know he's probably lying about this and a host of other personal identification issues.

So any questions you ask about SSN fakery must start with in what state and when did the person get his or her number. While it's certainly possible to get your SSN in one state and live in another, it's not possible to claim numbers for one state that don't match. Here are some geographic examples: 001 through 158 are for the upper East Coast, including New Hampshire, Maine, Vermont, Massachusetts, Rhode Island, Connecticut, New York, and New Jersey. The numbers 159 through 260 cover the middle East Coast and parts of the South, including Pennsylvania, Maryland, Delaware, Virginia, West Virginia, North and South Carolina, and Georgia. The numbers 261 through

399 cover Florida and parts of the Midwest, including Ohio, Indiana, Illinois, Michigan, and Wisconsin. The numbers 400 through 500 cover the South and southern plains states and parts of the Midwest: Kentucky, Tennessee, Alabama, Mississippi, Arkansas, Louisiana, Oklahoma, Texas, Minnesota, Iowa, and Missouri. The numbers 501 through 626 cover the northern border states, northern plains states, the Southwest, and the West.

Know also that the Social Security Administration refers to the first three numbers as "leading numbers" and the last four as "ending numbers." So typical invalid Social Security numbers include those with three or more leading zeroes, those that end in four zeroes, those that feature leading numbers 73 through 79 or any number of 8s. And rarely is the leading number 9 ever used to start the SSN.

More specific numbering styles include: 574 for Alaska, 575 through 576 for Hawaii, 577 through 579 for the District of Columbia, 580 through 584 and 596 through 599 for the U.S. Virgin Islands, 586 for Guam, American Samoa, and U.S. citizens from the protectorates.

If a suspect tells you he was born in one place and yet sports another number, dig harder. Have him repeat the number over and over and over again until he screws it up, gives you another one to check, or actually reveals his true SSN. It's tough to keep nine numbers memorized, especially if they're not really your own and if you're locked in the back of a less-than-comfy patrol car. Sometimes it helps to play dumb and act as though you didn't hear the number or wrote it down incorrectly. It's possible to get the suspect so frustrated with your "ignorance" that he gives you a real number by mistake ("For the last time, you dumb cop, it's 556 . . ."). By running every number the suspect offers up, you may catch his real name, real record, or another aka or alias that leads to even more warrants or evidence of past criminal records.

Since the SSN is such a widespread identifier in the criminal justice system, it's easy and popular for so many righteous crooks to misuse it. But while they may be able to memorize another ordinary/crime-free citizen's number so they can rattle it off during a routine stop or field interview, the stress of sudden incarceration may cloud their ability.

Look for mistakes and dig deeper. Most people know their numbers by heart, especially if they've ever held steady employment or been in the military. Stress may cause them to forget it for a moment, but they should be giving you the real number when asked. People who say they don't know a single number, or what it starts with, or what state they got their card in, or when and where their parents got their card for them, are probably pulling your leg. Start playing the numbers game with this additional knowledge of the Social Security system in mind.

The Police-Crook Magnet

Even after all this time, I'm still amazed each time a member of either the Career Criminals Club (CCC) or the Future Criminals of America (FCA) places himself or herself into the binocular vision of the average street cop. The old saw from homicide investigators about how the killer often reinserts himself into the crime scene, the follow-up investigation, or even the memorial service for the victim continues to prove true.

Criminal profiling experts suggest that certain "organized" serial killers or sex criminals (that is, more methodical and less dysfunctionally insane than their "disorganized" counterparts) will follow their crimes in the media or in even closer ways.

When the FBI whiz kids review an old or active homicide investigation that has the locals stumped, they often suggest that, based on certain indicators, the cops have already talked to the killer, perhaps even more than once. How can this be so, you ask? Why would any crook, especially one involved in a capital crime or a serious sex felony, get anywhere near the cops? Certainly the smarter ones would be leaving for parts north or east, or Mexico, or even Jupiter, just to be sure to put as much distance as possible between themselves and the authorities. And yet we know from experience that crooks go back home to the same old places, including their last known addresses on file in our computers. Getting out of town doesn't even seem like an option for them.

On the other hand, when we read or hear about one of those infamous armored car heists involving several million in cash, it's almost a given that the suspect(s) is either an employee (read that as guard-driver) of the firm or an associate of one. You would think that after getting away with that much untraceable cash, the crook(s) would bury the money in the backyard and lie low until it was safe to start spending it in small, unnoticed chunks.

And yet, the story is nearly always the same. A few weeks after the crime, we read in the papers that the FBI has arrested the armored car heisters in Hawaii, Las Vegas, Atlantic City, or the Bahamas. As the surprised crooks sit at the roulette wheel or by the pool, rum drinks in hand, the feds swoop in and gather them and what's left of the cash. We learn that various bartenders, cocktail waitresses, hookers, and Ferrari dealers have told the authorities that the crew in question was flashing big wads of dough and spending same as if it were about to go out of style.

The movie *Goodfellas* reminds us of this tendency not to lay low. After ripping off a huge airline payroll in New York, many of the mobsters, who were advised to do otherwise by their bosses, went out and bought Cadillacs for themselves and fur coats for their wives. All this excitement and newly found wealth generated plenty of police attention, especially when the mobsters started killing each other out of jealousy and rage for spending the money without "permission."

With regard to this inability to stay out of the eyesight of the cops, a few tales from my experience may dovetail with your own stories. One night, I was standing at the San Ysidro, California, port of entry with my partner, watching the flotsam and jetsam (drunk college students, assorted partiers, tourists, and cross-border workers). A woman approached my partner with a question about how the customs people could help her get her stolen car back from Los Angeles. It seems her teenage son "took it without permission" and headed south. She filed a stolen report with her local police and was concerned that if the kid took her car to Mexico, it and he would be gone for good.

My partner explained the intricacies of license plate numbers and VINs to the woman and suggested that if she had provided good information on the report and the locals had filed it correctly, the car would appear on the NCIC computers and customs would catch it and the son coming back to the United States.

As I stood watching this scene with several customs agents, the woman's boyfriend stood next to her fidgeting and shifting from foot to foot. He was carrying a plastic grocery bag filled with cartons of cigarettes. You can guess what happened next. The customs people said, "How many cartons you got in there?" When the man's answer came back as "five," they gestured him over and read him the riot act about two being the legal import limit. A few minutes later, following many questions, some paperwork and signatures of guilt, and a healthy dose of federal bureaucracy, the man was on his way, $15 lighter in the wallet for his cigarette "smuggling" efforts.

So what started as a simple car theft question by his girlfriend for the local cops turned into an enforcement activity that put his name into the vast federal computers for good. The dumb part of all this is that the guy admitted he knew two cartons was the limit and yet he still strolled up to the ever-vigilant customs bloodhounds with a bag full of smokes in plain sight.

This reminds me of the time in college when some of the guys in my gym went to Tijuana to buy and smuggle back some muscle-building "enhancers." As I heard the story, two of these barbell boys were sweating it out (literally) in line to cross back over when the customs officer asked, "Do you have any drugs to declare?" To which one of the fitness wizards replied, "You mean like steroids?"

This answer, of course, led to a search in customs secondary inspection, a seizure of pills and needles, an arrest, a hefty fine, and a conviction for smuggling. Oops.

Another common story amongst our officers occurs when the suspect they have apprehended refuses to either shut up or go along with the program. Therefore, a simple traffic stop turns into a felony arrest, a detention for public drunkenness turns into a trip back to state prison, and a radio call to a loud party ends up with stolen property, guns, quantities of dope, and many pairs of well-used flex cuffs.

One officer told me he and his partner responded to a call of a drunk, and when they arrived, the inebriate in question gave them more than the usual lip. It was clear that a trip to the county detox center was out of the question, and once the officers started digging, they found a parolee at large with a heavy rap sheet and a third strike candidacy in his history. Instead of sleeping it off in the drunk tank, this guy went back to the clink for more than a long time.

Again, the question resurfaces: Why don't these jugheads simply keep their mouths shut and take their lumps, that is, sign their taillight ticket and shut up or, better yet, work hard to avoid any police contact whatsoever? The simple answer is that many of them are too stupid to come in out of the rain. The more complicated response is that they're simply under the powerful draw of physics. That is, because of the magnetic attraction between cops and crooks, these people cannot help but to put themselves into our paths.

This is the gangster-shooter who cruises past the scene of his own drive-by just to admire his handiwork. An alert officer copies down his plate, and the guy goes to prison for life. This is the purse-snatcher or C-store robber who waits at the bus stop near the crime scene. This is the firesetter who likes to watch the Code 3 response and may even try to "help" put out the blaze. This is the murderer who "finds" the body and is happy to tell the cops everything he knows, except that he did it.

139

It's easy to classify the people we talk to as either little kids; the media; honest citizens who are either victims, witnesses, or varying participants in our activities and responses; CCC members, or FCAs. What is so amazing to me is how often the career crooks and the potential crooks pop out of the ground like weeds. In the heat of the moment it's hard to focus your attention on more than the here and now. Just be aware of how the smaller details or the "extra" people on scene who don't seem to fit may linger on the periphery, on the outer circumference, or in the background.

Remember that one of the many important roles of the Cover Officer is to watch the scene, the suspects, and the victims and gather as much intelligence information about the situation as possible while the Contact Officer is doing his or her important hands-on work.

The crook you need and want may be standing 5 feet or 105 feet away from you. So turn up the volume on your street sonar and start listening and looking for the pings.

Police and "Customer Service"
Citizens and the Moment of Truth

You go into your bank to deposit your paycheck. The line stretches near-ly out the door. It's stuffy and hot inside the place, and you can hear people grumble about the wait as they shift from one foot to the other. As you look around the room, you see deposit slips spilled on the floor, a shortage of ink pens (just empty chains), and an abundance of "This Window Closed" signs.

After an interminable wait, you get to the window and meet up with the winner of the Surliest Teller in Town contest. With a grunt of hello she stamps your deposit slip, slams your check into her drawer, and shoves a fistful of dol-lars in your direction.

You trudge off toward the exit door with your hard-earned money and a promise to change banks before your next payday. Why the thought of a switch? Because your bank failed in a number of critical moments of truth (MOTs).

For the sake of this discussion, let's define a moment of truth as "any episode in which the customer comes into contact with any portion of the organization and can form some kind of impression from it."

The bank failed in several moments of truth, from the shabby appearance of the place to the long lines to the poor treatment by the front-line employee. These negative moments of truth soured your experience as a customer. If it was bad enough or you were mad enough, you probably went home and bitched to somebody about the whole experience. Bad moments of truth stick in our minds, and rightly so.

Research into customer perceptions and opinions tells us that if a cus-tomer comes into contact with a front-line service provider and receives shabby treatment, he or she will tell more people about the poor service than if the situation was reversed. It's a strange paradox: poor service receives more word of mouth than good service. This experience is common to every industry, regardless of whether it's a true "service" field or not.

How does all of this apply to us? We're just cops. We're not running a business, so what's the big deal about all of this "moments of truth" stuff?

Next time you pass a police car, look at the decals on the doors and see if you don't see some variation on the theme "To Protect and Serve." We are in the service business, first and foremost.

New police officers like to think of themselves as true "crime fighters." Equipped with a badge, gun, and uniform, many new cops see themselves chasing "bad guys," making dozens of felony arrests, and solving major crimes on a constant basis. Unfortunately, this is not really how the job goes.

Studies of law enforcement tell us we probably spend only 20 percent of our patrol time actually in an actual enforcement position. The rest of the time we answer citizen complaints, questions, and requests; write reports; participate in administrative or training tasks; or just randomly patrol our areas waiting for calls.

The 20-percent figure that relates to enforcement—issuing citations, making arrests, and protecting life and property—is certainly an important part of the job as a police officer, but it's really only one of many functions.

Our society is a diverse and ever-changing place, filled with people who have different cultural backgrounds, ethical values, and moral standards. The residents of a city interact with the police on a variety of other matters, not just during enforcement situations. Since enforcement is such a small part of your job, you have to bring other "people" skills to bear. The citizens of this country look to the police for protection and service, and by its nature, police work is a reactive, service "business."

But let's get back to the "moments of truth" idea. Since we are service-providers, in a service business, *every* time we come into contact with the public or the public comes into contact with us, they form an opinion about us and what we do. Let me repeat this for emphasis: *Every time we encounter a citizen, he or she forms an immediate opinion about us and the level of service we provide.* Post this above your mental locker and let it sink in.

A well-known motivational statement among entrepreneurial people says, "If it is to be, it starts with me." The concept of moments of truth fits here too. Start with yourself and look outward. Ask these questions after every contact with a normal citizen you encounter in a nonthreatening situation: "Did I conduct myself in a professional manner? Did I solve that person's problem? And did he or she leave with a good impression of me and my police department?"

If you can't answer yes to these questions, then maybe you have to look at the way you do business in the field. Cops can get gruff when they feel they're not doing "real" police work but are stuck with handling civil matters, blocked driveways, and other noncriminal matters. They show this with bored expressions, negative body language, heavy sighing, eye rolling, and improper voice control. The officers who come home with a boatload of citizen complaints are not managing their moments of truth too well.

Note that I'm referring to encounters with "regular" people who need our help, not enforcement or control activities with known crooks, drug dirtbags, or street lizards. We have other less friendly ways of handling their problems.

An MOT case in point: You see a car change lanes several times without signaling. It doesn't involve a traffic hazard particularly, but the street is crowded with cars and you decide to make a stop. You hit the lights, and a middle-aged woman pulls to the side of the road. When you get to her car door and ask for her license, you can see her hands are trembling as she hands it to you. You ask if her signals work and she says, "No, they don't. I told my husband about it and he said a fuse was bad inside there. He was going to fix it tonight when he gets home from work."

What are your options? You can smile nicely and tell her to get the problem fixed as soon as she can. You can write her a "fix-it" ticket for the faulty equipment. Or you can write her a hazard cite for failing to signal and also for the faulty equipment. On paper, each citation option is perfectly acceptable (per your department or your sergeant's policy).

Generate some numbers and try to correct her driving habits, right? But what about the spirit of the law? What about those critical moments of truth? What would happen if you smiled, told her to fix the problem as soon as possible, and sent her along? What would she tell her husband when she arrives home? Probably this: "A police officer stopped me today because my turn signals didn't work. He (or she) told me to get them fixed right away."

Her husband will surely ask if she received a ticket. When she tells him you were polite and professional and merely warned her about the problem, how do you think that affects their opinion of you and this police department? Chalk up a very positive moment of truth for the both of you.

Let's back up a bit. Why was her hand trembling when she gave you her license? Because she was scared she had done something wrong! Most normal people have been conditioned since childhood to see police officers as the authority figures that they are. Think about what happens when people see you walk into business establishment, like a restaurant, on-duty and in uniform. You can see from their facial expressions that they think the same things, "How come the cops are here? I wonder what's going on? Did something bad happen?"

This is a normal reaction to your presence and one you probably exhibited before you became a police officer. It's no secret that cops make normal, law-abiding people nervous. It's built in to our role as an enforcer of society's laws and rules. Since we know going in that our mere presence can make people uncomfortable, what can we do? Above all else, we can show that we're human.

Most people rarely encounter the police unless they're victims or witnesses to a crime. If you talk to most good drivers on traffic stops, they'll usually tell you they haven't had a ticket in five or even ten years. Your stop with them may be their first contact with a police officer in over a decade.

Your arrival at their house to take a burglary report or, more commonly in most large cities, an auto theft report, may be one of the most traumatic events of their lives. But while it's traumatic, it also represents a critical moment of truth.

What kind of grade will you get on this critical moment of truth if you come to their house with a bored expression, take a few scribbled notes as if they're wasting *your* valuable time, give them a case number, and head back out to your car? A big fat F.

But how will you score if you arrive at their home, express true concern and empathy for their loss, ask them what you can do to help, take thorough notes as they tell you what happened, do a complete investigation, and explain what will happen over the next few days (follow-ups, detectives, etc.)? Will the people who called you still be missing their car or their VCR? Yes. But will they think you're actually concerned about their plight and that you'll do what you can to help them? Yes again. You'll get a high grade for creating a positive moment of truth.

Imagine this conversation: "You know, we got burglarized the other night and the cops came to take a report. I know they have a tough job and they're overworked and understaffed and all that, but the officer who talked to us really seemed like he (or she) was on the ball. He (or she) gave us some suggestions about home security and told us about engraving our stuff. I felt better about the whole thing."

Being a cop is not easy. We're constantly on the defensive from the never-ending barrage by our beloved media. We hear it from all sides from vocal minority groups to liberal civil and criminal rights organizations. And we hear the "Don't you have something better to do?" complaint when we write parking or speeding tickets. Why all of this? My humble opinion, after watching other officers for so many years, is that sometimes we fail to *manage* our critical moments of truth until it's too late.

Some MOTs involve small matters (e.g., a friendly smile to someone in a restaurant as you pass by), and others large (such as comforting the victim of a violent crime). Some of them represent opportunities you can control: your appearance, attitude, demeanor, empathy level, and especially your body language. And still others are beyond your area of control because not everyone will like you, no matter how hard you try.

Paladin Press author and veteran police officer Loren Christensen makes a great point when he says cops need to do a better job of "selling" what they do. When you arrest a dirtbag in front of a group of solid citizens in a public setting, take the time when the situation is under control to *explain* why you had to wrestle him to the ground or use pepper spray. It goes down a lot easier when people know why you had to use force. Loren suggests you start by saying, "Sorry you had to see that folks. This man was wanted on drug charges, and he didn't want to cooperate with us. We had to use some defensive tactics to place him under arrest. We hope everyone knows we were trying to make sure the situation was as safe as possible."

Is this overselling it? Sure. But is there a good chance that if the arrestee makes a complaint some solid citizen might step up and tell Internal Affairs or your sergeant how it really happened and that "you guys were just doing your jobs."

Did you ever arrest or cite someone who thanked you for it later? As strange as it sounds, it happens, probably because you treated that person with courtesy, dignity, and professionalism.

Remember the three questions to ask yourself during citizen contacts: Did I conduct myself in a professional manner? Did I solve that person's problem? And did he or she leave with a good impression of me and my police department?

Managing the moments of truth that surround police work is never easy, but you can strive to exceed someone's expectations of you and our department. Go the extra mile and do the things that help your reputation as a professional law enforcement officer. It all begins with you.

The Police Officer-Hostage
From Bad to Worse

When the pros at Calibre Press released their 1999 training video *Hostage Officer Survival*, it's likely that if you saw the publicity material on it you barely glanced at the brochure and the accompanying promotional photo (featuring a correctional deputy fighting with an inmate who has a knife to his throat). You probably weren't alone. Being taken hostage while on or off-duty is not the first nor the fiftieth concern for most cops.

When the people at Calibre Press sent me their new video, I put it on the top of a stack of possible police training column subjects and went about my business. After all, how often does stuff like that happen, anyway? It's an unlikely scenario, and the last time most of us received any training for it, we were still in the academy.

But once again, the newspapers help to tell the tale. On Friday, June 26, 1999, I found myself in the Atlanta airport, contemplating the five-plus-hour flight home with my usual dread (bumpy air, crying babies, middle seats, prison-like food, etc.). As I headed to the boarding gate, I passed a newspaper machine for *The Atlanta Journal*. The subject of the Calibre video hit me between the eyes when I saw the banner headline, "2 lawmen missing, 1 wounded after escape by Miss. Inmates: Manhunt focuses on Tuscaloosa."

Earlier in this book, I wrote about the poor handcuffing tactics used by the two Tampa detectives who were disarmed and killed by a murder suspect. Once more, let's turn our attention to the South and consider how and why the sheriff of Jones County, Mississippi, and his associate, a retired police officer, were overpowered the previous day by two prison inmates they were taking from the state prison to the county seat for a court hearing.

Without going through all the painful details, it seems the lawmen in this case picked up convicted burglar Jeremy Granberry, 19 (serving a six-year sentence), and his cohort, Marion Centobie, 32 (serving a 40-year term for kidnapping, burglary, and assault). Somewhere between here, there, and everywhere, these solid citizens managed to overpower the sheriff and his partner. At some period of time following this event, a Tuscaloosa Police captain saw the dented and damaged sheriff's car on the highway and pulled up behind it. As he approached it on foot, he was shot twice by one or more of the suspects, who drove off and left him, wounded but alive, at the scene.

Tuscaloosa police found the squad car later, abandoned—no lawmen and no inmates. You can imagine how apprehensive this turn of events made everyone feel. The wartime phrase "Missing and Presumed Dead" was probably bandied about, if not out loud then in the thoughts of the on-scene people.

On Friday, one day after the prisoners' escape, police found Sheriff Hooks and retired officer Butler "handcuffed to the posts of a dilapidated barn off a dirt road" about 60 miles from their original destination. Both men were alive with only minor injuries, although Butler was in bad shape because he was in dire need of insulin for his diabetes. A couple visiting a nearby grave heard their cries for help and called police.

On Saturday, June 27, a Moody, Alabama, police officer stopped what he thought was a stolen car. As he waited for a cover unit, he was shot and killed by the occupants, later believed to be Granberry and Centobie, who were thought to have stolen the car in Tuscaloosa. Granberry was caught the next day and charged with the officer's murder, among his other escape and kidnapping-related crimes. Centobie was finally caught eight days after the original escape and charged with similar crimes.

Perhaps the only positive thing that we can say about this saga is that instead of one officer dead and three wounded, it could have been four dead and suspects still missing.

So with perfect timing in mind, I looked at the Calibre video with much more interest in the subject than I had prior to my visit to Atlanta. Many law enforcement officers may remember the best-known Calibre Press video, *Surviving Edged Weapons*. This tape is now a standard in most police academies, and it was one of the first to hammer home the idea of the 21-foot "reactionary gap" that serves as the focal point and reason we must pull our guns and shoot at suspects who charge at us with knives.

That video showed officers with real knife scars from field encounters and others who received numerous "slashes" from rubber training knives whipped across their throats, faces, and arms by fast-moving "suspects." What the edged weapons and the hostage videos have in common is their high-value, Hollywood-style production. These videos are not your usual industrial-grade police videos we're accustomed to seeing (grainy video, lousy lighting, uneven sound, clothing and tactics from the 1970s).

The boys at Calibre (lead by Chuck Remsberg and Dennis Anderson) have done a nice job of mixing solid information with an entertaining production. (If you like seeing slow-motion blood splatter on the walls behind chest-shot dirtbag suspects, this is the tape for you.) The staged sequences are mixed in with actual news footage to keep you continually on the edge of your seat.

Here are just a few of the key points made in the tape:

- *Know the warning signs of a potential hostage situation.*

On or off duty, be aware of possible crooks in the area who may think they can get the drop on you. On duty, this might include arrest situations with potentially psychotic suspects; the presence of multiple suspects surrounding one officer; arrests made where the suspect knows the locale, the room layout, or the hiding places better than you; or botched or interrupted escape attempts in a correctional setting (think about the new jail and your arrival at a hostage event). Off-duty this might include carjackings; assaults while working out or jogging; home invasions; store or restaurant robberies; or stalking suspects who carry a big-time grudge and confront you at home or other places where your guard is down.

- *Practice the tactics of CONTACT & COVER to prevent possible disarming situations.*

Know when to say "when." Be ready to make a tactical retreat if you or your partner are suddenly outnumbered by violent unfriendlies. It's not fun to realize suddenly at a gang party call that your closest cover unit is 10 minutes and half a freeway away.

- *Hostage-takers usually fall into three categories: power-seekers, revenge-seekers, or attention-seekers. Any or all can be deadly to you.*

- *Stay as calm as possible and get the hostage-taker to see you as a human being and not just a faceless blue uniform.*

In terms of minutes or hours, the longer you are in contact with him, the better chance you have to survive, escape, or fight back.

- *Your best chance of escape comes at either the early "disorganized" phase, when fatigue has set in for the suspect, you've built some rapport, or he is momentarily distracted by something that allows you to fight.*

149

- *Your action is always faster than his reaction.*
  Go hard at your first opportunity to fight, and know which hand he is using to hold his weapon and/or control you.

- *Outhink these people.*
  Put your off-duty gun in your waistband, and give him your empty fannypack. Then pull your gun and do what you need to do to take control.

- *Any responding second (Cover Officer) should show up and provide immediate, fatal force* (read that as: point a gun at the suspect and tell him to give up) and not just stand there and become, in effect, a second hostage officer.

You can order the 82-minute *Hostage Officer Survival* tape from Calibre Press (666 Dundee Road, Suite 1607, Northbrook, IL 60062-2760). If you learn only one thing you can use on or off duty to enhance your survival chances or flat out save your life, it's well worth the investment. My guess is you'll learn more from this tape than you first thought possible. Instead of saying, "That stuff will never happen to me," change to a mind-set that says, "That stuff may not ever happen to me, but if it does, I'll be ready for it."

There's an old saying that goes, "All things being equal, most times it's better to know than not to know." When it comes to the subject of being overpowered, disarmed, beaten, or even killed, you'll want all the expert help you can get. (If you still need convincing, rent Quentin Tarantino's *Reservoir Dogs* or read Joseph Wambaugh's book *The Onion Field*, then call Calibre the next day.) Get this tape, watch it, and add these tactics to your memory bank.

The Police Response
to Domestic Violence
in the Workplace

Recent statistics tell us that nearly 20 percent of American working people have some sort of "significant" off-the-job problem that affects their productivity and performance at work. These problems are defined in a number of ways, including everything from car trouble ("I can't get to work") to cancer ("My health is in jeopardy"). They include substance abuse problems involving drugs and alcohol; physical health problems that cause excessive sick leave; mental illness problems, as with depression, paranoia, and suicidal tendencies; problems with children, including their illnesses, daycare worries, school or home problems; family problems, such as in-law or sibling troubles, elderly care situations; and marital problems involving divorce and, more specifically, domestic violence.

Domestic violence is a significant off-the-job problem. One battered women's shelter worker in Atlanta said, "If you have 20 women in an office, two of them are being abused by their partners." What makes domestic violence such a pervasive workplace problem is that it ruins productivity and work performance for the victims. They get no peace from their tormentors, even at work. The suspect (usually male) can control the victim (usually female) even if she is on the job and away from her home.

We have all seen the evidence of this stalking-type psychological and physical interference in the form of: notes left under her car windshield wiper ("Come back to me or else!"); harassing, threatening, or just plain annoying phone calls (asking "Is Darlene there?" 10 times per day and then hanging up when she picks up the line); unplanned, unannounced visits; or waiting in the parking lot for her to go home (otherwise known as "stalking").

151

What we did at home and what we did at work used to be separated by a clear line of rights, roles, duties, and responsibilities. This is not the case today. People bring their problems to work now; they don't check them at the door. An employee with a depression problem, a drug or alcohol addiction, or a violence problem at home will carry it to work. People with ill children, eviction notices, or bankruptcies don't stop thinking about those things as they sit at their desks, counters, or assembly lines.

What makes all of this even more disturbing is that some domestic violence suspects are not content to merely bother their victims; many of them are acting out their frustrations in public. Today we are seeing more and more examples of violence at home becoming violence at work. These two problems, which used to be, for the most part, mutually exclusive, now go hand in hand more times than you might think.

I have two perspectives on each problem. Not only have I been in law enforcement for many years (and so have seen some domestic violence cases firsthand), but I also cowrote one of the first books on violence in the workplace. And since I worked for six years as a Domestic Violence Unit investigator, I have seen an alarming rise in the number of incidents where some men have decided that it's perfectly within their scope of marital control to air their home problems in "public" and confront their partner at her workplace.

A case near Omaha, Nebraska, illustrates this disturbing trend. A distraught man—estranged from his common-law wife—waited outside the computer assembly plant where she worked and shot her and her new boyfriend to death before (as often happens) turning the gun on himself. This was the second similar incident in six years at this factory. This trend is not the fault of the factory operators; it points to the way some disturbed people solve their marital discords today.

The Omaha case is an example but it's far from the only one. A rental car agency in Dallas was the scene of a shooting when a terminated employee returned with a gun and shot and wounded his ex-girlfriend and her boss. Similar incidents are occurring regularly. Where once there were a few random instances, there are now many cases of men ending their partners' lives within the confines of their partners' workplaces.

A woman was shot and killed by her estranged husband as she worked at the La Mesa, California, branch office of the Southern California auto club (AAA). The surviving minor child of the woman sued the company for failing to protect the woman. The suit was later settled out of court. According to an AAA attorney, at issue in the case was the company's duty to protect the woman from known harm. In its argument, AAA said that the woman failed to notify them of the dangerous nature of her marital discord. Had she told her supervisors and other company officials of her husband's threats, the company would have taken a policy and procedural number of steps to protect her. "In theses cases," said the attorney, "it's not uncommon for us to immediately transfer the employee to an office in a new location. When employees tell us of restraining orders and the like, we keep track of that information and work with them to change their situation." In this case, AAA argued, the woman failed to notify her supervisors or ask the company for assistance. The company also pointed out that it offers employees access to counseling programs, legal help, and other family services if they need them.

It appears this tragedy might have been averted if the woman in question had looked more to her employer for the protection she needed. Triple A had a program in place to protect its workers from this kind of attack; many companies don't.

What do you think happens to a woman's productivity and performance at work if her partner either threatens to attack her at the workplace or comes in and does it? What message does a workplace homicide or other significant domestic violence event with injuries send to other women in the organization who have their own hidden relationship-abuse problems? And what message does it send to all the employees, especially if top management knew about it and yet failed to take appropriate action?

As law enforcement officers, it's our job to intervene in domestic violence incidents, no matter where they take place. In the "good old days," these kinds of problems might have been handled with no police involvement whatsoever. Companies and their leaders often took the position that said, "We'll handle this in-house," which is another way of saying, "God forbid that our customers, vendors, stockholders, the media, or our competitors found out about this."

This point of view is changing, thanks both to increased media attention and the real possibility that companies can be sued for failing to intervene with all available resources. (In other words, if they know about the problem and fail to offer a range of solutions, they can be held liable.) What saved the company in the auto club case is the fact that the firm *did* have plans, policies, and procedures in place to deal with domestic violence as it affects the employees.

Such intervention requires our expert help. Consider the following if you have to respond to a workplace following a domestic violence disturbance.

- *The victim has the right to request our services.*

We have to tell business people that it's proper, desirable, and legal for us to come onto company grounds and take reports or make arrests for domestic violence. Company property, although private, is not a save haven for suspects or victims. Further, any manager or supervisor who advises his or her employee to "take care of this on your own time" or "call the police when you get off work and are at home" should be educated as to how crime scenes work and the need for timely intervention by the cops and the employer.

In California, for example, a state law exists that mandates employers to allow victim-employees company time off to handle court appearances, such as to get a restraining order, without harming their jobs. If a company representative won't listen to your logic, suggest that he call an attorney right away and start planning for an appearance in civil court.

- *Go out of your way to listen to the victim.*

  Let the victim vent if necessary. When possible, reassure her that you will do what you can to take care of the problem. Having the cops come to your house is bad enough. Having them show up at your work is even worse. It can be extremely stressful for a domestic violence victim to have other employees see her and you sorting through her family dirty laundry. The presence of the police tells most people that something serious has happened and that the situation (and therefore, the victim) must be out of control.

  Recognize that some of the anger the victim has for the suspect may be redirected at you. We know from experience that our arrival at a domestic violence scene does not always bring cheers of joy from the victim. You may be seen as the person who causes the problem to escalate. If the victim fears retribution from her partner or her employer, she may be uncooperative and fearful of you.

- *Resist the urge to wash out a report.*

  In the interest of "corporate harmony," some frightened victims (and their employers) would much rather have you forget the whole thing. Often, your arrival on the scene in front of bosses, coworkers, peers, and customers can lead either the employer or the employee to change his or her mind and "not want to make a big deal out of it." Recognize that this sense of embarrassment is due to the way a private matter has suddenly become public knowledge. As such, take the victim to a secure, confidential place to gather the information you need to write a thorough report. If the facts of the case indicate the need for a report, write the best one you can manage. You should know by now that the penal code has already made the decision for you as to which reports need to be written and why.

- *Never forget: you're in the spotlight.*

  How you handle this particular incident at the workplace sends a strong message to the witnesses, coworkers, bosses, customers, potential or hidden domestic violence suspects, and anyone else who is on the scene and watching up close or from a distance. A positive, professional, and empathetic approach not only comforts the victim but tells other people that yes, your agency really *does* care about domestic violence, no matter where it happens. This kind of message pays obvious dividends. It makes for better witness statements, leads to more cooperation from management and the employees, and may give you that extra piece of information you need to solve the problem. Lastly, it tells other people, who may be gauging your response and comparing it to their own domestic violence episodes, that this is a serious, significant off- and on-the-job problem.

- *Your response may come under legal scrutiny.*

When responding to workplace violence crimes, make it a point to teach business people how to intervene safely and effectively into domestic violence situations. Just as law enforcement and the criminal justice system have intervened in these kinds of problems, businesses have to intervene as well. It's no longer possible to ignore these situations that start at home and get brought to the workplace. There are a number of things company managers and supervisors can do to shield the victim from continuing work-related domestic violence problems and help her stay productive (and employed).

Let's start with at one end of the domestic violence spectrum—workplace harassment by phone. Harassing, threatening, or otherwise "crank" phone calls offer a way for the suspect to control or terrorize the victim from anywhere he happens to be near a phone. In one case, a man called the office where his girlfriend worked every 10 minutes, like clockwork, for eight hours. And in an incident that belongs in *The Guinness Book of World Records*, a Tokyo man was arrested for making 6,500 crank phone calls a month to his former boss who had fired him. At one point, he was making as many as 1,200 calls *per day*. If you respond to this kind of problem, there are some immediate steps you can take to try and stop the problem and offer some relief to the victim (who may be in jeopardy of losing her job) and the company's owner or manager (who worries that this problem can hurt the business):

- *Call the suspect back and tell him to stop.*

As one sociologist I know puts it, "Some chronic phone harassers need to be confronted and threatened with legal action by an authority figure. Often, these people can't solve their problems face to face, so they choose the phone as a way to get nearer to their victims. They are scared of confrontation. In many cases, all it takes is for a police officer to say, "I know who you are, I know what you've been doing, and I'm telling you right now that it had better stop or we will do what it takes to arrest and prosecute you."

- *Help the victim and the company get a restraining order that forbids the suspect from calling the victim at home or work.*

- *Advise the company to sue the suspect in small claims court.*

  Most judges will be sympathetic to this case because they know what kind of effect it can have on a business. With the dollar limits in many states now at $5,000, this can really put a hurt on the suspect. If he fails to show up in court, the plaintiff wins by default and can start the collection process. Otherwise, he'll have to come to court and explain to the Small Claims commissioner why the business's telephone records show that he made so many calls and why it didn't cause the business or the victim to lose money or time.

* * * * *

Today, the employer and the police department have no choice but to intervene in some of the off-the-job problems some people bring to work. While we can't protect every domestic violence victim at her work, we can work with the employer to intervene, arrest, educate, support, empower, prosecute, and follow up.

Practicing with the Enemy
How Serious Crooks Operate

One of the things that helps to make law enforcement easy—and the list is not long—is the fact that most crooks are not too bright. There are few NASA University graduates out there doing burglaries, stickups, and dope deals. We often encounter people who think school is for sissies and books are good for blocking open doors or starting beach bonfires. As such, their lack of little gray cells above the neckline makes them fairly easy to catch.

These are the people who leave plenty of clear fingerprints on smooth surfaces, drop their wallets at crime scenes, or brag about their criminal escapades to strangers in beer bars. They also fall asleep in getaway cars, crash during police pursuits, and wear the exact same clothing, right on down to their "lucky" shoes, when they commit their capers.

I'm no statistical expert, but I'd hazard an educated guess that says 80 percent of the crooks out there are members of the Revolving Jail Door Club. These people get caught early and often. Most of the time, they stagger from one screw-up to the next, with a few down periods for jail time, random underemployment, and with luck, long visits to friends in other cities outside your state.

Perhaps another 15 percent of the criminal population represents an unbalanced mixture of occasional intelligence, luck, controlled insanity, and good timing. They get away with more criminal activities than their less fortunate brethren. It's harder for us to pick up their trail because they have either learned from past mistakes or they're lucky enough to get away unnoticed. I would put serial rapists, certain pedophiles, series robbery suspects, and car and home burglars who have passed the 100-case mark into this category.

The remaining 5 percent covers what one of my detective pals calls "serious thugs." These are the guys who work as professional, 9-to-5 criminals. When they wake up in the morning, their minds are on crime. They keep this thought in their heads until they hit the pillow at night. And these are not necessarily the glamorous cat burglars we see on TV or in movies, or the organized crime hitmen, or the armored car heisters. I'm talking about people who concentrate their daily efforts on the pursuit of one or more victim-specific crimes (as opposed to dope, gambling, etc.), that is, whatever works best for them. They have been smart enough to avoid long-term jail visits and extensive contacts with the cops.

You can usually tell you're dealing with serious thugs by the look in their eyes. They rarely show fear, and you'll probably have to look hard to see any signs of life at all. What makes them so dangerous to us is, like other people who work honest jobs for a living, they have developed their "job" skills to help their success rate. They practice many of the same things we do, if not more often, but possibly with more enthusiasm. If they fail, they can end up locked up or dead, so their motivations may be just a bit stronger than those of some of the cops they encounter.

Consider the following questions and answers: Can they shoot? Yes. If you'll recall the well-quarterbacked FBI shoot-out in Miami, Florida, those feds went up against two serious thugs. When the bullets stopped flying, there were dead and wounded agents lying everywhere. The crooks were killed too, but not before they managed to take a load of law enforcement folks with them.

The FBI investigation revealed that these suspects—professional, dedicated armored car and bank robbers both—spent nearly every weekend shooting their handguns, rifles, and assault semi-autos in the Florida swamps. One report says that these men shot more than *1,500* rounds per weekend and had been doing this every seven days for more than two years.

Were the FBI agents outgunned? Definitely. Did they go up against adversaries who had more training, experience, and range time than themselves? No question.

A parallel story: A story in an Los Angeles-based magazine described an outdoor ad-hoc shooting range along Lytle Creek Road in the San Bernardino National Forest. This homemade range, known as the "War Zone," is supposedly where San Bernardino and LA gun owners come to plink cans. But the photos accompanying this piece show groups of what looks like (to me) teenage gangsters hanging out their "moco rags," drinking beers, and shooting their handguns, sawed-off shotguns, and rifles. The ranger in charge of this area has arrested people for illegal possession of machine guns, fully auto assault rifles, and other swell weapons capable of causing serious "urban hunting accidents."

If you can only drag yourself to the police range every 4 to 12 months just to qualify, it's time to step up your number of visits. There are some heavily armed people out there who have a lot of trigger time under their index fingers.

Can they fight? Yes, of course. There are several million martial arts practitioners in this country. The vast majority of them are law-abiding people who use their respective fighting arts with discipline for physical fitness, self-defense, and body and mind control. Then there is that small fragment of the martial arts population that uses its fighting skills in a negative manner. People like this will take great pleasure in trying to kick your police butt hard, fast, and often.

And even if some serious thugs have no studio-trained martial arts skills, they are certainly no strangers to fist fights. Many of these people grew up in homes and neighborhoods where they saw other males—fathers, brothers, relatives, friends, or enemies—solve their problems by kicking the stuffing out of someone. They are no strangers to violence and may have fought more people in one month than some cops have fought in their entire careers.

If you grew up in a middle-class neighborhood far from the 'hood, your last teenage fistfight was probably in high school or even junior high school. There are people in this world who fight for their lives nearly every day. Who has the edge if you go toe to toe at the end of a long foot pursuit if you find yourself without a radio, baton, or a pepper spray can?

Are they physically fit? Most often, yes. I can't recall seeing a lot of grossly overweight thugs. Some of these people are large and mean, but they're rarely hugely fat. Living on the edge of society can give you a lean look. The abuse of drugs and missing more than a few meals can flatten the belly. Further, since much of their crime involves use of their body rather than use of their mind, serious thugs are often in good physical shape.

These are the people who don't waste time in county jail watching television or schmoozing during dominoes with their pals. They do lots and lots of push-ups, bed dips, sit-ups, and isometrics on the bars, and they lift water or sand jugs over and over until they get out.

With 30 or more pounds of gear—vests, back-up guns, radios, gun belts, etc.—it's hard for many of us to get up a good head of steam in a foot pursuit. Young thugs can run, jump, climb, and *evade* us, thanks to comfortable cross-trainers, loose clothing, and no extra weight. You may be in good physical shape, but can you run as fast in full uniform as you can in shorts and shoes?

Are they under the influence of various chemicals that alter their strength levels, endurance, stamina, pain sensitivity, aggression, paranoia, and fear? Why, of course. A San Diego Association of Governments study of county jail inmates shows nearly 85 percent of the new arrivals were under the influence of alcohol or illegal drugs. This means that over 8 out of the 10 people arrested were buzzing on some mind-altering substance.

And here's another scary thought: one of the two men involved in the aforementioned Miami FBI shootout still managed to drive his car several hundred feet from the scene, even though he had suffered *fatal* bullet wounds. What propelled him that distance in his car? Pure adrenaline. Autopsy reports show he was *not* under the influence of anything. On drugs or not, serious thugs can have a strong *will* to survive, thrive, and win. Police officers who brashly say, "If some crook tries to kick my butt, I'll just shoot him" are missing the big picture. There are some deadly, deadly people out there. I hope my statistics are wrong; I hope there are even fewer of the serious thugs than the 5 percent I think. But I wouldn't bet my life on it and neither should you.

Preventing Escapes

It's always a good time to review good prisoner control methods and offer some officer safety suggestions.

- *Search and remove any item that could be used as a handcuff key.*

  Even dumb crooks can make handcuff keys. Combs, melted toothbrushes, pens, straws, wooden matches, paper clips, sunglass frames, and any other small item that can be bent, twisted, or otherwise shaped into a tube with a small burr on the end will pop open any police handcuffs on the market today. Search for actual handcuff keys (these are usually found on the suspect's key ring if he's not too bright and his wallet or change pocket if he's only a little smarter).

  Look hard at any object that could be used to get cuffs open and off. Hard-core crooks who sit around in small jail cells have plenty of time to improvise and imagine. Remove anything that even remotely looks like it could crack a handcuff lock.

- *Check on your prisoner regularly.*

  There is a noticeable tendency among officers to get busy with the report writing and booking procedures once they reach the relative safety of the booking area, station, or jail. With so many reports to write, computer checks to run, papers to get signed, and forms to fill out, it's easy to forget about the person sitting uncomfortably in the back of the car. While you're hard at work with your pen, your prisoner may be looking for escape opportunities or just waiting for the right moment to cause big problems.

  Your police car, even if it is parked inside a semi-secure area, is not a fortress. If you were facing a long jail spell, a patrol car cage and few feet of chain-link fence wouldn't offer much resistance.

With booking procedures and report writing occupying anywhere from 30 minutes to several hours of your time, it's easy to forget that Mr. Suspect is in the back cooking up his own schemes. Prisoners are just like Thanksgiving turkeys, you need to check on them from time to time to make sure they haven't climbed out of the pan.

- *Use your interior dome light as a visual aid.*

This is another simple idea that can pay big dividends. In the field at night, the dome light tells you what your prisoner is doing while you're out of the car. When your car is parked (at your station, jail, booking areas, etc.), the dome light can serve as an early warning indicator of trouble. If you see movement, squirming, or other contortions, don't delay; get over there and recheck those always-temporary security devices known as handcuffs.

- *Designate someone to watch your prisoner for you.*

If you're going to be away for even a short time—doing impounds, making phone calls, etc.—try to get someone to keep an eye on your suspect. Asking a fellow cop, "Can you watch him for a few minutes?" will at least get you another pair of police eyes trained in your crook's direction. Do the same for other officers if you plan to be in the area for any good length of time.

- *Lock the back doors of your patrol car.*

Simple, effective and yet, hardly ever done. Locking both rear doors serves two swell purposes: it keeps your prisoner's dearest friends from "lynching" him out of the back—as can occur during arrests in neighborhoods where we aren't too popular—and it puts another physical barrier between your suspect and freedom.

Lock the doors as soon as your prisoner is safely inside the car and unlock them when he is ready to step inside the jail. Talk to him or her through the cage if you need to communicate.

- *Take another hard look at the handcuffs before you move your prisoner.*

Anytime you leave a semi-intelligent, escape-prone prisoner alone for even 30 seconds, he or she will try to manipulate body parts or handcuffs into a position of better comfort or advantage. This includes everything from switching the cuffs from back to front to hiding weapons or dope under your backseat. Before you leave for jail, and especially while you're still in the field, check the cuffs for position and security. The trip from your beat to the station or jail gives a smart crook plenty of time to wiggle around and get into mischief. Check them again before you leave for jail and make sure they aren't in the wrong position or causing your prisoner any unnecessary pain or injury. Keep in mind that the time he or she will try to bolt for freedom is usually during periods where you both must move on foot from one spot to another (especially outside).

- *Always put your prisoner in a position of physical disadvantage.*
As you can recall from academy and advanced officer training, moving with your hands cuffed firmly behind your back is not easy. Balance can be a problem. The thought that you might flop face-first on to the hard deck is another fear. It is possible and useful to exploit these same fears in your prisoner. Keep him slightly off balance when you move him from place to place on foot. Hold his arm tightly in a firm "escort" position. (Keep your soft, fleshy hands out of the way of the handcuff chain too.) Make sure your prisoner knows you have a good grip on him as you move around. Be prepared to shove him over or kick or sweep his feet out from under him if you feel the "resistive tension" that suggests he's going to bolt. This will help prevent the 50-Meter Dash for Freedom or a similar stupid stunt.

The back of your police car can serve as another good physical deterrent. You may want to sit real problem children so that their feet face one door and their backs rest against the other. This may prevent spitting sessions, squirming, and excessive rear-car movement.

- *If you were issued one, use your cord cuff more frequently.*
You could probably put an end to most prisoner-escape problems with the cord cuff. I think the humble cord cuff is one of the most underrated pieces of police equipment we carry. This ingenious device can hinder escapes on foot, prevent handcuff manipulations, and stop any other body-gyrating shenanigans your prisoner may try. Making a loop with the nylon end, wrapping the cord cuff around the suspect's waist, and attaching the hook end to his handcuff chain puts a quick stop to his Houdini the Contortionist imitations. Now, as he will discover, the handcuffs just won't budge. Wrapping a cord cuff loop around each ankle can prevent a foot pursuit, unless the prisoner happens to be a champion duck walker.

For added security, use the hook to attach the handcuff chain to a handy rear belt loop. In a real emergency, you can keep your prisoner inside the car (when it's parked of course) by attaching the hook to his cuff chain and closing the rear door on the cord cuff, leaving a short portion extending outside the car door. The cord cuff is light, compact, and easy to use, even under stress, as

163

when your prisoner is kicking and screaming under the weight of many blue-covered police bodies.

Too many cops think of using the cord cuff only during those rare times when a prisoner is high on PCP or attempting to kick out a rear patrol car window. Keep it handy and use it often, not just when the situation specifically calls for it, but to prevent serious problems from erupting. Make sure you follow your department instructions about using the cord cuff and, above all, keep it on your belt or in a close pocket. It won't help you much from the trunk of your car or stuffed in your gear bag.

- *Read his or her body language as a sign of escape or assault.*

Since the eyes are the window to the soul, keep your peepers fixed on your suspect's. Anyone who looks over his shoulder repeatedly, glances about for possible escape routes, or searches for other nearby officers is probably giving you a pile of visual clues. Similarly, keep your wits about you when you remove the handcuffs for any reason, such as for fingerprinting and so forth. Obviously, with your suspect unrestrained, his chance to fight or flee goes up markedly. Yet some officers actually relax their guard with unsecured crooks in what they think is a "safe" area, such as their own station house. Remember that cops are most often disarmed and killed in front of other cops. Look for the signs of impending problems and step in to counter them.

- *Search early, search carefully, search repeatedly, and search often.*

Some of our suspects are not the most hygienic people in the world. But body odors, filth, or the possibility of disease should not stop you from searching thoroughly for weapons. That's why we carry rubber gloves. Put them on and dig in, so to speak. Don't forget to run your hands through shaggy hair, look carefully at hats, backpacks, cigarette packs, belts, pagers, key rings, and wallets, and, above all, think like a crook. If you were about to be arrested, where would *you* hide your dope, needles, or weapons?

Hard-core crooks can make a weapon out of anything, from a comb to nail clippers to a belt buckle to a pair of sunglass frames. Don't let them keep anything that could be used later against you or an unsuspecting jailer or sheriff's deputy. If some item raises the hackles on the back of your neck, take it. Your prisoner can always get it back when he bails out of jail.

* * * * *

Escape-proof your prisoner control practices now, before it gets to the "I wish I had . . ." stage.

Professional Courtesy Part I
Yours, Theirs, and Ours?

In the spirit of generating some controversy, I'd like to address the issue of professional courtesy in law enforcement.

During any holiday or vacation season, many law enforcement officers have had the chance to attend some kind of festive social gathering. It may have been a Christmas or New Year's party, a football game-barbecue event, a baseball tailgate after-work thing, or an office party thrown at the workplace of a spouse or other friend or loved one.

Many of the ingredients at these shindigs are the same: some good food, some good friends, and, most likely, some good booze. It's easy to hoist a few adult beverages while under the protective awning of a party. Even if you don't drink, chances are good that some of the other party guests are busy imbibing at a somewhat brisk pace.

And as happens at social gatherings where people of different backgrounds get together, the talk (especially among men) turns to jobs and work.

"You're a cop?" says a partygoer to you with a knowing grin. "You know what that means!" he says, elbowing one of his cohorts in the ribs. "You cops can drink as much as you want and get away with it! Everybody knows cops can do all kinds of stuff like drink and drive, speed, and double-park." Here, everyone assembled usually smiles or laughs.

And then at this point in the festivities, another party member will launch into a story about his neighbor the state trooper or his friend the sheriff's deputy, or his wife's cousin's brother's nephew who is a cop and never has to answer to the same set of laws as the rest of the civilian world.

Many younger officers will make the foolish mistake of trying to debate party know-it-alls about the subject of cops and "breaking" the law. Most veteran officers, who have already realized it's largely useless to try to change the mind of a well-convinced (or well-oiled) taxpayer, usually excuse themselves and head for the safety of the chips-and-dip platter.

A variation on this theme is played out during the well-known, "Do you know?" game. This event takes place in similar social settings or, more commonly, during a traffic stop or even an arrest situation where the detainee says to the detainer, "Do you know Officer X? He's a real good friend of mine."

This attempt at pleasant conversation is more often linked to the stoppee's desire to get out of the ticket or handcuffs the stopper is about to administer. In most cases, where the officer mentioned works for some other agency, it makes little difference to the cop who stands there, ticket book at the ready. The majority of officers will just nod their heads and continue writing.

The vast prevalence of Police Officers Association, Police Benevolent Association, or Fraternal Order of Police window stickers has only contributed to this problem. Many civilians (and crooks) know what these stickers symbolize and may ask their police friends to "get me one so I can get out of tickets."

And while we're busy placing our officers into sticky professional traps, what about the people who flash the business card of an officer or detective and swear that they were told to "show this to the cops the next time you get stopped?"

What happens if the cop *does* know the officer whose name has suddenly and ceremoniously been dragged into the conversation? Haven't we all been put into this position at one time or another? Does this not place the officer in a bit of an ethical dilemma?

To resolve this thorny dilemma, we must first backtrack to one of the classic unwritten rules of street police work: "Cops don't give other cops tickets. It's called 'professional courtesy.'"

"Why is this so?" asks the taxpayer, his cheeks still smarting from his last 53-in-a-35 citation.

"Because," goes the long-held reasoning, "police work is a dangerous, difficult profession, and we all have to look out for our fellow officers."

No matter how many law enforcement ethics, management, or policy books you make cops read or how many agency training classes you force them to sit through, this rule has not changed and is not going to change in the future. The public at large can get as mad as they want; some things are just carved in stone. Or are they?

Have officers on your department received traffic citations from State Troopers? You bet. And have officers been ticketed by neighboring agencies?

Yes again. And have officers from your department signed a "Written Notice to Appear" given out by cops in other states? Yes once more.

As some officers can readily attest, if you get stopped by cops in other states, be ready for the fact that you might get a ticket. Is this right or fair? The answer depends upon whom you ask. Civilians may say, "Darn right!" while cops will surely say, "What? No way! I'd never do that."

One veteran officer explained it to me this way: "When I'm confronted with this issue by a civilian, I always admit that the 'no-ticket' rule might not be right, but it exists, just like other 'courtesies' exist in other professions. If you work for a large department store, you get an 'employee discount' that I'm not entitled to. If you work for a car dealership, you can qualify to drive loaner demo cars to and from work. And if you work as a salesperson for a roofing company, you'll get the 'family rates' when you need your own roof repaired."

So what about the phrase "professional courtesy?" What does it really mean and what do *you* do when it rears its ugly head?

Have you ever stopped speeding off-duty officers only to have them act like *you're* wasting *their* valuable time?

"What did you stop me for? I'm a cop!" they say, as they shove their badge at you through the window. If you let them go without a word (most cases) or a warning to slow down (rarely), didn't you also say under your breath, "If that jerk hadn't been a cop, I would've wrote him!"

And what happens if you're the guilty party who gets stopped for speeding? How do you respond when the officer walks up to your car window?

Personally, each time this happens to me (thankfully, it's an extremely rare event), I feel like a jackass. I'm embarrassed for myself because I was probably driving unsafely, and I'm even more embarrassed for the officer, who must waste his or her time on my traffic stop.

During the early days of courting my wife, I thought it would be more than advisable to make friends with her father, a then-assistant chief. I got a pair of San Diego Padres tickets and asked him to come along for an afternoon of baseball. On the day of the game I was running a bit late and my driving was less than careful. Coming from one part of town and driving like a bat to meet him at my station, I crossed the path of a motor officer and his radar gun.

Offering the best lame excuse I could think of ("I'm late for a Padres game with the assistant chief"), I took my good-natured tongue-lashing from the traffic cop and gratefully left. But all the way to the ball game and well into the evening I felt stupid. I wish I had paid more attention to my speed, and I wish I hadn't put the officer on the spot as a result of my behavior.

Now, I'm far from sainthood and I can't point fingers at other officers without having some of them aim back at me. But it's clear that in terms of professional courtesy, there are some of our law enforcement brethren who view their badges as if they offered some kind of diplomatic immunity. And God forbid some hardworking police officer, parking controller, or sheriff's deputy should try to suggest they might have broken the same laws they're supposed to enforce.

When I stop Officer Off-Duty Grouch or Deputy Uppity, I just shake my head and walk back to my patrol car without another word. It's easier just to drive away rather than explain to some cops why they can't drive 90 miles per hour just because they bleed the blue.

And what about, speaking of unacceptable behavior, the subject of drinking-while-driving cops? Do we deserve the same professional courtesy from each other? Not hardly and for good reason. Drunk driving is dangerous. Many officers feel strongly about the subject: "If you're drunk and on the road, you could injure or kill my family. I don't care if you are a cop. You, of all people, shouldn't have been behind the wheel."

Officers on departments all across the country have been arrested for drunk driving, some after an accident and others after a traffic stop. Responding to this event afterwards, some officers have told their court-ordered alcohol counselors that the arrest certainly identified a real problem and probably saved their lives. It must not be easy to arrest another cop for DUI at the scene of an accident, but it must be done.

How about this frightening-but-true scenario? Last year, an off-duty New York Police Department chief was spotted by a young patrolman staggering out of a convenience store. As he fumbled for his keys to leave, the officer stopped him and offered him a ride home in a cab or his patrol car. Allegedly, the chief cursed at the officer, pushed him aside, and then got into his car and drove away.

When the apprehensive patrol cop tried to complain to his supervisors, he was told to mind his own business and forget about it. Now how do you think this new NYPD officer feels about the concept of "professional courtesy?" Had this incident happened in your town, would this case end up on the desk of someone at your Internal Affairs bureau? How would you bet?

How we treat each other in an on- or off-duty capacity can lead to difficult moral or ethical decisions. The possibility for double standards certainly exists. What *you* do in a certain situation involving an off-duty officer may be completely different than what your partner, squad member, or fellow officer might do. We are taught to enforce the letter of the law, but we are also given the latitude to recognize the spirit of the law when we see it too. As with most difficult ethical decisions, you can only do what you think is right.

Professional Courtesy Part II
Dealing with Other Agencies

I wonder if the phrase "professional courtesy" isn't itself an oxymoron. You know the ones, things that don't sound like they go together, like "jumbo shrimp," "affordable housing," or "honest politician."

Is it possible for officers to be civil to each other in the most trying of circumstances? A few stories from the ol' Albrecht historical files may raise some thoughts and remembrances in your own mind.

To wit: During the achingly brief period in between my graduation day from the academy and my first real day on the job, I decided to fly up to San Francisco to visit a buddy. He was an old school chum, whose father was, at that time, a San Diego PD homicide detective. As a military police officer (MP) in the army, my friend was taking Russian classes at the Defense Language Institute on the Presidio near Fort Ord. I went up to relax and take a look around.

My plane landed late at night, my friend picked me up, and we went straight from the airport to a great seafood restaurant on the wharf. We parked a few blocks away and started to hoof over to the place. Along the way, we passed a uniformed San Francisco Police officer struggling frantically to get his locked police car door open with a Slim-Jim.

"Do you need any help?" I asked, flashing my brand new gold badge and proudly announcing my affiliation with his sister city to the south.

"No!" came the less than polite reply, as the officer rooted around the inner workings of his car door to no avail. My friend, who knows a thing or to about Slim-Jims and car doors (but that's another story), tried to tell him the best way to use the device. This too was met with a hearty, "Why don't you guys just mind your own business?"

Shrugging, we left the cranky cop to his problem. About two hours later, filled with good food and other mealtime essentials, we left the restaurant to walk back to our car. Officer Friendly was still at it, only this time, we walked by without exchanging another word. For all I know, his keys may still be locked inside his patrol car.

I'll quickly concede that the officer in question was certainly upset at his mistake and probably embarrassed to be in such a spot, in front of the public, and maybe even in front of other cops. (This probably includes his own squad pals, or otherwise he would have called them for help, right?) But why the bad treatment aimed at us? We only wanted to help this officer into his car and get him on his way. So much for the "fellow brothers in arms" idea.

Two San Diego officers I know—a male and female who are married to each other—left town for a short vacation in Las Vegas. Arriving at their hotel on the Strip, they checked in, dropped off their bags in their room, and then went right back downstairs to make a few donations to the city's economy.

When they came back to their room only a few hours later, the worst had happened. You guessed it—a burglary. Some jewelry, cash, and a handgun had been stolen from their room.

An inside job, you say? It certainly sounds like it, what with no forced entry, and their room a dozen stories above the street. Unless the culprit was Spiderman, it's probably safe to assume someone who worked for the hotel or a related accomplice got in and out with the aid of a pass key.

So you would assume that in a situation like this the Las Vegas police would send over some cops to conduct a thorough burglary investigation, maybe try for some prints, interview some hotel people, and actually attempt to solve this one.

Close, but no. Arriving quite a bit later was a Las Vegas PD Community Service Officer who, by all accounts, was polite and professional but was basically there to do little other than collect the bare facts and take a report. Apparently, Las Vegas has so many of these kinds of hotel capers that they use sort of a roving Telephone Report Unit to document them. No LV cops ever came to the crime scene.

Of course, the attitude of the hotel people was, "Hey, it's not our fault." Their total show of indifference makes you wonder if this kind of thing happens at the joint all the time. To his credit, a plainclothes investigator from the Gaming Commission did respond to the call and helped the San Diego officers by running some computer checks and entering the stolen gun data. His assistance was the only ray of sunshine in an otherwise dreary trip.

All of this is not to pick on the cops in either San Francisco or Las Vegas. They work just as hard as you do, if not harder, on their own crime problems.

And having met and worked with some of them, I know there are fine officers in both places. But if you look at your own experiences, can you say that you were treated well by cops in other cities when you came into contact with them, or not? And is it possible that just like in the movies and TV, other small police agencies don't really like cops from the "big city?" Some officers can tell stories of being stopped, frisked, and even made to sit through a field interview by cops who nabbed them on their way through some small-town burg. So if it has happened, what can you learn from it?

- *Don't assume anything.*
  The help, advice, or assistance—verbal, physical, or otherwise—that you might find welcome from other officers, no matter where they're from, may not go both ways. If you're out of town and the situation warrants it (e.g., a pending, in-progress, or just-occurred crime you've seen), you'll certainly want to protect yourself, identify yourself, and help the responding officers. But if discretion is the better part of valor, you might want to see how the whole situation unfolds before you offer your two cents worth.

- *Gun laws differ from state to state and even from county to county.*
  What weapons might be fine for off-duty cops to carry, conceal, or transport in California could be vastly different in Arizona, Nevada, or New York. Many police administrators counsel their officers, "If you have to travel, leave your gun at home." I've heard of situations where officers have even had their guns confiscated by overzealous cops in other states.

- *Regardless of what it says on your badge, you should go into any situation outside your city with the belief that it might not carry much weight.*
  Retired officers, some of them with high rank, have told me they have run into complete indifference, apathy, or even rudeness when they've had to deal with cops in other states. And plainclothes officers with long hair and beards or those from obscure federal agencies (e.g., Food and Drug Administration [FDA] investigators, welfare fraud investigators, agriculture inspectors) say that many times the local officers they contact don't even think they're "real cops."

- *If you're a crime victim in another state, don't expect the red-carpet treatment from the responding officers.*
  If you get some good help, consider yourself fortunate, cooperate as best as you can, and then head home with a lesson learned. If some out-of-state oaf

goes out of his way to make your sad situation worse, you might want to shoot a letter to his command or chief to tell your story and express your frustrations.

- *And always keep in mind that your off-duty response to a crime or pending crime in another state or town may not be welcome or requested.*

Being a polite, professional witness can often pay more dividends than being perceived as an Officer Know-It-All. We'd all like to think that the badge and the uniform mean the same thing to all law enforcement officers everywhere. Experience tells us this isn't always so.

Cops watch for things, no matter where they are. As you travel in other cities, counties, and states, you're probably casting a wary eye around you just as a matter of habit. As such, you'll probably see more than the average person will just because of your training. This vigilance may give you the opportunity to run into your law enforcement brethren in various ways. Do what you can to help them, but realize you may find yourself in that odd gray area—not really a civilian, but with no jurisdiction there—that many officers find discomforting.

* * * * *

Think about your own on-duty encounters with out-of-city or out-of-state officers. Was it always pleasant and helpful, or did their presence at your scene cause more problems than it solved? Professional courtesy is clearly a two-way street. Give some to get some, and so on.

Protecting Homicide Scenes

The best way to catch any murderer who has beat feet—cop killer or otherwise—is to respond quickly, protect the crime scene, and let your department's homicide experts examine the evidence. Short of an eyewitness found on canvass who saw the suspect run into a house and hide, crime scene evidence offers the best hope of finding the culprit. As any veteran investigator will tell you, a crime scene is a fragile thing, filled with trace evidence, small and often hidden clues, and a wealth of information if you know what to look for.

A review of good murder scene protection rules might be in order. Sergeant Bob Manis retired from the San Diego Police Homicide Team #2 after a 30-plus-year career. He offers some helpful advice for patrol officers who respond to calls where someone's life has seeped away.

"First," says Sgt. Manis, "don't hesitate to call Homicide if you go to a dead body call and the circumstances seem suspicious. We would much rather respond to the scene and determine that it's *not* a homicide than to have the coroner call us a few days later and tell us it is."

He adds that officers who call for Homicide are usually always justified and correct in their decision. In other cases, the coroner or the deputy coroner can make the same judgment and ask that Homicide detectives come out to take a look.

Manis remembers a case where officers went to a dead body call at a downtown hotel. It appeared that the victim had died of alcohol poisoning, but the lividity (pooled blood in his body cavities) was inconsistent with his position. The blood had settled into the back of his legs, and the victim was found face down, indicating that somebody had moved him after death. In

173

this case, homicide detectives rolled to the scene and were able to determine that, although the evidence pointed to a murder, it was not. (A friend had repositioned the body to protect the victim's dignity in death.)

"Secondly," says Manis, "do everything you can to protect that crime scene. Leave everything in its original, untouched position, especially firearms or other weapons. Don't cover the body with anything, and don't allow anyone at the scene (e.g., the firefighters or ambulance personnel) to cover the body either."

While Sergeant Manis admits officers may feel compelled to cover a dead body to spare the witnesses or family members, it usually destroys valuable evidence, such as blood, semen, dirt, or fibers. (Look to the JonBenet Ramsey case as a perfect example.) Don't cover the body; move the family members away from it. The only exception here pertains to rainy weather. In these cases, you should call an evidence technician to the scene to take the appropriate evidence protection measures.

In nearly all cases, however, the rule is clear: Leave everything alone and untouched. Secure the scene, set up a safe perimeter around it with crime scene tape, and guard the area until the detectives can arrive. Don't let anyone, including other cops or supervisors, into the area around the body. The evidence you protect may solve the case.

Sergeant Manis adds that once you've protected the body and the crime scene, remember that "you're still a cop." One thing that upsets him and his fellow detectives is the "rope off the scene and wait for Homicide to get here" attitude.

Recalling one incident, Manis says that after a shooting, officers on the scene found three eyewitnesses and carefully "stored" them away in police cars to await the arrival of the detectives. When he arrived, Sergeant Manis asked what the witnesses said about the crime, only to hear that no one had interviewed them during the several hours prior to his arrival. (They were not happy about being sequestered in police cars for that amount of time, needless to say.)

"Be a cop out there," says Manis, "It's a good idea to separate the witnesses, but make sure you interview them and get their stories. They may be able to tell you where the suspect went, where he lives, or some other piece of valuable information. Don't wait for us to get there. Ask questions, get some good statements, and follow up on their information."

Dealing with the suspect at a homicide scene, however, is a completely different matter, says Manis. He cautions patrol officers *not* to admonish the suspect and avoid talking to him (or giving him anything, such as cigarettes or food) unless it's necessary. "If he wants to talk and gives you unsolicited statements, let him talk all he wants. Just don't admonish him, encourage him to talk, or try to question him about his involvement in the crime. Take accurate and complete notes of what he says and give them to the detectives."

As with most major crimes, anytime you respond to a homicide scene, you'll be asked to write a short report describing your actions, duties, interviews, and so on. If you take witness statements, get complete personal information, including addresses, pager numbers, and telephone numbers.

Homicide suspects arrested at the scene or later are processed by the detectives. Typically, a suspect will be taken to the Homicide office for photos and fingerprints, as well as myriad other tests, including, gunshot residue (if applicable), a blood draw, an Intoxilizer test, and, in rape-murder cases, semen samples.

Just before the suspect goes to jail, the detectives take him or her to the hospital for a complete medical exam. This protects the detectives from harm later if the suspect tries to say they coerced a confession. The medical exam can also reveal injuries, wounds, or other evidence that may change the nature of the case.

Crime scenes in remote areas like dirt roads, canyons, or parks can cause problems with evidence retrieval. If you're the first officer on the scene, make sure you walk carefully to and from the location of the body. Keep other officers away from the scene so no one will destroy any suspects' or victims' footprints. Sergeant Manis says that when the Homicide team arrives, the detectives will talk to the officers who found the body and have them show where they walked. Later, an evidence technician will take pictures of the officers' shoe prints to compare them with others found at the scene.

Lastly, Sergeant Manis echoes a belief expressed by many patrol supervisors that officers at a homicide scene should always remember that the media is usually there with video cameras running. Keep in mind that any inappropriate behavior by officers guarding the scene (e.g., laughing and joking, and so on) will probably show up on film somewhere. Manis suggests that you be as professional (and tight-lipped) as possible if you're dealing with the media or they are working around the scene.

A homicide represents the worst of our society at work. Homicide teams are made up of veteran detectives and supervisors with much training and experience. Help them to do their job by doing yours as best you can.

Putting Crooks on Foot
Safe Tows and Impounds

The 1996 shooting death of a rookie California Highway Patrol (CHP) officer in Orange County, California, during a traffic stop and attempted vehicle impound brings up a number of interesting officer safety issues. Sadly, as with other police murders that have come before and with ones that will no doubt follow, we must try to learn from the events that took this officer's life.

From media, witness, and investigators' accounts, CHP Officer Don Burt, the 25-year-old son of a CHP officer, stopped a late-model white BMW near a restaurant parking lot in Fullerton. Burt, who had been a CHP officer for only 15 months, spoke to the lone driver, an Asian male, long enough to get his driver's information.

After running his name, Burt must have determined that the driver either had a suspended or revoked license or somehow did not match the name he had given. For this reason, Officer Burt did what any other cop would do—he ordered a tow truck and prepared to impound the vehicle and cite the driver for driving without a valid license.

Early witness accounts say Burt began a cursory search of the trunk while the suspect still sat in the driver's seat. Other investigators have said that Burt had the suspect sit on the curb next to the BMW while he searched the trunk. In either case, Officer Burt may have discovered items of contraband—reported as stolen or phony traveler's checks—in the trunk.

Before Officer Burt could confront him about the checks, the suspect ambushed him and shot him seven times. The last shot hit was an execution-style blast, which hit Burt point-blank in the head. The suspect was armed with a handgun, and, prior to his escape, he also disarmed the officer and fled with not only his service weapon but his marked patrol car as well. (As the tow truck Officer Burt had called approached the scene, the driver saw the CHP unit go by at a high rate of speed with its overhead lights flashing.) The suspect abandoned the CHP car about seven miles away in Anaheim.

Using the physical, trace, and ID card evidence at the scene, the investigators were able to trace the suspect through his aliases and prints. Within two weeks, the suspect, Hung "Henry" Thanh Mai, 25, was arrested in Houston by Fullerton Police, FBI agents, and the Houston PD. (He was convicted in April 2000 for Officer Burt's murder; not a hard choice for the jury, especially since the defense did not present *any* rebuttal to the prosecutor's case.)

Mai, a Vietnamese immigrant, is supposedly connected to an Asian gang with national and possibly even international ties. He has an extensive criminal record, including arrests and convictions for assaults, possession of automatic weapons, robbery, and, not surprisingly based on the contents of the BMW's trunk, forgery. Some investigators said that Mai had been arrested before wearing a bulletproof vest and carrying automatic weapons.

This sad situation should give you much to think about. Specifically, the way we handle encounters involving traffic stops that turn into vehicle impounds.

Some questions come up: What is your mind-set once you discover that a tow is required? What is the traffic violator's mind-set—and when does he or she change status (into a "suspect") and become a potential threat to your safety?

Typically, these field encounters begin normally enough: you see a car with missing or expired plates or tags, no front plate, or a cracked windshield. Following the stop and during the contact, the driver usually says, "Uh, I left my driver's license in my other pants," or words to that effect. Having heard this many dozens of times before, we know it is a coded phrase that really means, "I'm truly sorry, officer, but I have no legal right to be behind the wheel of this car. For you see, sometime in the not too-distant past, I was dumb enough to lose my license for failing to appear, getting too many DMV points, or pleading out to my third drunk driving apprehension."

And so the drill begins. You hear those fated words "No ID," and, having confirmed the appropriate dates, times, and lengths of suspension through your trusty MDT, order a tow truck and pull out your impound report forms. It's time to step forward and break the bad news to the soon to be ex-driver. Or is it?

What do we know so far about this contact? For one, the car is officially "under arrest." It's now yours to hand over to the police tow company that works your beat area. In other words, its ownership has temporarily changed from the driver to your city's treasurer.

For another, the driver is now eligible for a misdemeanor citation for driving on a suspended or revoked license. The key word here is "misdemeanor." In other words, we've moved up a notch on the "Police Seriousness Scale" from an infraction like running a stop sign to a bona fide arrestable offense.

These are not just semantic differences here; these definitions should tell you that its now perfectly legal for you to detain this person, place him under misdemeanor arrest, write him a misdemeanor citation, and then release him on his written promise to appear.

So if you feel it's necessary to conduct a pat-down prior to this misdemeanor arrest process, do it. If the driver-suspect resists your efforts to get your paperwork finished, it's within your power to treat this hostility like any under misdemeanor, especially since you happened to have witnessed the driving portion of this one.

Always remember that the driver has not followed the rules of the road or of good common sense, i.e., "Don't drive with a suspended or revoked license, stupid." Should this lead you to believe he or she is likely to play hard and fast with other laws (as in being drunk behind the wheel or in possession of drugs or an illegal weapon) as well?

Your safety is important throughout the contact, but especially from the moment the driver figures out or learns from you that he or she and the car will not leave together. As such, keep alert to the driver's attitude, statements, or furtive movements as you record the report information. Once the driver and any passengers are out of the car and standing on the curb, you should have a cover unit to stand by while you inventory the car's contents, search the trunk, or get the odometer reading or keys. Keep your head out of the driver's window unless there is another officer watching the driver..

Back to the vehicle impound process. Some officers like to tell the drivers right away, so they can begin preparing themselves for the fact that the car will soon be separated from the underside of their laps. This allows them also to get their belongings out of the car, surrender the ignition keys, and start thinking about what to do next and how to get there to do it.

Other officers prefer to order the tow, start the paper with the hopes of getting all or most of it completed, and wait awhile to spring the bad news. The benefits to this approach is that it delays any possible verbal confrontation with the driver until the last moment, when the tow away is inevitable. Further, it finalizes the process when then tow truck appears and the driver suddenly realizes he cannot begin to try to talk, bully, plead, fight, or cry his way out of the tow.

With the first approach—tell 'em, then tow 'em—you run the risk of the driver starting the Great Debate as to how he needs his car to get to work, or he was just on the way to the DMV office when you stopped him, or he needs his car to sleep in or otherwise he'll be homeless. Here, the driver might start off by being cooperative ("Maybe if I give him a 'big bucket of worms' story, the officer will let me slide without towing my car, searching it, or searching me"), but then turn hostile once he realizes the officer will not listen or bend.

With the second approach—tell 'em when the truck arrives—you run the risk, to put it into service terms, of "surprising your customer." His sense of outrage or hostility may rise exponentially if he realizes you have not given him what he deems to be fair warning about the tow.

In either case, make sure *you* understand what the removal of his car means in terms of the disorganization that will be the next week of his life. If necessary, politely explain to him what the removal of his car will mean to him in terms of fines and fees, locations, and retrieval methods.

In most cases, the driver may turn hostile when he or she suddenly realizes, "I'm now on foot; I won't get this car back anytime soon; I'll probably get socked with heavy fines, penalties, and DMV fees; and I'm going to need a ride to the storage yard, the DMV, or the city treasurer's office." No driver will be too pleased with any of these realizations.

Some officers try to smooth oil on the roily waters by showing the driver the vehicle code section for storage and impound. They wrap up this "It's required by law" statement with a brief explanation about police civil liability if they were to let the driver go with just a warning. (This may or not help, but it makes for a good notation in your report: "I showed the driver vehicle code section 1234 and explained how he was in violation . . .")

You can lay it out immediately or use the element of surprise. It may depend upon the situation, the time of day or night, the presence of potentially hostile passengers, or your perception of the driver's capacity to cooperate all the way through the contact.

Lastly, stay alert and stand by until the car is hooked up and rolling away. Keep your head out of your report and on the driver. Is he standing by with an increasingly angry look on his face? Has he already left the scene? Or is he lurking nearby? It's not unusual for truly erratic drivers to take out their anger on the poor tow truck driver who's just trying to do his job.

As we attempt to learn from the death of a brother officer, the Fullerton CHP murder should prove one critical point: there are no routine stops in this job. Treat an occupied vehicle impound like the *legal detention* it is. Be ready for that time when the driver changes from traffic violator to misdemeanor (or worse) suspect.

Rape Investigations in Patrol
Don't Be First, Be Right

The two books discussed below deal with sex crimes investigations. I had hoped to be writing about them during a time that would coincide with the arrest of a suspect or suspects in one of the most recognizable murders of the modern era. I'm referring, of course, to the notorious JonBenet Ramsey case in Boulder, Colorado.

As the parent of a young daughter myself, I found the news of her death even more disturbing than usual. It's common for people in and around law enforcement to steel themselves to even the most sadistic of sex crimes in adults. We cling to a hope that adult victims will somehow be able to put their painful event into some kind of context; that is, to be able to say, "As horrible as this was, someday I will start to feel normal again." We try to believe that with counseling and support from others, including the criminal justice system, these people will learn how to cope.

It's hard to convince ourselves of that in cases involving little kids, who don't understand why adults do these things to them. Most children have no grasp of the rather abstract concept of time. Today is the same as yesterday, as tomorrow is the same as next month or next year. It's nearly impossible to tell a sexually injured child, "You'll feel better about this later," because he or she doesn't know when "later" will arrive.

Of course, in the Ramsey case, there will be no "feeling better later" for anyone, because JonBenet is dead. As all patrol cops and detectives can attest, the best time to catch any crook is immediately following the commission of his crime. The in-custody clock begins ticking as soon as the act has been completed and doesn't stop until the suspect is safely captured in the backseat of a

181

police car. While it's true for all crimes, homicides, rapes, shootings, and robberies lead the list of capers that demand a hard combination of both police officer speed and police department accuracy. It's no secret as to why we bust our chops to get to crime scenes and nearby vicinities; we want to make an arrest while the scene and the situation are still fresh. The longer the wait between crime and the arrest, the more problems we will face with either catching the true culprit or making the charges stick.

Witness the handling of O.J. Simpson. On the day of his wife's murder, the first LAPD patrol officers to contact him trusted their field-tested instincts and put his wrists into a pair of handcuffs. It was only after the brass hats and attorneys arrived on the scene that they were convinced to remove them. We know they thought they had the right man for the crime, but other forces prevailed, and the hook in O.J.'s mouth was removed, and he was placed back into the water to swim away. Days later and a few hours of slow Bronco-driving on television, and we had a big fat mess on our hands.

It's not necessary to rehash the Ramsey case. Suffice it to say that as hard as the Boulder authorities have tried, they have not been able to make an arrest or arrests. At this writing, we are as yet no closer to closure on this case as we were on the day after it happened. I have officially given up hope on the possibility that any person or persons will be taken into custody for this crime.

To me, getting to a crime scene quickly is not nearly as important as knowing what to do once you're there. In the stress of the moment, you've got to think like 10 different types of people, not just yourself. At any significant event, you may have to play a combination of roles, including crowd container, scene coordinator, quasi-detective, evidence protector or collector, photographer, media manager, witness transcriber, victim protector, interviewer, family counselor, first-aid provider, hostage negotiator, handcuffer, transporter, or deadly-force user.

With any of these tasks, it's easy to get bogged down in the details and miss the importance of the overall response. Our function is to catch crooks as soon as humanly possible and, barring the immediacy of that effort, to protect the environment in and around the crime scene so that others can respond or follow-up on our reports and catch the crooks themselves.

This last statement is not merely a restatement of the obvious or an attempt at "No kidding" sarcasm; it's an attempt to keep us all focused on doing the right things for the right people within the first five minutes of our response to serious crimes or within the first five hours or the next 50 days. What we do, alone and together, at any crime scene, sets the tone for what will happen to the involved parties for anywhere from one day after the crime to a span that covers the rest of their lives.

The suspect's footprints you obliterate with your police boots won't come back. The supposed "witness" you let slip away from the homicide may be the killer. The blood or semen stains you miss, contaminate, or destroy can't be brought back by stopping the hands of time.

We have all had moments of clarity in our lives where we review our response to a situation in the bright light of hindsight and say, "If only I had done this, said that, asked this, took that . . ." You have to think that the participants in the Simpson saga and the Ramsey misadventure are mentally flogging themselves with a long list of "shoulda, woulda, and couldas."

It's easy to fall back on the "I'm only human" response to a serious error in judgment, an omission of duty, or a missing element in a police report. As an old saying goes, "Doctors can bury their mistakes. Architects can only tell their clients to plant lots of ivy." None of these comments work when it was your crime scene, your radio call response, or your case.

It is because we are all human that good cops and investigators develop systems for doing the right things the right ways. Under stress, we revert back to how we have been trained. If you are methodical when responding to a garage burglary, you can transfer that same precision to a robbery scene. If you know how, why, and when to protect the scene and its evidence at a hit and run case with injuries, you can use the same methodology to respond to a rape investigation.

Regardless of the crime or the scene, it's not necessary to reinvent the wheel. The majority of the response, reporting, and investigatory protocols you will ever need are found in your policies and procedures (P&P) manual and in your past experiences and those of your partners and colleagues.

Several football teams carefully map out the first 20 or so offensive plays of every game. They print these on a laminated card, which every offensive player gets and studies. They make few deviations from these plays once the game starts, even if the other team changes its own look on the field. The coaches want their players to respond on instinct under stress, safe in the knowledge that they know what's coming next, where to be, and what to do. In other words, when in doubt, use a checklist. And since I began this discussion with the importance of the right responses to a rape scene, what follows are brief reviews of two new books that will help you prepare for such a call.

I suppose I should find some small comfort in the fact that (reported) rapes are not a common police call. Some officers may work months or even years over day, midwatch, or graveyard shifts and never get sent to one. Depending on where you work, you could go to no rape cases in several years or two valid rape cases in two days.

I'm not naive enough to think that we have successfully tackled the problem of rape. I'm painfully aware of how rape is our most underreported violent crime and how often it involves young victims, predatory or opportunistic suspects, and casual dating situations and results in long-term psychological damage. So while we may not go to one every day, when we do get the call, it's critically important to handle it right from the start.

In his Paladin Press book, *Rape Investigation Manual: A Guide to Investigative Procedures, Victim Care, and Case Development*, Det. Sgt. James R. Powers, (Ret.) sums it up best, "The only difference between a violent forcible rape and a homicide is a heartbeat. You must deal with the 'living dead' without the benefit of an autopsy."

Using this chillingly accurate statement as his credo, Powers provides a powerful prescription for law enforcement officers at all levels who must respond to rape situations. With chapters for the first responding patrol officers, for patrol supervisors, evidence collectors, and the primary and secondary detectives, this book serves as one of the most definitive manuals on the subject to date. Powers gives knowledgeable advice based upon his long experience as a sex crimes investigator, a position he admits is not for every cop, even those with an iron will and a strong stomach. His use of highly detailed and well-organized checklists makes this book an indispensable guide to every patrol officer's and detective's response to rape scenes. Powers literally leaves no stone unturned in his treatment of the crime scene, the victim, and the location, arrest, and successful interrogation of the suspect.

In his Paladin Press book *Sex Crimes Investigations: The Complete Investigator's Handbook*, F.D. Jordan recounts a nearly two-decade career as a sex crimes investigator. With chapters on interviewing the rape victim, crime scenes and warrants, locating serial rapists, interrogating rape suspects to get confessions, child victims and pedophiles, and even repressed memory syndrome, his book serves as an effective companion to the more encyclopedic Powers title.

Jordan discusses what makes a good first-responder to a rape scene and, subsequently, what makes for a good detective. It's not enough, he suggests, to just have good police skills; you must be able to "interact professionally with the victim, or she is likely to withdraw her cooperation and drop out of the investigative effort. When this occurs, a sex offender escapes justice. He is free to continue his criminal acts, reinforced in the belief that law enforcement is powerless to stand in his way."

There is no doubt that responding to rape calls is nearly as stressful for the officers as it was for the victim. We may overidentify with the victim (who may remind us of someone we love), and in our efforts to comfort her or ease her pain, we may miss important pieces of the puzzle that is the crime and the crime scene. There is much to be said for doing the right thing in situations as emotionally and physically disturbing as a rape. There is more to be said, however, about doing things right in these cases. Just as you only have one chance to respond the right way to a homicide scene, you only have one chance to respond to the needs of a "living and breathing homicide victim" who has been sexually assaulted. These books should become a permanent part of your police library.

Sex crime cases can be some of the most disturbing and demanding police calls you will ever respond to in the course of your career. The more you know now about what to say and what to do, the better chance you will give the victim of seeing some form of justice again.

Responding to Workplace Violence Incidents
On the Suspect's Turf at Work

Late on Tuesday evening, May 27, 1997, two plainclothes detectives from the Glendale, California, Police Department went to a Chatsworth, California, warehouse to find and arrest a man accused of domestic violence and the attempted murder of his live-in girlfriend.

Eight hours later, one of the detectives had been shot dead at the scene, two LAPD officers were injured by gunfire, and the suspect either had killed himself or was killed in the subsequent firefight and SWAT stand-off.

What this tragedy demonstrates is the critical importance of understanding a suspect's mind-set and frequent tactical advantage when we go to his workplace.

According to news accounts, Israel Chappa Gonzalez, 28, allegedly assaulted his girlfriend of eight years with a stun gun, knocked her down, handcuffed her, and gagged her with cloth. She apparently lost consciousness during the fight, only to come to as he was trying to drown her in a bathtub full of water in their home. She was able to talk the suspect out of drowning her, and after he fled the scene she called the police.

Glendale detective Charles Lazzaretto and his partner learned that the suspect worked at the warehouse facility of an adult video business. They decided to do a follow-up at his workplace to see if he was inside.

Arriving late in the evening at the building, the detectives met another employee, who lied and told them Gonzalez was not there. The detectives either didn't believe the employee or heard a noise in the back and decided to look for themselves.

According to police accounts, Detective Lazzaretto entered a doorway

187

and found himself in the well-known "Fatal Funnel." The suspect was standing or hiding in the shadows or in darkness and fired a handgun (either a .380 or a 9mm) at Lazzaretto, striking him in the head.

As the partner detective took cover, the suspect allegedly took Detective Lazzaretto's duty gun from his holster and prepared to engage in a firefight.

SWAT officers arrived to surround the building and communicate with the barricaded suspect. He refused to surrender or negotiate with them, so they fired tear gas rounds into the building.

By the time SWAT officers could make safe entry into the building (about eight hours after the initial shooting), they found Det. Lazzaretto, a 10-year veteran, fatally wounded in a hallway inside the facility.

The suspect had either shot himself or was shot during one of many exchanges of gunfire with officers. He managed also to shoot two responding LAPD officers, inflicting wounds to the arm, leg, and buttocks of one and the arm of another.

This incident raises many questions. Did the detectives have prior knowledge that the suspect might be armed, either at home or work? Did they know any details about his workplace, e.g., the size, number of rooms, exit doors, etc.? Did he have a record of prior violence? Did his girlfriend tell them of his demeanor, both before and after the domestic violence/attempted murder incident? That is, did she perceive him as suicidal, homicidal, intensely antipolice, or willing to "take other people out" with him?

And this case further reinforces my belief that we must view the suspect's workplace as being just as dangerous (if not more so) as his home.

We are often taught in academy and in-service domestic violence training that because "a man's home is his castle," we must respond to his residence carefully and recognize that he knows the ins and outs, the location of any hidden weapons, and the "backstory" or history of his life and/or that of his partner, spouse, or family. Since we're not privy to that information, we take great pains to keep him away from the things that can hurt or kill us, facilitate his escape, or cause the destruction of evidence.

And yet some officers still feel that contacting a suspect at his workplace is somehow different than that same contact in the streets or at his home. It's my firm belief that many violence-prone suspects will fight even harder at work than they will at home.

Take our response to a domestic violence-related crime as an example. While the suspect may see his love relationship as unsalvageable, he may reason that it (or, more accurately, "she") can be replaced with another. But because his workplace represents his sense of economic viability—his meal ticket—he may view it as being much more fragile and worthy of protection.

In interviewing several perpetrators of workplace violence homicide, my sense is that these men saw any threat to their jobs—discipline, termination, an at-work arrest by the police—as a direct attack on their sense of self, emotional well-being, and hope for the future. Their mind-set seems to have been, "If I lose my job, then I lose my identity. If I lose my identity, I might as well take my life or those of the people I see as responsible for my loss."

While this suggests some of the psychological dilemmas faced by the suspect, the tactical considerations for a police response to the workplace are even more significant.

As with the suspect's home, the workplace provides a frightening variety of hiding places, entrances and exits, hidden weapons or tools, locked doors, and certain "sacred" or off-limits areas he deems untouchable by the police.

And like home, work may also contain certain people who the suspect feels make his life miserable—his bosses, his coworkers, the security guards, the guy who fills the soda machines, and so on. These people, along with the police, may be participants in forming the suspect's sense of general outrage at the world. His contact with any of these people, either on a regular or accidental basis, can serve to put him on edge.

And when the "rule makers" seek to put him down or keep him down, he may reach what many psychologists call a "dynamic moment."

In cases where the suspect has committed a serious crime and fled to his workplace (as in the Glendale incident) or has injured or killed someone at work, the stakes are just as high as if you were to initiate a high-risk ped or car stop on this person in the street. But remember that mobility and familiarity with the facility are usually on his side.

From seeing these types of workplace violence homicide or suicide cases either in your own city or in media accounts from across the country, we know that the suspect may "overarm" himself with everything from semiautomatic or automatic weapons to bombs; move around the building at will; and seek to target specific bosses, coworkers, a spouse or partner, a stalking victim, a security guard, or, as we see in "suicide by cop" cases, newly arriving law enforcement officers.

All this is not to suggest that our workplaces are fast filling with homicidal maniacs. However, we know that some people bring their home problems (domestic violence, stalking, drug and alcohol excesses, suicidal thoughts or actions) into the places where they earn or used to earn their pay.

Our responses to serious crimes will continue to take us to their workplaces, either for report writing, follow-up, investigations, or arrest duties. It's time to start seeing these places as requiring just as much vigilance and tactical awareness on our parts as we use in the mean streets.

Running out of Gas
Police Officers and Compassion Fatigue

We know police officers and stress go together like mobile homes and tornadoes. Our knowledge of this subject comes from an ongoing study of how people react to high-intensity stress in public safety/public health jobs (cops, firefighters, paramedics, emergency room personnel, etc.) and mental health positions (crisis counselors, social workers, child protective personnel, etc.).

Most of us are familiar with the concept of Post-Traumatic Stress Disorder (PTSD). In lay terms, it's the mind and body's reoccurring psychological and physical responses to a highly stressful event from the recent or distant past. After World War I, soldiers were said to suffer from "shell shock" and the term has evolved into PTSD as a way to categorize the ways many people feel after being exposed to life-threatening events.

Police officers who have had to shoot someone or otherwise inflict serious or fatal injuries on a suspect (or a victim or a bystander) know PTSD quite intimately. It surfaces in their daydreams and nightmares, or what is correctly called their "intrusive thoughts." In other words, although the event may have happened months, years, or decades ago, they still can replay every detail.

To give a "pre-police career" example from my own life, when I was 15, I was robbed at gunpoint by two suspects who took over a small drive-in milk store where I worked. One of the crooks forced me to lie face down on the floor and put the barrel of his gun against the back of my head. Today, nearly 25 years later, I could reenact the major and minor details of this crime and not be wrong by much. For three or four years afterward, just seeing a large male with a red beard (as one of the suspects had) would trigger the trauma of the robbery for me again.

191

While the clinical definition of the actual "disorder" portion of PTSD is more than a bit complicated, it's safe to say that those who have experienced the impact of past exposure to violence and death know it when they feel it. The physical and psychological feelings can range from mild and irritating to severe and incapacitating.

At this point, the news does not get much better. The fact is not only are we in law enforcement more susceptible to the impact of PTSD in ourselves because of our own life-threatening, life-protecting activities, but we are also vulnerable to the traumatic events of others.

Another form of PTSD is called "compassion stress," and it occurs when we are exposed to the trauma experienced by others with whom we come into close contact. As Dr. Charles Figley, a psychologist and researcher from Florida State University, has defined it, compassion stress comes from "the natural behaviors and emotions that arise from knowing about a traumatizing event experienced by another person and the stress resulting from helping or wanting to help a traumatized person." In other words, just because you did not personally experience a physical assault like a rape, a gunshot wound, or a debilitating car accident, you can, by coming into close contact with the victim(s), feel many of the same physical and psychological "pains."

For many of us, this is a difficult concept to discuss or explore. We are trained to respond to the terrible life situations of others with calm, emotionally controlled professionalism. I'm aware that some officers have come from backgrounds that include significant work in military, medical, or service careers that have already exposed them to trauma. And related to this is the fact that many people who go into law enforcement have exactly the right temperament for effectively dealing with other people's pain.

In other words, from a preemployment screening perspective, the fact that you are doing this job indicates that you have the emotional stability and coping skills to survive in highly difficult environments. But as the old sages always say, "Knowing about something in advance doesn't always mean you'll be able to fix it up right."

And the fact that we chose a law enforcement career means we have at least a propensity for wanting to help people. After all, we know from street experience that we do more helping than crime fighting, more serving than protecting. So it is from this unique position of "police officer as helper" (just like a physician, nurse, paramedic, firefighter, psychiatrist, psychologist, social worker, or counselor) that we can experience burnout, emotional and physical exhaustion, and a disturbing concept known as "countertransference."

According to the definition, feelings of countertransference "occur when the wounds of the helper are triggered by the victims they are trying to help, by similarities between the victim and the helper, or by recent traumas in the life of the helper." This can occur along two levels, sort of like a sliding scale. At one end, you respond to the trauma of another person by becoming overly detached, using a "Just the Facts, Please" approach that serves to distance you from the person and what happened to him or her. You may also seek to minimize the traumatic event as "not that big of a deal" or express "bystander's guilt," as if you could have prevented the act by driving faster, arriving sooner, or being in the right place at the right time. At the other end of the spectrum, you may feel partially or completely overwhelmed by the severity or details of the victim's traumatic event, or so numbed or horrified that you're unable to respond "normally" as a law enforcement officer.

Events that will trigger either of these responses can take you quickly out of the mode of the helper and into thought processes, actions, and feelings that seem almost as if you're experiencing the same event as the victim. In effect, you can become a second victim. Most of us become hardened to the painful reality that some human beings have a sickening knack for injuring, maiming, or murdering others in unique ways. And still others of us have figured out various positive (and perhaps not so good) methods of coping with a specific range of "acceptable" crimes or traumatic events, as long as they don't cross our own personal boundaries.

What might horrify the average civilian with no experience or knowledge of your city's traumatic events (e.g., the presence of a dead body in their neighborhood, a neighbor injured in a car accident, or a robbery that happened at their local bank branch or favorite convenience store) does not usually invoke a traumatic response in the average police officer.

But other events that can take us out of our training and experience-created comfort zones include the brutal rape of a young child, the murder of a person who reminds us of a family member or close friend, a multicar accident involving people we know, or a mass murder event, like a workplace or family violence case, or any multiple-victim homicide scene. In these cases, the sheer size and immense pain of these traumas can cause us to doubt our once rock-solid belief that we can cope with anything, anytime, anywhere.

Other, less severe, examples might include the officer who responds to the battered woman with inappropriate feelings that she should "fix her own problems" (or, at the other extreme, a desire to go out of his or her way to assist the victim in getting her life back in order by helping to "get" or "punish" the abuser) or the officer who has an alcoholic or drug-abusing family member and can't separate his feelings of anger or anxiety toward this relative when forced to deal with similar people in the field.

Countertransference symptoms can appear as rage, dread, horror, revulsion, shame, grief, mourning-like responses to death, overattachment or inappropriate "bonding" between the victim and the officer, and a desire by the officer to take on the role of "liberator" or "hero" for the victim. It seems highly unlikely that any of these responses will help the situation for either the officer or the victim.

It's time to look at possible solutions to feelings of countertransference if you experience them to any degree in yourself or see them in a family member or a close colleague who has expressed some signs or mentioned some symptoms as a prelude to increasing problems. The first and best solution is one that therapists, counselors, social workers, and other mental health caregivers use themselves: they get immediate counseling from other caregivers who know about PTSD, countertransference, and the related feelings of loss of control.

Many law enforcement agencies have excellent psychological services for department members and their families, available on a confidential, immediate, and 24-hour basis. Make the call when you feel you need to talk to someone who is sympathetic, empathetic, and qualified to help you cope more effectively with the demands of this job.

Besides some therapy sessions, other helpful intervention techniques might include more and varied physical exercise, more contact with friends and family who live and work outside law enforcement, and taking reasonable and timely breaks from your work (up to and including changing assignments, divisions, shifts, partners, or squads). You might want to find new hobbies or interests outside police work, write down some of your feelings for later rereading, get involved with religious services in your neighborhood, adjust your eating and sleeping habits to maximize the rejuvenating benefits from each, monitor your energy level throughout the day, and, finally, know your limitations with certain "hot button" subjects, events, suspects, or victims.

We're all human. Feelings of PTSD and countertransference are entirely normal and, given the right kinds of qualified, professional help, very treatable. Because you're currently subject to the demands of so much physical and emotional trauma in the lives of others, it's possible to see these events impact many parts of your life as well. Recognizing these feelings is an important first step toward feeling better about them.

Shotgun Safety Specifics

In some police departments, it's hard not to hear a nasty rumor about the use of patrol car shotguns. It seems that some officers, using fuzzy logic, make the occasional or permanent decision not to load their shotguns for the field. Stories have arisen about shotguns being left unloaded in the trunks of police cars, or worse yet, in the designated rack.

The reasons for this behavior speak to the many complicated issues surrounding the police shotgun as a tactical tool. It's awkward, unwieldy, and heavy to carry around on calls. It's hard to use in close quarters and small rooms. It's too intimidating to civilians; they expect to see our handguns, but the shotgun calls bad guys, riots, or urban terrorism to their minds. And because is not an everyday tool for us, it's hard to remember what to do with it in a stressful situation (Is the safety off? Did I already rack a round into the chamber?).

For many officers, the mere presence of the shotgun at a high-risk scene certainly conjures up thoughts of increased civil liability. Whereas most officers know their rounds will leave the barrels of their guns one at a time, they're concerned that the double 00 rounds they use will send nine pellets (approximately .33 caliber) downrange in a willy-nilly fashion. And then there is the accompanying belief that the usual police-sized 18-inch barrel fires pellets in an overly wide spread, which gets wider as it moves away from the barrel. Some officers believe the spread pattern is so v-shaped that the shotgun is useless at a distance.

In his many years with the San Diego Police Department as the rangemaster, Sgt. Reggie Frank has seen and heard of officers going into the field with unloaded shotguns. This habit caused enough concern for Sergeant Frank and his range staff to rewrite their department's firearms policy concerning shotguns. (You should take this time to review your own department's policies on both use of force and shotguns. As Yogi Berra might say, "You should look it up.")

Sergeant Frank said that the old SDPD policy allowed for some gray area concerning loading or carrying shotguns in marked patrol vehicles. The new policy spells it out explicitly: *Officers will load and carry a fully functional police shotgun in their marked patrol cars.* Their choice to use that weapon, of course, it still up to their discretion and the nature of the situation.

Sergeant Frank recapped some of the important points for us all to remember about shotguns. The spread pattern for the shotgun ammo most police agencies use is about one inch per yard, just as it always has been with double-ought buck. This pattern is subject to several factors, such as the weather, wind, and condition of your rounds. (Don't forget to exchange your shotgun rounds for fresh ones whenever the plastic casings start to develop nicks, burrs, or other imperfections that could affect the way they feed, fire, or eject.)

According to Sergeant Frank, the important thing to remember about the shotgun is that it's a highly effective protection weapon at most *distances not farther than 30 to 45 yards.* Beyond that distance, the skill of the operator must be very high. In other words, the shotgun can be an effective weapon when dealing with armed suspects at distances where you would usually use your handgun. Just as you don't "spray and pray" with your handgun at longer distances than you can see comfortably and hit your targets accurately, you must use the shotgun with the same caution.

After most major shooting incidents involving determined, armed suspects and the police (e.g., Columbine High School, the North Hollywood bank robbery shoot-out in Los Angeles, the Rodney King riots), there is often a clarion call by police agencies for "more firepower." Some departments in this country have switched from shotguns in their squad cars to .223, .30-30 rifles, or even assault weapons.

The belief here is that these long guns will give officers more protection from equally armed crooks. Other agencies have not bought into this idea, perhaps because the police shotgun is a powerful, multiround delivery weapon. Within reach in your car, you have access to a weapon that has plenty of firepower and, just as importantly, more stopping power than your handgun. Armed crooks who are shot with shotguns tend to stay down, unlike their colleagues who can take multiple 9mm rounds to the body and still break into a 100-yard dash as they head for the hills.

Consider the scenarios where the police shotgun is an effective protection tool for you and your Cover Officers.

It's certainly quite useful during high-risk vehicle stops, as when the Cover Officer covers the Contact Officer's commands and control of suspects. And its use in these situations should emphasize dramatically to you why you need to keep it loaded. How would you feel if you were the cop who ran to the passenger door of a fellow officer's car, removed his or her shotgun from the rack, jacked in a round, covered the high-risk stop, and later discovered you had chambered nothing but air? No one wants to point an empty wood and metal tube at a suspect.

A shotgun can be a useful tool during robbery-in-progress calls. It's a good weapon for controlling the escape of multiple suspects. From a position of good cover, you can use the shotgun to prone out the crook (or crooks) during the mad dash for the exit and getaway car. Stupid, brave, or stupidly brave criminals may call your bluff and turn to run if you're pointing your handgun at them, but they usually know the show's over when the shotgun is aimed at their flesh and bones. Even the dumbest robber has seen TV and knows that the shotgun can fill his hide with several bullets in a hurry.

And while it's true the shotgun is not the best choice for a foot pursuit, crowd work involving more friendlies than hostiles, and your average domestic violence call, it should move to the front of your mind for many felony crimes involving armed suspects.

Speedcuffing

Handcuffs are odd-looking devices. I often wonder whether the people who invented them ever had to use them as often as the average street cop does. We certainly put a lot of faith in them as prisoner control devices. In the dead of the night, in the darkest of alleys, and in the worst part of your beat, you reach for them and hope you can get them quickly fastened onto the thick-banded wrists of Dino the Boxing Rhino.

Even after you get them on, the game of "keep me under control" has not ended. The wiry, the drug nut who feels no pain, and the escape-prone suspects will see your application of steel bracelets as a mere inconvenience, something to defeat and bring home as a souvenir of the encounter.

In these days of multiple-arrests, many officers carry two sets of handcuffs. Some use both the hinged type and the standard swivel type. Each has its advantages and disadvantages, as I learned one night long ago.

A woman and her boyfriend rushed to the police station late one night. They flagged us down as we were leaving to say their female roommate had used a kitchen knife to slash up her clothing and generally terrorize the apartment.

She had apparently locked herself in the bathroom with the knife and was threatening suicide. We arrived, jumped back into our trusty car, and zipped over to the address. We did indeed find an upset female locked in the bathroom. After a rather heated conversation where she not-so-politely told us to take a hike, we were still not sure if she had a knife in the room with her. When our boss arrived, we all took turns trying to talk her into coming out, all to no avail.

Finally, we noticed that the bathroom door lock could be picked with a screwdriver, so we decided to open it up, grab her, and put an end to this mini-standoff. My partner played Houdini with the door lock, and we rushed in when it sprang open. We snatched a very surprised woman up and off of the floor and brought her gingerly out into the bedroom. She had had quite a few drinks and did not think much of the Men In Blue. With one burly sergeant holding one arm and one burly officer holding the other, I applied the cuffs, using my hinged set since I reached for that one first on my belt.

I spun the cuffs in place and let go of her. The next thing on my mind was to go back into the bathroom and look for the knife or other similar goodies. As I turned my back on her to walk into the bathroom, I heard a *thud* followed by the *tink* of metal hitting metal. I turned to see two things: her struggling with the cops again and my handcuffs on the ground.

In my haste to get them in place, I had failed to notice how small her wrists were. I was using my hinged cuffs with the larger-than-normal wrist openings for male suspects with arms like truck tires, not for women with dainty ballerina wrists and butterfly bones.

As the struggled continued, I whipped out my regular-sized swivel cuffs and recuffed her. Paying more attention this time, I tightened them down to the proper setting. Good thing my boss was there to witness my complete lack of handcuffing skill at that moment in my long and fascinating career.

We all have stories to tell where the handcuffs came out and failed to achieve their assigned objective. In bar fights and alley tussles they can end up 20 feet away from the conflict. Some people built like Gumby will just not stay cuffed behind their back. I suppose they feel more comfy with the cuffs in front of them; it makes it easier for them to pick their noses, comb their hair, adjust their ball caps, or scratch themselves.

In most cases, however, our handcuffing problems occur because we just don't get them on fast enough. How many times have you heard the story about the guy who finds out he has a felony warrant and appears to give in and say, "Okay, you got me," only to take off like a rabbit set on fire when the cuffs get a few inches from his wrists? What about the people who start fighting as soon as you get only *one* cuff on their wrist? Now armed with a sharp, hook-like piece of metal, they can make for a quick emergency room visit if you should happen to get raked across the face. Lastly, what about the guy who manages to twist and turn and gyrate so much during the handcuffing process that by the time you get done with him, he looks like some piece of modern art sculpture? There are hands and wrists and handcuffs facing in fourteen different directions. After all this movement out of the "standard" handcuffed position, the crook starts wailing about the pain in his wrists, as if *we* were the ones who hurt him.

The key to safe and sane handcuffing lies first with *speed* and then with *accuracy*. Get them out fast, get them on fast, and get them on correctly later. Experience tells us it's always easier to readjust twisted cuffs once they're already in place.

Some officers get into the habit of having cooperative suspects place their hands behind their backs in the palms-together position. They grab the suspect's fingers, slap on the cuffs, and they're done. But if you'll notice, the palms-together position unfolds perfectly into the hands-in-front position. If you're arresting the Amazing Rubber Man and you take your eyes off him for even one minute, he will pull his cuffed hands from back to front in no time. In the palms-together position, he can use his mitts to bend police car cages, operate steering wheels, and remove himself from the scene.

But if you cuff in the reverse-palms position, with the *backs* of his hands together, you can still grab the fingers and get the cuffs on PDQ. And with the backs of his hands touching, it's quite hard for him to get his hands to the front. Even if he could pull his hands to the front (which sounds like a physical impossibility unless he wants to intentionally break his own wrists in the process), he can't do much with the backs of his hands facing each other, except perhaps wave to you in a humorous way. If you're still using the palms-together position, try switching over to this method. You can still get control of his fingers, but you lessen the risk of his moving the cuffs to his front side.

In all cases, even with the elderly lady that looks like your grandmother, cuff quickly. Get in the habit of pulling them out and putting them on as fast and as accurately as you can. The faster you cuff, the safer you are. If you know that a handcuffing situation is imminent, get them out of the case and stick them in your belt in front of you. Better yet, put them into the correct facing positions in your off hand and stand by until you have to use them. Just like the old saying that goes, "The fastest drawn gun is the one already in your hand," the fastest applied cuffs are the ones that are so near the suspect's wrists that the next sound he hears is the click of the notches.

Stop Talking Like a Cop!
Avoiding Media Manipulations

It's time to discuss a national problem: lousy police communication practices, either on paper or on the screen. Why is it so hard for some plain-speaking officers to get their thoughts down on paper? Were they asked by a partner or a supervisor what happened and what they did in response, they would have no trouble articulating the events in a solid chronology. And yet on paper, they struggle.

And why, when the lights of the television cameras turn toward their faces, do normally well-spoken, articulate street cops or plainclothes law enforcement agents become tongue-tied jargon-heads? On TV screens from here to Jupiter, seemingly simple situations become exceedingly complex. Plain and easy-to-say English words and phrases like "person" and "climbed out of the car" become "perpetrator" and "exited the vehicle."

Let's look at the paper side of police communication, then we'll switch to the TV cameras. We can use a rule of thumb that might help you deal with both situations.

The "Triple-A Rule" (AAA) doesn't stand for "Automobile Association of America," but rather, these three important memory-joggers for better communication: Active Voice, Avoid Jargon, and Average Sentence Length 15–20.

Violation of the first rule, active-voice writing, is an epidemic in law enforcement circles. We see sentences like, "A gun *was recovered* from the vehicle and the suspect *was taken* into custody and later *transported* to county jail for booking." Immediate questions arise: *who* recovered the gun and from what part of the car? *Who* actually put handcuffs onto the suspect? (This is nice to know when a subpoena for allegations of police misconduct shows up six months later.) And did the reporting or arresting officers actually drive this guy to jail, or did they have another unit do it for them?

Passive-voice writing is irritating because it makes it hard to figure out who did what, when, why, and to whom. Put the subject of the sentence up front (the "doer" or the "actor," then the verb (what action took place) and let the other information trail after it. From the previous example, it reads better if you say, "*Officer Jones recovered* a loaded, 9mm pistol (serial number 123) from the suspect's glove box. *She arrested* the suspect for being a parolee in possession of a firearm. *We booked* the suspect *and took* him to county jail."

The second Triple-A Rule is to avoid jargon. Jargon is specialized, coded language that helps us shorten the time it takes to describe something (often technical, repetitive, or highly structured). The caveat for jargon is simple: If you and the other person know the jargon you're both using, no problem. But if one person uses jargon the other person doesn't know or understand, that's when the head-scratching starts.

Since we know most of the people who read our reports know our language (supervisors, attorneys, judges, etc.), we feel free to use a fair amount of jargon. Law enforcement, like most complicated fields, hobbies, or endeavors, is filled with jargon. We use code words, code numbers, and other official or nonofficial phrases or slang to help us speak with others in a way that's common to them and us.

The balance point should be taken more toward the idea of less jargon versus more. Keep in mind that your reports may be read to juries (think O.J. trial here), who may not understand your lexicon, even if it makes perfect sense to you. So if you say in your report, "We did a hot stop on the vehicle and took the driver and two passengers into custody," you won't find too many people outside law enforcement who know what all that means.

The last part of the "Triple-A Rule" deals with a writing habit that's easy to control: average sentence length 15–20. This means you should try to keep your sentences to about 15 to 20 words in length. Studies tell us this number leads to the highest comprehension among your readers. Shorter than this and you sound like a telegram; longer than this and people have to reread your work to figure out what you're trying to say. An even simpler rule of thumb is to only write one action or idea per sentence.

Look at this awkward construction: "I removed and recovered a small plastic baggy with approximately 10 grams of marijuana from his left front jacket pocket, which I later impounded at the Central Station on Tag #123." (Does this mean you impounded the jacket or the dope?) Try to smooth it out a little with two sentences and fewer words: "During a search incident to the arrest, I found a plastic baggy of marijuana in his left front jacket pocket. At

Central Division, I weighed the marijuana (10 grams) and impounded it on Tag #123."

The "Triple-A Rule" can work just as well should you find yourself trapped in the glare of the media lights. Follow the same guidelines as if you were communicating on paper. When speaking to the camera hounds, use the active-voice style. Say what *you* and/or *your partner(s)* or *the suspect(s)* did, specifically, using "I," "we," "him," or "they" language.

When on camera, describe things as they are, not in police language, but in common terms. It's not "vehicle," it's "car." It's not "discharged the weapon," it's "fired a gun." You shouldn't feel like you have to use Joe Friday-speak terms like "affected an arrest," "initiated a pursuit," or "subsequent to the officers' arrival." People reporting or watching TV news want to know what happened in plain terms. Cops who use too much police-speak can come across as officious, bureaucratic, and robotic.

I always like it when some officer says, "We chased this guy down through all these canyons and finally caught up to him as he was climbing over a fence." That's short and snappy and offers the perfect sound bite for the media and public, who don't want to hear police jargon anyway.

So if you find yourself on camera, don't use the passive voice, tell us what happened in terms of the actions the specific participants took. Keep the police jargon down to a bare minimum. And try to keep your sentences short and to the point. (And by the way, don't forget to hold still; they hate it when you move your head, hands, or body all over the place as you're talking and they're filming.)

Stop Thinking Like a Cop!
Think Like a Crook!

From the first day of the police academy we are taught to think like cops. We are educated as to the ways to develop that all-important "sixth sense" about crooks and their crimes. We are also schooled, if not formally then informally and as part of our police culture, that some people lie when stopped by us.

The old adage "You can tell a guy is lying to you when you see his lips move," becomes a part of our understanding of the borderline-honest people under the stress of an encounter with law enforcement. As such, once we leave the academy environment, it's hard not to feel as if the world is out to get us.

The new field officer's head is filled with officer safety horror stories, traffic stop nightmares, and radio call violence. For the first year, and perhaps longer, depending on the division worked, the new officer is hypervigilant, putting all of those newly learned patrol theories to work.

But like many jobs involving long periods of relatively "routine" activities followed by short bursts of highly stressful or dangerous movements, it's easy to get into a workday rhythm. After much time passes where we haven't had to put our more intensive police skills to work, our minds can start to play tricks, saying, "Nothing bad happened yesterday or nothing happened the last time I did this or went there."

With low-margin-of-error jobs such as nuclear reactor technician, air traffic controller, or coal miner, it can get mentally and physically tiring waiting for the one time when the screws really do come loose and it's time to activate Plan A. And so it can go with police work, where the hours turn into days and the weeks into months, and suddenly you look back and realize (again, depending on where you work) that it *has* been a long time since you took a gun off someone, it *has* been a while since you stopped a stolen car where the driver and several passengers rabbited, or that there *has* been quite a spell between your last felony dope arrest, your last heavily resistive suspect arrest, or your last high-speed failure-to-yield pursuit.

In this vein, it's probably too late to go back to those early post-academy days where you thought the woods were full of bogeymen and the streets were thick with thieves, liars, and homicidal maniacs. But you should be ready to review some basic primers about how real crooks think and how we need to walk a few miles in their Nikes to be more prepared to catch them, either before, during, or after their various capers.

So if you were a burglar, when would *you* strike? When and, more importantly, how would raise your chances of getting in and out without being caught?

When are we, as a police patrol force, the most vulnerable? How about during those last few graveyard hours before the sun comes up and before first watch officers hit the field? Are not many officers parked in their cars, trying to stay awake and warm? How about when it's extra cold, snowing, raining hard, or totally socked in with fog? How hard do we look for casers, burglars, or robbers when the weather is bad?

The point: when the urge to sit is the strongest, get out of your car and get on foot in your high-burglary areas. Walk the alleys behind closed businesses. Go behind the buildings of stores and offices to see who might be back there with a crowbar, safe hoist, or pickup truck. Find a safe, hidden area where you can watch a whole street full of parked cars. If the guy on foot in the area is not the paperboy or milkman, you know he's up to no good.

And speaking of burglars, what is the first thing we do at a burglary call once we reach the building? Most cops check to see if the doors and windows are unlocked or damaged, and if all perimeter checks are secure, they leave. So if you were a smart burglar, what would *you* do once you made entry without damaging the doors or windows (coming in because either or both were left unlocked)? Lock the doors or windows behind you, make sure the curtains or blinds were down, and go about your business without making much noise.

The point: get out of the habit of just rattling the doors and leaving. Stop, wait, look, and listen for those sights and sounds that are out of the ordinary. Look for evidence of entry beyond broken locks or windows, such as visible foot, hand, or fingerprints; signs of rooftop entry (e.g., tools, broken tiles, noise from above, etc.); trash cans or Dumpsters moved or pushed up against the building; still-warm parked cars nearby, and so on.

So if you were an armed robber, when and where would *you* strike?

What types of businesses would you hit? How about a bar right at closing time? The patrons tend to be somewhat liquored up (thereby reducing their effectiveness as witnesses), the staff may be at skeleton levels, and the cash drawers are usually full.

When could you hit a convenience store late at night without much fear of an immediate or surprise police response? How about 20 or so minutes after a cop has gotten his or her coffee and driven out of the parking lot en route to another call or a safe place to drink it and finish writing reports? Most cops head away from their favorite late-night coffee stop with their minds on other things.

The point: be willing to play hide and seek. Find an unobtrusive spot near a bar, restaurant, or convenience store and see who comes by. Check or stake out the rear doors of these establishments; the places where the employees step outside to smoke, take a break, or empty the trash cans offer a smart robber easy and unnoticed access to the business, its customers, and its cash.

What is the best time to steal an expensive car, and where might you want to do it? How about 7:30 A.M. in front of the local convenience store? Don't we still see people who "only leave the keys in their cars for a second" while they run inside to buy coffee or lottery tickets?

Are people who park near a curbside mailbox and get out with their cars running not ripe for a carjacking? The carjacker gets the best of all worlds in this scenario: a distracted driver, a driver out of the car, and a vehicle with its engine already running.

The point: go to those places where people are less than vigilant with their cars. Watch to see who loiters around high-traffic areas with no legitimate business. The guy sitting on the nearby bus bench may be waiting for an easy auto theft opportunity.

And speaking of stolen cars, stop running only the broken-down-looking cars with the cracked windshields and the missing trunk locks; look harder at the occupants of more expensive cars. Smart crooks like Jaguars, Range Rovers, and Corvettes just like the people who can afford them. After they steal these costly rides and before they take them to their fence or chop-shop connection, they like to go for a little spin around town.

Watch for people who seem unfamiliar with either the car they're driving or the area they're in. They guy who doesn't know how to operate the power windows on a hot day in what is supposed to be his own car should have some explaining to do. And this includes the guy who claims to live "just around the corner" and yet can't remember his ZIP Code or mispronounces or can't recall what street he is on.

What are the best disguises to wear to commit felony crimes? How about an expensive business suit, the colors of a delivery driver's uniform, or jogging clothes? There is an odd paradox attached to our definition of who "fits" into an environment and who does not. The best thief I ever met always wore his finest business suits into his retail store targets. He knew a lot of security guards saw a "white male wearing a suit and tie and carrying a clipboard" and visually and psychologically dismissed him as having a low theft or threat potential. They knew from their "experience" on the job that young kids were the biggest shoplifters.

It's part of human nature to take women with babies, guys carrying briefcases, and people dressed in work uniforms for granted. They are part of the scenery, and it takes a broader mind to think that their choice of dress may be part of a deliberate effort to get *you* to overlook them as well.

Smart crooks have realized that the guys with the visible jailhouse tattoos (full body suits, teardrops over the eye, etc.), gang colors, long hair, multiple piercings, and ratty clothes get stopped more often by patrol cops. Some of our brighter organized crime members (with prison, biker, drug, or street gang affiliations) *do not* want to draw any law enforcement or public attention to themselves or their activities. They seek to fit in with the rest of society by blending.

How about the presence of sexually oriented devices, videos, or printed pornography in a subject's vehicle? Is it carried by a kid on his way to a fraternity party, or does it represent the "warming up" tools of a potential sexual predator?

We know from the high recidivism rate of sex offenders that a number of serial rapists and serial pedophiles carry certain kinds of pornography and sexual devices with them as precursors to their fantasies or actual deviant acts. Even the person who offers the most glib explanation as to why he possesses unusual quantities or types of sexual material is worth a photograph and an FI slip for your detectives working sex crimes.

And what do some serial arsonists like to carry in their cars? Anything that relates to the fire department, like a portable scanner tuned to fire frequencies, firefighting equipment, or fire-starting or fire-related paraphernalia.

Are there not certain people who know how to overwhelm inexperienced or unaware officers with piles of DMV-related paperwork about their cars? How many of us have been so confused by the dates, names, vehicle identification numbers (VINs), and fees on questionable ownership stops that we just threw up our hands and let the guy go with a stern warning to "Go to the DMV and get this cleared up right away"?

And what about that fraction of people with seemingly valid excuses for missing ID, being in certain odd places at certain odd times, whose little speech to us sounds too practiced and too smooth to be right?

The point: be willing to take the extra time and dig deeper. Unless you have an immediate priority call to go to, it's well worth your effort to ask tough questions during your legally justified 20-or-so-minute stop.

Start thinking outside the boundary lines. If you were a crook, what kinds of tools would you need to bring along with you in order to operate successfully? Most law-abiding citizens don't carry the following things around in their cars on a regular basis: burglar tools like lock picks and dent pullers; drug paraphernalia such as scales, balloons, or baggies; dark clothing that includes bandannas, ski masks, or hoods; more than two pagers or multiple car phones; lots of bullets or shotgun shells; more than one knife; handcuff keys; several forms of ID under different names; lots of wristwatches; women's jewelry, purses, or women's clothing if they're male; more than one car stereo; license plates, tags, or papers for several different cars; many sets of car or house keys; several checkbooks, wallets, or credit cards in different names; or bulletproof vests.

Don't just rationalize their reasons for owning these things. Trust your intuition and gut feelings. If it looks, talks, walks, and acts like a crook, it must be a crook.

Always look for that second ID card, the second gun, or the second bag of dope. Smart crooks know most cops are neat and clean freaks. We don't like touching filthy or soiled things, so we might not search a filthy bag that contains dope, a knife, or some other fruits or tools of crime.

There is a scary percentage of people in your town who spend a lot of time in the dark, waiting and watching for what they perceive to be the perfect opportunity. Our knowledge of their habits—that is, their tendency to do the same things over and over again as they prepare for or commit their next crimes—is what can help us catch them.

Street Talk
Mastering the "Double Huh"

One of my favorite police columns from yesteryear was accurately titled, "Mastering the Double 'Huh.'"

The "Double 'Huh'" was about police-public communications at its finest. Coined in Chicago, the city of big shoulders, the "Double Huh" plays out as follows:

Patrol Cop with FI pad to guy walking in alley at zero-dark hundred: "Hey, what are you doing here?"

Alley Crawler: "Huh?"

Cop: "Huh?"

Alley Crawler: "Nothing, just walking home . . ."

Here's another version of the same:

Cop: "You ever been arrested?"

Street Hood: "Huh?"

Cop: "Huh?"

Hood: "Yeah, a couple of times . . ."

You get the point. As described by the Chicago PDers, the Double Huh works best when you repeat their "Huh?" back to them and then wait for their catch-up reply. If you simply try to repeat the question, the person just looks at you with that MEGO expression (as in "My Eyes [Have] Glazed Over") when they are asked toughies like, "Where do you live?" or "What have you been arrested for?"

Of course, those of you who pay attention to these things have realized already that the Double Huh does not much apply to "normal" people. When they are asked a direct question by a cop, they nearly always give back a direct answer.

No, the Double Huh technique works best for those less-than-honest folks who are trying to think up ways to get around your question by coming up with an appropriate near-truth, half-truth, or complicated lie.

Officers less familiar with the Double Huh waste time asking different versions of the same question or, worse, complicated questions in general. Here's an example:

Cop: "Have you ever been arrested, and if so, what have you been arrested for?"

Street Urchin: "Huh?"

Cop: "I said, have you ever been arrested, and if so, what have you been arrested for?"

Urchin: "Well, what do you mean?"

If it was me in this situation I would have fallen back on the trusty Double Huh or even better, not asked a "compound question." For those of you with children, you know that compound questions or two-task questions usually result in only one answer or one completed task. If you tell your teenager to empty all the trash cans in the house and bring in a bottle of water from the garage, the odds are good you'll get water but full trash cans, or empty cans but no help for your thirst problem.

Under stress, people revert back to the path of least cognitive and conversational resistance. This means if you ask them complicated, multianswer questions, they'll goof it up for sure. Go back to your last few difficult FI encounters and decide whether it was your fault or not if the suspect didn't, couldn't, or wouldn't understand you.

The other fact of stress-laced communications is that most people are not listening to us; they're just waiting for us to stop talking so they can tell their story. This means they are only paying attention to a fraction of what you're asking as they play out the possible response scenarios in their heads.

And remember, too, that many of these people have already scrambled their heads with drugs, alcohol, front temporal lobe damage, lousy or nonexistent educations, and adrenaline-driven fears of being caught, found out, or arrested.

To put it in simple terms, you must speak to your audience. Most of us know instinctively how to shift our conversational style; the bank president on a traffic stop gets one kind of conversational method, approach, and vocabulary, and the dazed transient lying on the sidewalk gets another.

It may sound high-hatted to say that sometimes we have to speak to adults as if they were children, but it's no secret that simple, short declarative questions and phrases have the highest comprehension level for the listener. This is why we say, "The guy who hit you, which way did he run?" rather than "In which direction did the suspect flee from here?"

Keep it simple is good interviewing advice for suspects, witnesses, or victims. Each has his own agenda and his own view of the current situation. It may be some incident that you've experienced quite a lot of, but it may be a once-in-a-lifetime event for any or all of the participants.

As such, don't ask hard questions when easy ones will cover the same ground better and faster for all concerned. Be prepared to repeat them for scared or stressed people (you could fall back on the Double Huh when conversing with street lizards).

And don't make the mistake I've made many times, when I've *assumed* *something*. Don't forget to ask the seemingly obvious questions, such as, "Did you see the accident or just hear it?" (This divides up the earwitnesses and eyewitnesses.) "Did you pull the trigger? (This shouldn't be a pre-Miranda or spontaneous question, of course.) Or, "Tell me, exactly, what you've been arrested for."

There are really only two types of questions we should be asking anyway: open-ended questions and closed-ended questions. By definition, open-ended questions consist of the who, what, when, where, why, and how variety. They are designed specifically to both extract information and keep the other person talking. Variations include "Tell me where you were standing when you saw the car hit the curb?" and "What happened just before the police got here?" and "Describe the guy for me, starting with his race and age."

Closed-ended questions are usually answered with a yes or a no. They tend to be "is/do"-type questions, such as, "Is this the guy who stole your purse?" or "Do you want me to arrest your boyfriend for stealing your VCR?"

Closed-ended questions are designed to bring "closure" to the conversation for one, as well as to help you move quickly from Point A to Point B. The difficulty with either of these two types is that sometimes we get them confused. When all we know how to ask is yes/no, is/do, closed-ended questions, we make more work for ourselves. Getting a boatload of yes/no answers forces us to come up with even more questions to keep the conversation going, especially with less-than-helpful people or suspects.

Get used to using more open-ended questions, such as, "And then what did you do?" or "Then what happened?" Remember, too, that silence works just as well in some situations as continued questions. Asking a tough question and then following it up with a facial expression that says, "Well? I'm waiting," doesn't use any more of your words and can help to put a lot of social pressure on some people who can't bear to have any lag in the conversation. They may fill the awkward gap in the discussion with some blurted-out statement that gives you more room to probe.

Phrase your questions in simple, single-idea, one-thought forms, to avoid the compound questions that bamboozle any undereducated or conversationally deficient types you encounter. Ask the obvious ones first and then the less-obvious ones later, after you've filled in most of the gaps in the story. Tailor your style and terminology to who is standing in front of you and be ready with your patience pills to repeat even the simplest of requests. ("Huh?" "Huh?" You get the idea.)

Until we perfect the mind-reading equipment the ACLU is already convinced we have, we'll just have to ask better, smarter questions.

Surviving Group Attacks
Staying Vertical in a Crowd

In days of old, as the story goes, the sheriff of a small Texas town was having a pile of problems with the local crook population. A labor dispute was brewing, and some of the more opportunistic bad guys set out amongst the union members to stir up trouble between all sides.

Fearing the worst and knowing he was badly outnumbered, the sheriff sent a frantic telegram to the Texas Rangers district office nearby. "Expecting riot," it read, "Send help immediately."

He received his reply from the Texas Ranger office: "Help arriving on next train."

When the sheriff went to meet the train, he was surprised to see only one rather large Texas Ranger step out of the passenger car.

"Where are the rest of you?" cried the sheriff, looking around for his reinforcements.

"Don't need 'em," said the sturdy lawman. "One riot, one Ranger."

With the nervous sheriff in tow, the Texas Ranger strode into town and headed right for the center of all the trouble.

Spotting the hard-faced leader of the instigators, the Ranger walked right up to him and said, "I think it's time for you and your boys to clear out."

Legend has it this tough hombre took one look at the Ranger, his badge, and his six-gun, and decided to go home and finish knitting lace doilies for his grandma's coffee table (or something like that).

To this day, you can still see a bronze statue of a Texas Ranger in Houston. "One riot, One Ranger" reads the engraved inscription on the front.

The point to this story is that sometimes, even in the face of overwhelming odds, you *can* talk your way out of a big ol' mess and survive with all your parts intact.

I always think of this story when I hear about how short-staffed we are in law enforcement. These days, with budgets at microscopic levels and police bodies in short supply, it's becoming painfully common to wait for a cover unit. In high-crime parts of your city (just about everywhere you look, these days), the request for service is high and the number of uniforms is low. More of our cops are finding themselves in the unenviable "one riot, one Ranger" position, only in this case, it's more like "one cop, several angry street lizards, and oiled pistols."

We've heard more stories across the country of cops being involved in fights with multiple suspects. Either one officer is getting shoved around by a group of thugs, or two or more officers are taking some lumps in a crowd. The prospect of more scary crook/cop ratios is real. You can have just as many problems in five-on-ones as you can with three hundred-on-twos.

An old rock song by Stealers Wheel, "Stuck in the Middle with You," accurately defines the tactical problems officers face with multiple suspects:

> *Clowns to the left of me*
> *jokers to the right*
> *here I am, stuck in the middle . . .*

With this subject in mind, I looked at a defensive tactics videotape by kenpo karate black belt Larry Tatum. The tape was produced by martial arts video leader Panther Productions and covers Master Tatum's views on dealing with multiple assailants.

He offers the following tips to keep you vertical and in possession of your gun and your faculties:

- *Stay in constant motion.*

Move so that you keep all of the suspects in front of you, with at least 180 degrees in your peripheral vision. Don't ever let anyone get behind you. Move anywhere and any way you can to keep everyone in front. Never let them circle around you. Far better to have your back against a wall than to have several crooks get behind you, ready to rain heavy blows onto your unprotected skull.

- *Move when they do or before.*

In any apparent multiple-suspect confrontation, take the initiative immediately. Don't wait for them to make the first aggressive move. It could be too late. Catch them off guard and, better yet, off-balance.

- *Make one suspect an example of your aggression.*

Move quickly, choose who you will fight first, which targets you will strike first, then do it. Nothing like the sight of the ringleader writhing on the ground in bloody-faced agony to send the other guys packing.

- *Don't try to make an arrest just yet.*

This is a fight with multiple assailants who want to do you harm. Getting one of them into handcuffs, while certainly admirable, should be your last step. Worry about who goes to jail only after sufficient cover has arrived on scene and the fight is officially over. Stopping to handcuff a downed suspect leaves you vulnerable to another attack from the ones who remain.

- *Use whatever weapons are at your disposal.*

Be rapid, aggressive, and on-target with your fists, feet, baton, OC spray, flashlight, or, if you are in real fear for your life, firearm.

- *Use your feet early and often.*

Most street hoods still fight in the Marquis of Queensbury manner, that is, fists cocked near their faces. If you can, use your feet first to fight back. You can always punch, parry, or grab with your hands, but several well-placed boot kicks to their knees, shins, abdomen, or (as a last resort) groin will sit even the toughest guy on his rear. The key to these kicks, as Tatum so aptly demonstrates, is speed. You must move faster than fast. Tatum is so quick during the demonstrations on his tape that if you blink you'll miss him. I wore out my thumb holding down the rewind button and watching him move like a bee on speed.

- *Grab and pull or grab and push.*

Don't be afraid to put hands on. Fights are notoriously unbalanced affairs. With people moving in several different directions, it's easier than you might think to shove one person into the other and send them both to the pavement. By putting more than one attacker on the ground, you save your own energy, burn precious time so help can come, and force the suspects to use more effort in getting up. In the right circumstances, you can keep two people down by circling around them and using hard pushes to their backs.

- *Use the motions of others to protect you from punches or kicks.*

If you remember the old *Batman* TV series, the men in tights were good at this. Use the body of one assailant to block the attack from another. Most people will instinctively not hit their own pals, especially in a pressure situation. Use your awareness of this to tangle them into each other.

- *If you have to, protect your gun side by fighting one-handed.*

In a worst-case encounter, fight back with your off hand and use your strong hand to cover your holster. Better to take a thump or two than lose your gun.

- *Keep your radio on your belt, not in your hand.*

Stressful situations like these make us forget that the radio will still operate even if it's not two inches away from our mouths. With the radio on your belt, you can still press the transmit button and shout out a request for help. Holding the radio chin side only helps to distract you and limits your side-to-side vision. (Break yourself of the habit of looking at your radio when you transmit; some officers still do this and lose sight of their suspects in the process.)

You may never have to fight two or more suspects, or you could do it tomorrow. You may never face a fistfight ambush alone, or you could walk into one next week.

The key to your success and survival in any multiple-attacker event is to be faster and tougher and be able to safely protect yourself until help arrives.

SWAT Calls
What to Do before the Big Shots Arrive

It seems like the woods are always full of nuts, and not the kind that grow on trees. You can't sit in a patrol car, pick up the newspaper, or turn on the local and national news without hearing about the latest in what seems like a series of SWAT missions. All over our country, the boys (and female SWAT officers too, on some progressive departments) in black or camo have been busy.

Sometimes, the need for SWAT help is unmistakable; they'll come out in force for a high-risk warrant service, an armed and barricaded suspect firing at will from a building, multiple suspects hiding in a house filled with dope and guns, or an armed robbery gone bad.

But the decision to call for SWAT is not always an immediate one. There are several levels of threat and danger surrounding a potential SWAT incident, and patrol officers and patrol supervisors may have to make certain hard decisions on their own.

Bringing in SWAT is not something that occurs by chance. A number of factors enter into the decision, and nearly all of them are critically important (and potentially expensive and time-consuming). Usually, a street situation will deteriorate into a life-threatening incident, and the on-scene patrol officers will back off, call for supervisors, and cover the scene until they arrive. From there, the supervisors will usually make the call and initiate a SWAT response. However, sometimes the first arriving patrol officer can quickly scan the scene and, realizing that he or she will definitely need help from SWAT, call for their help.

Here's how it works in some cities, according to a veteran SWAT officer: "Once patrol officers have made the decision to call for SWAT, they should immediately contain the inner perimeter, near the suspect, and the outer perimeter, near the public. While patrol officers are protecting the perimeter, keeping the suspect in sight or blocking any potential escape routes, a citywide Primary Response Team (PRT) will head to the scene to evaluate the incident."

The highly trained and well-armed PRT members can either handle the incident themselves or make the judgment to initiate a complete SWAT call out. The PRT group will gather intelligence, prepare the SWAT Command Post area, and continue to monitor the situation as they wait for the complete SWAT team to assemble.

Intelligence gathering, say SWAT team members, is an extremely important part of any mission. Patrol officers should be ready to brief arriving SWAT officers on a number of factors, if they know them, including the reasons the police were originally called, the type of crime, the exact location of the suspect(s), a detailed layout of the building (number of floors; number, size, and shape of the rooms; number and location of the windows, etc.), any specific things the suspect has said or done prior to SWAT's arrival; any prior police contact with the suspect (history of violence, drugs, weapons, etc.), and any other information that will help SWAT end the incident quickly and safely.

Even something as simple as which way a door opens can change the way SWAT officers approach a building. (Remember the old rule of thumb: If you can see the hinges, it opens towards you. If you can't see the hinges, it opens away from you.)

From their perimeter-guarding positions, patrol officers should always keep the "field of fire" concept in mind. Where is the suspect now? Where are you in relation to the suspect's position? What kind of weapon does the suspect have? And can he reach your position with it? If he has a knife, a position 50 feet away may be relatively safe, but if he's equipped with a high-powered assault rifle, even a quarter mile may be too close for safety.

Even if you only see one gun, keep in mind that the suspect may have access to a dozen others. Keep your distance and keep your head down below good cover, not just concealment. Does your current position even offer adequate, safe cover? Engine blocks surrounded by police cars may offer good cover; newspaper racks or mailboxes may not. Can you see more than one area where the suspect might be, like using a corner position to watch two sides of the building?

Can you fire your weapon safely and accurately from your perimeter cover position? Do you have the proper firearm for the situation? Sometimes a shotgun is the best choice, other times your duty weapon is more appropriate.

For more information about SWAT call-outs and the decision to use SWAT, review your own department's instructions or policies. In most cases, your police safety and survival instincts will tell you which situations you can tackle alone or with partners and which ones require the presence of SWAT. When you make the SWAT call, protect the perimeters, don't let the suspect(s) escape, gather as much useful information as possible, and be prepared to help the team achieve its mission of protecting officers and civilians from harm and getting the suspect(s) into custody.

The Tactical Approach

We need to think about the way we get to the door and meet and greet our suspects, victims, witnesses, and those who waffle back and forth between being all three.

Nearly every law enforcement agency has lost good patrol officers as they answered radio calls and walked up to meet the reporting parties. It's easy to get into bad habits on so-called regular radio calls.

Answering your fifth burglary call of the night, you park, walk up to the business or house, hoof the perimeter with your partner, rattle a few doors, look for obvious signs of a break-in, and, if you see none, put out an "all secure" over the radio and head back to the car. We've all done it, especially if it's been some time in between valid burglaries. But just because we all do it from time to time, that doesn't make it right.

The time to think tactically is *before* you realize some hot-prowl nut is waiting behind a side garage door with a gun. Just as real estate is all about location, location, location, officer safety on radio calls is all about the tactical approach, the safe approach, and, most importantly, the *planned* approach.

Even under high stress, if you can at least think of one thing, remember this: They can't hit what they can't see. Make your presence known to suspects on *your* terms and when you're ready. They don't call it the "element of surprise" for nothing.

For proof, just think about the number of times you've served as cover officer on a traffic stop. As your partner or Contact Officer talks to the driver, you watch the driver and the passenger. The passenger is usually so intent on watching the contact officer that he or she forgets to look for you over his or her shoulder. The immediate shock of recognition that follows once it registers who you are can give you a tremendous tactical and "force presence" advantage.

It's the same with your approach to a house or business. If you can get to them before they even see you, they'll lose valuable time making the connection that says, "Oh no! The cops are here!" And often, those extra seconds on your side can mean the difference between your life and their death.

Keep the following approach ideas in mind as you plan your next radio call response. And these are not just for radio calls of the pulse-racing variety; they can apply to all of your response activities.

- *Park far and walk.*

The first thing we learn in Patrol Theory 101 in the academy is "park away from the scene and walk up." So why is it that, as experienced officers, we start to park closer and closer to save us that long walk from the car door to the front door? There are more than enough good reasons to add that extra 100 feet to your journey, the main one being that you have extra time to judge what is going on around you in terms of safety.

I know it's a pain to walk half a block with a handcuffed suspect who is kicking and screaming. If he or she is too uncontrollable, stop, get a better grip, or send another officer for your car. I also know it's no fun to walk forever when the rain is coming down in buckets, or it's ice cold or boiling hot outside. But why advertise your arrival before you need to? Unless you routinely drive an undercover car, the good guys and bad guys all know you've appeared on-scene when your big metal cocoon sits a few feet from their front window.

- *Stop, look, and listen.*

This is another gimmee. If you pause for just a few seconds at the hood of your car and cock your ears in the direction of the house in question, you can often get an idea of what's going on inside. What you hear can range from voices arguing to crockery breaking to shotguns loading or guns firing. Give yourself some extra time to get a feel for the street, the design of the house, the people, cars, mean dogs, and solid cover-type objects around you.

- *Stay out of the light; stay out of their sight.*

This first one is critical at night, and the second is good advice anytime. A true tactical approach will put you right on top of the location without anyone inside knowing it. Untrained people tend to look for movement in lighted areas, not in unlighted ones. Use darkness as concealment; stay in the shadows and out of the street or house lights whenever possible. Leave your flashlight off. Your night vision should be sufficient for you to get from Point A to Point B without falling over anything in your path.

- *Use hand signals.*

Whether you and your partner are approaching or already at the door, use hand signals—finger pointing and other universal gestures that say, "I'll go here and you go there." All of this cuts the need for unnecessary talk that spoils your approach and gives your position away too soon.

- *Be quiet.*

Keep your keys under wraps, your radio piped into an earpiece, and your footfalls muffled. And this goes for your driving approach as well. Nothing spoils a good police surprise better than a loud radio, squealing tires, or slamming car doors.

- *Be especially careful on balconies, small landings, and other areas covered by railings.*

It's hard not to get tense when you and a partner have to respond to a domestic violence call in one of those two-story apartment buildings where the architect has graciously included about three feet of space between the front door and the balcony railing.

With two cops near the door and screaming people everywhere, it can make for a bad case of concrete poisoning should one of them fall against you and send the whole party to the hard deck below.

Any location with balconies, short porches with railings, or other places where a rickety set of steel bars (probably installed before you were born) is all there is between you and solid ground should make you wary. Keep away from these things, and don't make them support your weight or balance under any circumstances.

- *Create a gap on stairs.*

I'm reminded once again of the final scene in the Joseph Wambaugh movie *The New Centurions.* An LAPD cop played by Stacy Keach is walking up a very narrow flight of outside stairs to get to an apartment door. Inside, he and his partners can hear an argument. Before he can get all the way to the top, a man bursts through the door and shoots him in the stomach. He falls against his partners and as they wrestle the gun from the suspect, dies at the scene.

I'm a firm believer in creating a safety gap on staircases, especially narrow ones leading straight into doorways. I've always felt that on staircases where two cops cannot stand comfortably side by side, one of us should wait near the bottom while the other one knocks. Tactically, the lower spot still gives you clear sight of the door and your partner, puts you in a good position to return fire if necessary, and keeps you out of any wrestling match that could send *two* cops and/or one suspect tumbling down the staircase keister over apple cart.

- *Don't stand in front of windows on the door side.*

This design is common in many apartments and houses, where one side of the door is walled and the other features a window. Standing on the stucco side gives you at least some small concealment protection, but standing on the window side not only offers no protection—it puts your head and upper torso right into the line of fire from inside. Even if the window has curtains, don't stand in front of it; your silhouette can still appear in the frame.

- *Use callbacks if you can't approach safely.*

The dispatch-to-do-a-callback system is great for bank robberies, convenience store stickups, hot-prowl burglaries, and the like, but it can also pay dividends with radio calls where you want suspects or victims to come to you rather than go to them. If you can't get in, have them come out. During our search for a cop killer, we surrounded a house belonging to the suspect's relatives and used a cellular phone call to get them to come outside.

- *Take approach "shortcuts" to cut distance and come in from different angles.*

To any homeowner who reads this, I'll apologize in advance: "I'm sorry, but if you call me to your house and I don't know you or what's going on inside, I may walk across your grass instead of the concrete walkway to get to your door."

Since the shortest distance between two points is assumably a straight line, don't let natural or manmade barriers stop you from approaching in a tactical manner. This is not to say you should trample people's property with abandon, but neither should you let bushes, shrubs, or other garden items prevent you from making a safe approach when the situation dictates it.

- *Come from where they don't expect you.*

The majority of bad guys who want to do us collective harm do not think much past the usual, "Let's shoot 'em when they get to the front door" scenario. This is all the more reason to come in from the side or approach from the rear.

The best ambush-beater is the one that ambushes the ambusher. If you can make entry from a rear door during a hot call, do it. If you're going to a bar fight, come in through the back door. Start your burglary door checks from the backyard. As old-time Baltimore baseballer Wee Willie Keeler used to say, "I hit 'em where they ain't." You should follow his advice in reverse and not let anyone hit you where you are.

Be creative in your approaches, using safety as a rule but flexibility, inventiveness, and tactical experience as your guidelines.

The Tactical Cover Call
Second-Officer Roles and Responsibilities

Even in police work, with armed, trained cops all around, there is not always safety in numbers. Two cops can get killed just as easily as one.

Cover calls, with one officer responding to a request by the on-scene officer, is an event that goes on literally thousands of times per day in law enforcement. And it's because we respond to each other's needs so often that we can forget we're usually driving in "blind" to a situation we did not initiate. And neither do we know all of the details, since the dispatcher updates or MDT screens provide scant information at best.

When we first became umbilically attached to the MDTs, other officers suggested that for all their power, convenience, and accessibility, the screens have helped to replace some of our more practical patrol habits.

This includes the simple radio command "On Scene" (usually a 10 or 1 code for many agencies), which used to go out over the air and now goes out over cyberspace. In the days before the widespread use of police MDTs, we used to know by the sound of the officer's voice that he or she had arrived on scene. Today, on the other hand, it's a guessing game. When the responding officer uses the MDT only, he or she tells the dispatcher that he or she is on scene, but the officer needing cover may not be aware of it. When responding to some of our more high-risk calls, some officers will call for a meet with their Cover Officer a few blocks away from the scene and then drive in together. They may talk over a tactical frequency or use the MDT while waiting or en route, sharing information as needed.

This makes good sense, especially when the call is hot and the Cover Officer is coming from a distance. There's simply no reason to be in a huge hurry to get to a scene by yourself if it involves armed or multiple suspects. Arriving alone and jumping into the situation without sufficient cover could make you suddenly part of the problem instead part of the solution.

231

This is not to suggest that we should always hang back on every call and wait for the other officer to arrive on scene first. Do too much of this and you can quickly develop the reputation of being a call-dodger. While we shouldn't dawdle around and wait for another cop to get there before we drive up, we also don't need to rush into dangerous situations alone.

Just to make the point clear, there are numerous examples of officers who stumble upon hot crimes, violent assaults in progress, and other potential cover-now calls. I'm not suggesting we ride around with felony blinders on if we don't have an in-the-car partner, only that you have to weigh your ability to take control of every potential high-risk situation when you are the first and only officer to arrive on the scene.

Shouting, "I've got one at gunpoint and one by the neck in a carotid restraint and two in sight as they run away!" suggests that maybe you're in over your head and in need of immediate help.

Most tactically safe officers already have a good idea where their potential Cover Officers are with relation to their locations. You should already know when and how to stay close and when to swing by when other officers are making car or ped stops. Most cops have developed a sixth sense about how far away they are from other officers at any given moment. It's common to have conversations in your head that say, "I just saw Dave on a stop two blocks away. If I stop this group of gangsters cutting through the park, I know he's still nearby."

If you're paying close attention to your radio or, if applicable, your MDT and the work status of your nearby beat partners, then you'll know who is where and how far you are away from each other within a few miles.

All this leads back to the concept of cover call protocol and your duty to provide clear, current, and immediate information to any responding officer(s).

It's not just the *type* of information you provide that's important—your location, suspect descriptions, weapons, direction of travel, entry points, etc.—but the *quality* as well.

You cannot make the dangerous assumption that your responding Cover Officer will know what you know about the situation, the participants, or even the exact location. Be fast and specific at the same time. If you say over the air, "I'm in the laundry room!" during a fight with a coin box burglar in a large apartment complex, three cops may go to one of the two other laundry rooms they know, none of which contain you.

Officers who get shot on arrival at a cover scene may have lacked the one piece of critical information they needed to respond safely. "He has a gun!" or "The suspect is heading north through the west alley!" should tell cover units what they need to do or where they need to go when they arrive.

If you assume your Cover Officer knows you've arrived on the scene, you might make decisions under the mistaken belief that he or she is right around the corner. This might include confronting enraged suspects, getting into a foot pursuit, or making an arrest with a "No" person.

There are times when it's perfectly acceptable to hit the "On Scene" button on your MDT and answer the service call. There are others when a simple on-the-air mention of the same code will send a valuable message to whoever is en route to you. It says, "I'm here and I'm about to get involved in this call. Monitor my progress as you drive toward me."

And if and when it's time to call for more help fast, don't confuse other officers with mixed messages. When things look really tough and you're outnumbered or alone and need the cavalry, say, "Cover now!" not "Could I get a unit for my location?"

It's common to hear many officers say, "Could you have an officer meet me at my location?" when they want a report form, some extra tickets, or a piece of advice. Yet some officers will use this as their request for more urgent cover and then act surprised when the cover unit arrives with only normal, routine speed.

Don't make your partners guess what you *really* want them to do. Size up the situation and act accordingly. If you need urgent, immediate help, ask for it quickly and correctly, using language or codes (Code 10 or 11) that we will not misinterpret as routine.

The key to protecting your arriving Cover Officers is to provide ongoing, updated information over the radio. We know how sensitive our portable radios or cable microphone can be for voice use. You don't have to hold it right up to your mouth to talk. In a pinch, press the button and shout out what you need. If you're running, fighting, or pointing your gun at someone, let everyone know the significantly important details so they know how and where to respond and what to expect visually as they arrive on the scene.

Once things settle down and you and the other officer(s) have gained control, be quick with your use of "All Secure" (or "Code 4" in many agencies). Remember, other officers are moving toward you, often at high speeds, under the assumption that you still need help.

It's not easy to talk, think, fight, and defend your life all at the same time. Your cover partners don't expect a long speech, just the facts. Don't rely solely on the MDT as your means of communicating with your Cover Officers or the dispatcher. Think back to the good old days before we had computers in the car and we had to tell everyone else what we were doing, seeing, or needing. Don't assume the touch of a keyboard button is enough to replace the sound of your voice.

Street Lizards
and Tunnel Vision

If you're one of the few people in the galaxy who has not plunked down part of the $500-plus million earned worldwide by the makers of the movie *Jurassic Park*, please skip ahead a few paragraphs so I won't spoil part of the plot for you.

In the film, the main bad-boy dinosaurs are a group of claw-toed, razor-fanged demons called velociraptors. These scaly beasts roam around for most of the movie, eating people and chasing after two small children. They can open doorknobs, see like hawks, smell like bloodhounds, and eat like college football tackles.

They have another frightening talent: the ability to attack in groups, and often from opposing sides. In one especially chilling scene, one of the game wardens comes across a raptor and gets him in his gun sights. Before he can squeeze off a round that would turn it into lizard mush, another raptor sneaks up on his blind side and, to sugarcoat it a bit, eats him.

The game warden made a fatal mistake under the extreme stress of the hunt—he got tunnel vision. He forgot to keep looking around when things got really intense. The enemy you do see may be a part of the one, or the three, or the fifteen you don't.

The parallels to high-risk suspect encounters are similar, although most of the ones we encounter don't have scales and a tail.

In football, the story is the same. Watch the highlight films on the sportscasts when some NFL team's star quarterback gets whacked. If he doesn't blow out his knee when some behemoth falls on it, chances are good you will see him get dragged off the field in a daze after a particularly hard blindside tackle.

We see the QB fade back to pass. At the point just prior to his release of the ball, he gets smeared in the back or the side, (or the head) by an opponent he never saw.

If the smelling salts don't get him back into the huddle after a few downs, it's probably because his shoulder is separated, his ribs are cracked, or his noggin feels like a plate of cooked spaghetti floating on a bowl of lime Jell-o.

The point is that blindside attacks, whether on the movie screen, the football field, or the police officer's field, can be dangerous.

One of the many symptoms of extreme stress is that our bodies shut down, stimulate, or protect our vital organs. As our heart rates zoom and our muscles fill with energy, other physiological changes take place that may not always be so helpful. For one thing, our field of vision narrows. The body says, "Hey! We've only got two eyeballs and we're gonna need them for quite a few years more. We're gonna close up shop so we can save this precious natural resource."

In some respects, this "hooding" of the 'ol peepers is a good defense mechanism. In others, it can limit your field of view unless you consciously train yourself to prepare for it.

I'm reminded of a bank robbery story. Officers responded to a valid bank alarm and got into a position to take the suspect down as he came out of the bank and headed for the parking lot. A female officer was ordering the suspect to approach her position near some cars in the parking lot. When the suspect got near her, she was ready to make the arrest. Guess what? There were actually two suspects. Out of her blind side, the hidden suspect tackled her, the original crook ran off, and she found herself in a fight for her gun. The second suspect wrestled and scrapped with her before fleeing himself. She was not badly injured in this fracas, but I'm sure it was quite a shock for her to be ready to put hands on the first idiot when his partner came out of the shallow weeds like a pouncing hyena.

It's easy to lose sight of the potential for attack. Los Angeles cops and sheriffs have been shot at by passing gangsters as they wrote tickets or, worse, tried to conduct high-risk stops in police-unfriendly neighborhoods.

And as some chagrined patrol officers or detectives can attest, their cars have been lifted out from under them by light-fingered crooks who are either tremendously desperate to get away or tremendously stupid, or both.

"How could that have happened?" other officers listening to their radios ask as a stolen police car pursuit begins. The answer lies back in *Jurassic Park*—tunnel vision.

In the heat of the moment, we can get so caught up in one task—watching for velociraptors, avoiding defensive linemen, catching bank robbers, foot-

pursuing auto thieves, or dodging bullets aimed by homicidal gangbangers—
that we forget to look around.

What's the remedy? Start by forcing yourself to becoming aware of your
immediate surroundings. When the grease is well into the fire, make an effort
to stop, regroup, take several quick "combat" breaths, and look around you.

In times of stress, your peripheral vision intentionally narrows. Counter
this stressful response by breathing deeply, making an effort to move your
head and not just your eyes, and look hard around you.

This is difficult for a variety of reasons, but it's an important tactical skill
to develop. If you take a quick moment to focus your attention back on to your
position, you can suddenly see what's in your peripheral field of view and
reorient yourself so you can change to a new position if necessary.

Speed kills, goes the old saying. Moving too fast or focusing too quickly
on one area of vision makes you vulnerable to the blindside attack.

Vehicle crash studies make an interesting point here: The faster you
drive, the less you see to the sides of your car. So the deadly paradox proves
that driving fast in a pursuit may get you there quickly, but you may miss
things to either side of you, like obstacles, bad road conditions or, worse,
oncoming cars passing through the intersection to your left or right at the
exact moment you arrive.

This tunnel vision driving problem is particularly heightened at night.
You may become so focused on the suspect's tail lights in a pursuit, or so
engaged in getting to a high-risk cover call quickly, that you fail to see what
else is going on around you. This is how suspects can leave the scene and drive
right past you.

In high-stress scenes like domestic violence calls, bar fights, or out-of-
control parties, you may be so involved with one loudmouth that you fail to
see the other one coming from a back bedroom, a rear door, or a parked car.

The next time you're at a relatively low-stress call, practice breaking the
tunnel vision habit. Get used to looking around and try to make like you have
eyes in the back of your head.

This is especially true during felony arrest situations where you and your
partner may become so engrossed in the suspect in front of you that you both
miss his two cohorts who may be ready to flee, fight, or shoot. If you can both
get into the habit, so much the better. Two pairs of eyes can see four times as
much, in all directions.

Save your tunnel vision for the next time you can use it safely—like inside
a tunnel.

Trouble from Above
Rooftop Attacks

At a recent gathering of officers, stories of choice patrol escapades abounded. Somehow the subject turned pleasantly to drunks who throw up, not near you, but *on* you. One fellow copper told me of a time when he was talking to a staggering inebriate at some loud party. The souse in question looked strangely at him and said, "I think I'm gonna be sick!" And in the blink of an eye, this yo-yo heaved the beer-based contents of his stomach all over the officer's clean uniform. Had he been using a spray paint machine, his aim could not have been better—the uniform pants, the boots, and even a little backspray onto the gun belt. Ugh!

Police work is filled with chance encounters with people who pour adult beverages into their gullets like kayaks racing down a waterfall. Too much booze usually leads to a whole host of police-related problems, all of which are bad for the drunks and the cops.

Thanks to any number of bars, dance joints, and your ever-popular "private party," where the hosts have invited 600 of their nearest and dearest friends, things can get out of hand fast. Besides the fights, other assaults, stabbings, shootings, car accidents, and drunk drivers, there comes to our attention the person who seems to feel that it's okay to act like a jackass who has leaned over the pasture fence and nipped at the fermented fruit hanging nearby. (In an odd police paradox, obnoxious behavior actually *increases* when we arrive on scene.)

I recall standing on the porch of this narrow three-story house filled to overflowing with partiers. I was trying—in vain, of course—to lecture the host of the event as people spilled into the streets, the alleyways, every room of the building, and indeed, even onto the rooftop.

Unfortunately for me, I had observed every category of drunken reveler except the last ones listed above. As I stood screaming into the ear of the party-giver, a cascading tidal wave of beer hit me from above. It seems some of the party animals on the roof thought it would be fun to pour the remaining contents of their keg into a 33-gallon plastic trash can and then spill it down onto my unsuspecting self.

Now, if you're like me, you can take verbal abuse, ugly language, and even uglier people and their problems. But I will *not* take a beer soaking lying down. After I recovered from the initial shock (and thanked God my contact lenses weren't washed out of my head), I did what any other self-respecting police officer would do—namely, I threw a tantrum.

Looking skyward, I saw a number of laughers and pointers on the roof. I roared through the front door with a full head of steam and stomped up three flights of stairs in search of my prey. Bursting onto the rooftop, I attempted a single-handed arrest of about 50 people all at once. Many people bounced down the stairs headfirst at the hand of my gentle touch. The rest of them stomped on their fallen comrades as they fled. It was not a pretty sight, and, in retrospect, I certainly overreacted.

And in the end, it did seem like we took the whole building to jail. Returning to my patrol car with several young revelers under my arms, I noticed that one friendly partygoer had taken a key and scratched several lines all the way around my car. Ah, but all's well that ends well.

Before I could fly into yet another fury and dig through my gear bag for my trusty flame-thrower, another officer said, "I caught the guy who keyed your car. He's handcuffed and sitting in my car over there." Thank God for small favors.

So it was back to the station with our 17-year-old tagger scratch artist so I could write a detailed report, complete with swell accompanying photos, and then call his mommy at 0200 to come and get him. I assured her the city's cost-recovery people would be in immediate touch.

The point to this crusade is simple: keep your head up. Don't get so locked into what you are doing or saying in front of you that you miss some of the less-than-obvious signs of activity above.

If you have a number of industrial parks, office buildings, or retail establishments in your patrol area, I'll bet that you have had at least some activity from a rooftop burglar. Many of these cases have come from series crooks who do these kinds of capers all over town. Yet how many times do we look on the roof when we check ringing alarms? I know it's not always feasible, safe, or easy to get on top of them, but the roof is where some of your better burglars make their entries and escapes. Any goofball can come in through an unlocked door or throw a brick through a window. The real pros come and go from the top.

And although it's not always easy to spot a rooftop burglary until the hoods are long gone, a few signs should tip you off, including the obvious presence of extension ladders, cars parked directly under building fire escape ladders, ropes, cables, stacks of pallets or boxes piled higher than normal, or Dumpsters moved near the building's edge, outside piping systems, or second-story windows.

A quiet, careful, and tactical approach is critical. Even from a distance and at night, you may be able to hear sawing, banging, prying, or other sounds of forced entry. Many of these thieves use lookouts, who sit on the roof itself or on other high-ground areas where they can see you coming and warn their pals.

And trouble from above is not always burglary-related. Juveniles, who are out late and up to no good, also seem to be natural-born climbers. They can get onto rooftops and run around with what seems like golf shoes on. While vandalism and general noise-making seems to be their plan, they may be into other crimes and can usually see you coming long before you get there.

Worse yet, they don't seem to have much in the way of a fear of heights and will attempt jumps down from high-flying areas that a guy like me, with a mortgage and mouths to feed, would not attempt on his best day.

Lastly, your low-rent apartment types and downtown flophouse hotel dwellers are not immune from dropping the occasional hard object onto an unsuspecting cop's skull. These single-room-occupancy garden spots can offer shade and comfort to a whole platoon of disturbed people who feel no shame about aiming rocks, trash, assorted heavy things, and even feces and urine at responding officers from above. And the full or half full can of beer makes a great propellant when aimed from a third-story window at cops and nearby patrol cars on the street.

All this is not to say that you need to walk around wearing your helmet or like you have a stiff neck from staring at the stars. Just be a bit more cognizant of the fact that in certain places and under the right conditions—multistory parties, rooftop burglary calls, disputes at hotels, and so on—there can be just as much trouble above you as there is in front of you.

How to Be Smarter
Than a Drunk

In the days prior to the death of Princess Diana, a local attorney appeared on a San Diego radio talk show, decrying with all his might law enforcement officers who lie in wait for their "only-had-a-few-drinks" prey. This lawyer, whose practice is limited to helping the unwitting drunk driver beat his or her rap in court, feels strongly that the deck has been stacked against every poor sap who has even one adult beverage and then gets behind the wheel of a car.

Less-aware radio listeners out there might perceive this attorney's message as, "Drunk drivers of the world unite! Under our no-tolerance temperance laws, you have nothing to lose but your cars, freedom, or lives!" I believe his message to hapless and impaired motorists is "Come to me with your drunk-driving arrests and I'll attempt to fix what ails you."

And so goes the new and disturbing mantra from various sources on our newsstands and radio and TV that says, "If you're going to drink and drive, at least do it 'responsibly.'" This fallacy is similar to the suggestion offered by one nut playing Russian roulette with another: "Aim carefully." I've had it with these diatribes about our God-given right to drink booze and get behind the wheel of the car if we feel up to the trip home. "As long as we don't have 'too much' to drink," say this theory's supporters, "then we should be allowed to drive home in peace."

Statistics from the emergency room community tell us that at blood alcohol levels between .09 and .15, you're more than 200 times more likely to get into a fatal single-car accident. Recall that the deaths of Princess Diana and her boyfriend involved a car moving at 121 miles per hour, seat belts being used only by the lone survivor, and a blood-alcohol level nearly three times most states' limits of impairment. Alcohol-related highway fatalities numbered more than 17,000 in 1996, and while that figure is down from the well-proffered "Nearly half of all deaths on the road are related to alcohol," the numbers are still too high. Just ask the many surviving family members of nondrinking residents in your town killed by drunk drivers.

Here's a short excerpt from a conference presentation put on by the National Association of Criminal Defense Lawyers. It appears that one or more defense attorneys offered a session called "Defending DUI Cases: Insights from the Masters." (Oh to have been a fly on the wall at that presentation. The things we could have learned. . . .) I've transcribed the following words of legal wisdom in quotes and then add my own comments to the advice.

- *"Do not take a quick blast of breath spray or mouthwash. These contain alcohol and can spike test results."*

We've all seen drunk drivers' feeble attempts to cover the alcohol on their breath by shoving everything from mints to cigars into their chops. Good cops aren't fooled by odor masks. We know the telltale signs—they light up as soon as you light them up, pop candy mints into their mouth, try to suggest it's toothpaste or mouthwash that's making them smell like they fell mouth-first, into a distilling tank.

If you stop a smoking driver, ask him or her to put out the butt or stogie, and wait for the air to clear for a few minutes. Once your nose is acclimated, get a whiff of the violator's breath. If your probable cause is good enough to initiate the stop (i.e., equipment violations, hazardous movements, an accident, etc.) and you smell alcoholic beverages, you can go to work on his or her impairment. The old police maxim suggests, "If it walks like a duck . . .", so obviously, booze on the breath of the driver is the best first indicator. If you saw them smoking or eating as you approached, add it to your report.

- *"Do keep your own counsel. When the officer asks if you've been drinking tonight, politely refuse to answer any questions until you speak with an attorney."*

Besides sounding like advertising for criminal defense attorneys, this advice is just plain dumb. As we all can attest, anyone who plays "mum's the word" always piques a cop's interest, and then his or her desire to dig deeper for the real truth. This certainly could lead to these kinds of conversations:

Officer: "So, is there a logical explanation as to why you swerved all over the road, hit some parked cars, and spilled out of the driver's seat onto the ground with a can of beer in one hand and a bottle of Jim Beam in the other?"

Alleged Drunk Driver: "I want my lawyer."

Make the proper notations in your report. We know that hostility, interference, and a general lack of any cooperation are the hallmarks of the alcohol-impaired. (Where do you think the phrase "Beer Muscles" got its origins?)

- *"Do not cop an attitude. Cooperate, but do not feel obligated to perform any roadside contortions. You can usually refuse to take a 'field sobriety test'— standing on one leg, walking a straight line, touching your finger to your nose—without repercussions. A failure to pass, however, will be used against you in a court of law."*

  Great! I'm happy when a deuce refuses to perform our Field Coordination Tests. I can skip all of the demonstrations—which usually fall upon deaf and intoxicated ears anyway—and write "Refused" across the box on the report and continue with the arrest process in harmony. We've all had drunks fall over, run off, dash into the street, argue belligerently, throw up, pass out, whine, or cry while we were trying to get them to say the alphabet, so thanks for making it easier on all of us by refusing. Just add their exact words to your report. They'll often say swell things like, "Honest officer, I can't even do those moves when I'm sober."

- *"Do provide a sample. Refuse to give up urine or blood and at trial it could be used as evidence of your guilt, add to your jail time, and cause your license to be suspended instantly. Take the test—and attack its validity later."*

  Fine and dandy with me. Many city or district attorneys won't prosecute a drunk driver without a chemical test as evidence of over-the-legal-limit impairment. In other words, if they won't blow in the tube or fill the plastic cup, it's no sweat off our brows. We can and will take a blood sample, using the usual and humane method of needle and blood draw technician.

- *"If you do think you might be legally intoxicated, do opt for the urine test— it's more unreliable and more easily challenged than a blood test. But consider: drug use shows up on blood and urine tests but not on Breathalyzers."*

  So if you suspect your driver is also into the nose goodies or other unseemly legal or illegal drugs, take blood to be sure. One study in a large city revealed that nearly eight inmates out of ten booked into the county jail had drugs in their system upon arrival, so based on those numbers it's not hard to extrapolate that over half of your drunk driving arrests might involve drugs as well.

  In other words, take blood when the arrest situation suggests it's a good idea. Good clues might include the existence of the driver's long drug arrest rap sheet, obvious signs of street drug use inside nostrils, pupils, and elbow

245

joints, and the presence of any filled or empty prescription bottles in the front seat of the car or in the suspect's pocket.

I recall one drunk driving arrest where Party One got into an accident on the way to a veterans' hospital. Not only did he smell strongly of alcoholic beverages at 0800 hours, but he had a big bottle of prescription drugs in his front shirt pocket. After a warning from Mr. Miranda, the driver admitted that he drank booze and took pain pills to prepare himself for his back surgery at the VA hospital in a few hours. It occurs to me that we might have saved his life by arresting him. I'm assuming his doctors would not have cut him open had they known he was stewed to the gills, but who knows?

- *"Do phone home: call someone, anyone, even if you have to wake them. Later, they can testify that you sounded sober."*

This is my favorite from the list. Imagine how happy you would be, as Mr. Drunk Driver's pal, to receive a zero-dark-thirty call from him in the drunk tank and then be subject later to a subpoena and a courtroom visit to tell everyone what he said. Is it not possible that the prosecutor will ask this pseudocharacter witness how much formal medical training he has in determining sobriety over the telephone?

- *"Do prepare to pay—a lot. This should go without saying. Get a damn good DUI lawyer. And next time, remember this: You could call 2,500 cabs for the cost of his fee."*

Besides offering another less than subtle commercial for the defense/DUI bar, this advice begs the question, "Why don't defense attorneys spend their time telling people why they shouldn't drink booze and get behind the wheel of a car?" The simple answer is this: You don't kill the geese that lay golden eggs. Teaching people not to drink and drive shrinks the potential client pool. Any attorney who wants to buy that summer beach house or a new speedboat knows this. Better to have people think they can bamboozle the average dumb flatfoot with tricks and tactics than to urge them not to engage in this kind of behavior in the first place.

The severe injuries and deaths of officers across this nation at the hands of drunk drivers should reinforce one point: people still aren't getting the message.

Using Your Intuition
Trusting Your Gut Feelings

Midway through your graveyard shift, you begin to notice that your portable radio is starting to act up. "It's probably the battery," you think. "I'll swing by the station and get a new one." But then, one call after the other appears on your MDT screen, and you get busy.

Now, with but a few hours to go before the end of your shift, your radio is deader than a frozen wharf rat in Alaska. You definitely need a battery, and soon. As you're heading in, a speeder buzzes past you on the freeway with hardly a look in your direction. After a short chase, you pull the car over, get out, and walk up to the driver with a nonfunctioning radio . . .

Here's another one: Your pepper spray can is empty, and you've forgotten about it until you're already in the field and it's too late to get resupplied. You don't have your straight baton or PR-24. It sits, not on your belt, but nestled safely between your driver's seat and your door or, worse, in your trunk or back in your locker.

You stop at a convenience store on your beat. It looks as if a transient is inside the store giving the clerk a hard time. As you get out of your car, you see your baton in its usual place near the floorboard. You think, "I don't need my stick to handle this guy." As you enter the store, the confrontation inside escalates . . .

Consider this: You've just arrested a doper for being under the influence of his drug of choice. As you begin to search him, you notice he stinks, his clothes are completely filthy, and worse yet, he's wearing pants and a jacket that seem covered with pockets. You don't want to put your hands in any of these places, even with rubber gloves in place. The more you search, the more clut-

ter you find—photos, paper clips, keys, scraps of paper, matches, bent cigarettes, etc. He's squirming all over while you attempt to dig through his many
crowded pockets. Finally, you say to yourself, "This is a mess. I'll finish searching this guy later." He goes into the back of your car half-searched and wired
on crystal meth . . .

Each of these scenarios is all too common for some patrol officers. It's
easy to fall into a work routine that says, "I know what I should do, but I'm
too busy, distracted, lazy, tired, or 'experienced' to worry about it right now."

Veteran officers fall prey to many of the above because, for the most part,
nothing has ever gone wrong to justify any change in their behavior. In these
three examples, many officers could well say, "Nothing bad happened the time
when I made a traffic stop with no portable radio or went into a store and
dealt with a nut when I had no baton and no pepper spray," or, "The last time
I did a half-baked search, the guy didn't have a weapon or more dope."

For many officers, the past becomes their driver for the future. Because
the last 99 burglary calls have been from a false alarm, what's to say the hun-
dredth one won't suddenly be valid?

The downtown drunk who always goes along with the program each
and every time he's arrested certainly won't cause a problem this time, right?

The last week, month, or year you spent behind the wheel of a police car
was accident-free, so why wear that always-confining seat belt? You've never
had an accident before, so why bother with a seat belt that just gets in your way
anyway? Besides, it's the "other guy" who gets in accidents, not you, right?

My friend, Los Angeles security expert Gavin de Becker, is well known
for his work as a protection consultant to Hollywood's brightest stars. He also
is one of the leading behavioralists in the area of threat management, threat
assessment, and, ultimately, threat prevention.

He is a big believer in a simple motto: The past is absolutely no indicator
of the future. And in police work, this should hold especially true; what did or
didn't happen to you yesterday must not serve to influence your behavior today.

This is not to say your experience is not valuable in the streets; we know it
is. Experience is what makes good cops, what makes good FTOs, and what
pulls our bacon out of the fire in times of great stress and danger. It's just that
you shouldn't let any lack of past problems lull you into a false sense of security.

While working in San Ysidro, California, I drove past the former site of
the 1984 "McDonald's massacre" regularly. Each time I passed this tragic place
where nearly two dozen people lost their lives, I was reminded of the incident,
and the scars surely still remain for every cop, victim, and other civilian or
emergency service worker who survived that entirely unpleasant day.

The point to this remembrance is this: Do you think any of the on-duty police personnel who became involved in that incident actually believed something that bad would ever happen to them, especially during their work shift?

What about our officers who have survived being shot or had to shoot someone? Do you think they ever drove to work with thoughts in their heads that said, "I may get shot today," or "I may have to kill someone today"?

But while they may have never consciously considered being shot or having to shoot prior to these life-changing events, you can bet those thoughts are in the center of their minds as they prepare for a patrol shift today.

In law enforcement, we can no longer afford the luxury of relying on the past as an indicator of future events, especially when it comes to the behavior of the people we meet on the streets. Start looking at the so-called routine things you do in the field with more of an eye toward what could go wrong, rather than what hasn't gone wrong.

If your gut feelings have gotten rusty, take them out and give them a psychological polishing. Your first instincts are usually your best ones, especially when it comes to your survival.

Go back and get that radio battery, take your baton into that store, and dig deep into that doper's pockets. You know in your heart and in your head that there are certain shortcuts you just shouldn't take, ever. The time to make the right decision must come long before harm arrives on the scene.

Using Your P&P Manual
Cheat Sheets for the Streets

When I was a young officer going through the phase training program, I had a Field Training Officer (FTO) ask me if I carried my department-issued P&P manual (then known as the "yellow sheets" and now called the "tan sheets") with me.

I remember staring at him for 30 seconds while I considered the magnitude of that question. "Carry my sheets?" I thought to myself. "In my police gear bag? Why would I do that? Those things are heavy and bulky and full of bits of mostly useless information I'll never use."

And so, grudgingly, I admitted that no, I did not carry my five-inches-thick department binder with me. His response was, "Why not? Nearly every answer to nearly every question you'll have about doing this job is in that book."

And, even more grudgingly, I had to admit that he was correct. So the next day found my police car trunk filled with the usual police bric-a-brac in my gear bag and, next to it, my copy of the department P&P manual.

Leaving phase training and going out on my own, I eventually lost the habit of carrying the big brown notebook from my locker to my police car. The reasons for this were based mostly upon general laziness, not the original wisdom of the idea. It *is* a hassle to lug such a fat lot of pages to and from your trunk, and it *is* a struggle to fit such an awkward item into your ever-filling locker. But is there any patrol officer out there who can honestly say that he or she has never encountered a situation in the field where the options, answers, or solutions weren't crystal clear?

The presence of your P&P manual is for those times when you say, "I've heard about this procedure, problem, or response, but I've never had to act on it . . . until now."

251

Your P&P manual usually appears on scene when you or your colleagues begin the hard work necessary to take a promotional exam. For those of you who are preparing to take this test, I'm sure your first thoughts, as you pulled the dusty binder from some long-forgotten shelf, was something near to: "Oh great, I bet I don't have all the updates or the most recent pages in here. Now what am I going to do?"

And here I can empathize, having taken the sergeant's test and wondered—as I read the sheets straight through for the third time—if I had all the necessary new pages, not wanting to trudge to in-service training to get the right ones.

I'm willing to bet that those officers who keep their sheets completely up to date, including all the new update packets, are in the minority—the exception rather than the rule. The spectrum probably spans from this end—fully stocked and updated—to the other—cops who lost their P&Ps years ago and never bothered to replace them. Then there are those somewhere in the middle (and in the majority, perhaps) who could find their sheets (in their garages or closets) if asked and may have managed at least to keep the various updates in the vicinity.

I'd also argue that the minority that does keep fully updated P&Ps comprises cops who see the P&P manual as a living and breathing resource to be cracked open and consulted on a regular basis. Your sharper field lieutenants, sergeants, and patrol officers know that the sheets are what holds your organization together, offering complete descriptions of rules of conduct; arrest, cite, and reporting procedures; patrol and investigation recommendations; traffic issues; and emergency responses.

Even experienced detectives look to the P&Ps for guidance in new narcotics, firearms, or property-handling procedures. Since these practices change frequently, good investigators know that with the threat of civil liability as a constant, it pays to know what to do and how to do it.

And those sharp patrol officers or detectives who find themselves working as acting sergeants see the sheets as a good information source for those areas where they may not have much hands-on experience.

Put yourself in the following situations and see how the P&Ps could give you accurate legal, and even life-saving information on various difficult, complicated, or time-intensive events. (For the sake of discussion, we'll say that there are no available supervisors or knowledgeable partners to help you respond to these incidents; you're on your own.)

As either a patrol officer or an acting sergeant, how would you respond to the report of a bomb threat at a movie theater on your beat? And whom do you call first if someone finds a suspicious-looking device when you arrive?

What if the device was to go off and injure dozens of people? What procedures would you initiate after calling for paramedics?

Let's say you work near an airport. How would you respond to a small plane crash near the runway or near a residential area? What if it was a military jet? What then?

Suppose you're the acting sergeant when one of your officers gets involved in a shooting. After the paramedics arrive, whom do you call next?

Again as the acting sergeant, how do you investigate and document a citizen's complaint or a sexual harassment charge against one of the officers on your squad?

What's your departmental policy for working with agencies from other bordering cities or counties? Federal or state law enforcement agents? Ridealongs?

How do you impound $10,000 cash found at 3:00 A.M. at a dope house? A fully automatic and loaded machine gun with a defective trigger guard? An expensive stolen painting recovered while searching a storage center and too big to fit into your department's property room?

What are your duties or responsibilities, on and off duty, following a major earthquake, a large fire, or a full-scale riot?

What are the duties, responsibilities, functions, and limitations of: a police helicopter? Police K-9s? SWAT? Reserves?

And with so many changes in things like your booking, juvenile, or injured suspect arrest policies, the answers to these tough questions and more just like them are found in your P&Ps.

Does this mean you should run to this book every time you start a traffic stop, answer a radio call, or make an arrest? No. But it's always better to know a little bit about a lot of things than a lot about only a few things.

Only you can be the judge of your overall body of knowledge about police work, your department, and your policies and procedures for doing things safely, legally, and effectively.

Looking at the seemingly endless number of policies and pages in the manual, it can be daunting and far too time-consuming to start with the goal that you're going to sit down and read the beast from cover to cover in one sitting.

But since most P&Ps are logically divided into sections and subsections, it helps to break the total number of pages into a sum of their parts. Start by quickly reviewing the department policies you know well and spend more chunks of your time on those areas where you might have some gaps in your knowledge. At a minimum, if you make it a habit to read a few subsections per day, you can get through the whole book in a few weeks.

And if you encounter a situation, problem, report-writing, or procedural question in the field or station and you don't know or can't get the answer, jot yourself a note to review the related sheets (at work or at home) later to refresh your memory for next time.

Your Use of Force Continuum

As the Paul Newman movie *Cool Hand Luke* so accurately described, perhaps what we have in law enforcement is "a failure to communicate." Perhaps now is as good a time as any to all stand, in uniform and in unison, on the roof of our police stations and shout out, "Attention Citizens! We Carry Guns!"

The reason we need to make this announcement seems suddenly clear to me; too many suspects seem to have forgotten the fact that we are armed with deadly weapons and given the sworn duty, powers, training, and rights to use these devices to protect ourselves and others from certain serious injuries or death.

Nearly every law enforcement agency has or will have its share of fatal shootings. As difficult and painful as these incidents were for the officers and others involved, they were suspect-driven, not officer-created. We showed up wearing police uniforms, police badges, and openly displayed guns on our hips. This gun thing is not new; we've been wearing firearms for a century or so.

In the glow of hindsight, how is it that seemingly intelligent citizens are amazed that when we engage armed suspects, we try to make it work out that we go home alive? I'm still amazed that people who don't understand why deadly force rules of engagement exist get their "knowledge" from Hollywood movies and TV cop shows. In these safe environments, the good guys and the bad guys always act accordingly and respond in ways that even children understand. On the screen, the cops can wing a heavily armed bad guy in the arm and save the day. Or, they can use some handy Chuck Norris moves to swiftly disarm a knife-wielding psychotic without breaking a mild sweat. Were any of that actually possible, our jobs would be much easier, well defined, and less subject to public scrutiny.

Recent police shootings and others that have occurred (and will certainly occur again and again in the future) lead to the usual spate of letters in the newspapers and television stories. We see the requisite on-scene interviews with "earwitnesses," distraught family members, or cohorts of the dead suspect who loudly complain that we shot first and asked questions later.

When it comes to deadly force, we should offer no apologies for what we do, because the suspects dictate the outcome at every step. Given the opportunity to drop the knife, put down the club, or not reach for a firearm, they make the choice to escalate to the next, more deadly level. We're constrained by laws and ethics and a powerful sense of protecting ourselves, our partners, and nearby civilians. Armed suspects are hedonists in the extreme; they often don't care about anyone but themselves. Who they hurt or kill is secondary to what's controlling their own emotional states. Sometimes, we must become the life-or-death decision-makers for them. It's not a pretty picture, but they hold the brushes, the paint, and the canvas. We can only react to the scenario they're trying to create.

After police shootings, the accompanying media stories follow the usual themes, "Are the Cops Shooting Too Soon, Too Often, or Too Many Times?" The follow-up stories usually show some earnest-looking reporter down at the police range, watching us practice with our guns, or up at the academy, hooked up to a shoot-no shoot system like Firearms Training System (FATS), and walking through the scenarios. These stories carry the usual statements that say, "Police only have a split-second to make a life-and-death decision. Still, some questions about the latest shooting remain . . ."

It's this last statement that gives the media members and other not-at-the-scene citizens the "out" they need. It's always easy to say we should have waited, called for a psychiatrist, jumped on the suspect with capture nets, or talked him into a deep sleep. It's always easy to question our methods, motives, tools, techniques, and reasoning processes in the cold, bright light of day, not the dark of the alley or the white heat of the moment.

Our use of deadly force starts and ends at the discretion of the suspect and with his actions. We've all been trained in our agency's use-of-force policy (often called a "use-of-force continuum" today) that starts at with our mere presence in a police uniform and escalates and ends with the business end of a firearm. Since every contact, citizen, or suspect encounter is different, our responses must vary as well. The fluidity and time pressures of each encounter make it hard to find the "perfect" solution to every potentially high-risk contact. Situations go from "Shoot" to "Don't Shoot" and back to "Shoot" again, all in a matter of seconds.

Thankfully, for the sake of our safety and survival, we don't have to participate in every single step in the use-of-force continuum. If we did, armed suspects would be busy dancing the tango on our skulls while we chose the right "stop-right-there" words or the proper pain-compliance technique. We can and should move up the levels, rapidly and effectively. If it goes from, "Wait a minute, I want to talk to you" to "Drop the knife!" to a loud percussion sound, then the suspect had every opportunity along the spectrum to give up and give in.

And speaking of knifes, never forget that the well-defined and well-described reactionary gap for knife-wielding suspects is still a robust 21 feet. Watching the "reality cop" shows on TV, you can still see cops standing at arm's length near people holding knives.

A friend of mine who was a sheriff's deputy in New York and who owns a martial arts studio offered his assistance during the filming of a knife protection video for law enforcement. Even when the uniformed officer knew my friend was coming at him with a visible knife, the "attacker" still managed to "stab" him more than 50 times with the rubber training knife. The safety equation with knife-carrying suspects must be: Distance plus firearm accuracy plus center mass targetry.

It's the use-of-force continuum's flexibility that makes it so effective for us, both as a defensive tool and as a life-saving device. And it serves as a powerful civil protection shield as well. Since we know that many fatal police shootings will end up in civil court, we will need to explain, in great detail, why we chose the options we did and why others were not brought to bear. While this is difficult enough to do in front of a jury, it's even harder to depict to a plaintiff's attorney who truly believes we took his client's life without provocation. To him or her, no suspect-created circumstances will ever justify our deadly force response.

As such, every law enforcement officer is obligated to know his or her use-of-force continuum policy from bow to stern. You should know it from two perspectives: an instinctive, internal one, and an external, communicative one. In the former case, you need to know how to apply it—quickly, legally, ethically, humanely, and safely. In the latter, you need to know how to justify your actions, out loud and on paper, in your reports. It's not just enough to use it, you've got to be able to explain your actions to the many interested parties who will scrutinize the timing, legality, safety, and risk of your every move from the moment you contact the suspect.

As cops, we know why we went from talking to pain compliance to pepper spray to a firearm. We must be able to articulate the reasons to the myriad investigators, attorneys, or courtroom participants who will follow any use of deadly force. Your use-of-force policy is there for a reason. It should give you the peace of mind and the tools and techniques needed to survive any high-risk encounter.

50 Ways to Stay Alive

I recently attended the always-popular Calibre Press "Street Survival" seminar. As usual, I came away impressed with the high quality of instruction, the never-ending supply of patrol car or news media videotapes that show good, bad, and ugly police work, and the fresh supply of new survival techniques.

On the one hand, the Street Survival seminar is great for encouraging patrol officers to stay motivated, legally aggressive, and safe. On the other, it's also great for infusing the participants (okay, at least me) with a healthy dose of paranoia. I watched a slew of state trooper videos showing cops in hats getting beaten up, kicked, cursed at, shot and wounded, and, sadly, shot and killed.

As a founding member of the Paid Paranoids Club, I don't need much to get me thinking suspiciously about most people anyway. Seeing two days of cops getting whupped by "Yes" people who suddenly turn into raging "No" people is enough to get the gravel in my guts rolling like a rock-polishing machine on overdrive.

Many of the videos in the seminar point out two problems: one, cops who make stupid tactical mistakes run a high risk of being beaten or shot; and two, cops often *assume* that suspects who are cooperative at the start of the contact will stay that way throughout.

It's easy to watch these segments and say what every other participant near me said aloud: "*That* would never happen to me." In the shining light of hindsight, let's hope so. But if the presence of a patrol car video or a TV station cameraperson didn't stop these assaults, think about what might happen to your blue body, out there all by its lonesome, without the benefit of a permanent record.

Huddled in the near dark with my course booklet and my pen, random street-handy ideas came to me, one after the other, for two days. As such, here is a cornucopia of officer safety and survival tips, courtesy of my noggin and the two veteran instructors from Calibre Press, Dave Grossi and Bob Willis. (For more information about the Calibre Press Street Survival seminar schedule, go to www.calibrepress.com.)

1. Watch for hard-core crooks with handcuff keys in creative places, like their pockets, or, more accurately, neck chains, taped to their belts or belt loops in the rear, or in their socks. Search as if you expect to find a handcuff key.

2. Almost anything can be bent, twisted, or melted into the shape of a handcuff key. This includes combs, wire, paper clips, ink pens and caps, zipper pull tabs, hair barrettes, and safety pins. While searching, when in doubt, take it out.

3. Regardless of their injuries or *apparent* death, (save for decapitations or actual, verifiable total paralysis) handcuff *everyone* when the action is over. Head-shot suspects have run off, body-shot suspects have continued to fight, and suspects involved in seemingly "fatal" police pursuits or similar car crashes have driven away, run away, or fought or shot arriving cops who thought the battle was over.

4. Have the presence of mind to call ASAP for an ambulance for any armed suspect call. Chances are even money that a good guy or a bad guy is going to get hurt in the ensuing encounter. If it happens to be you or a partner, you'll be glad the paramedics were on scene or close.

5. Keep in mind that many county jail and prison inmates watch *Cops*, *LAPD*, *America's Most Wanted*, and *The Justice Files*. They view the tactical mistakes as training opportunities and the tactical successes as techniques they'll have to learn to beat. Keep ahead of them.

6. Shoot at the range at least once per month. Since most police shootings happen at the 3- to 5-yard range, focus on your close-up accuracy.

7. Don't refer to your opposite hand as your "weak hand." This creates a failure mind-set that one hand is "stronger" than the other during shooting practice or real combat. Call it your "off hand" and practice, practice, practice until you can shoot with speed, accuracy, and confidence with it.

8. Pepper spray can solve a lot of problems that empty-handed grappling can't. Aim accurately and don't stand too close or too far away.

9. Remember that in terms of threat assessment of suspects you've dealt with previously, past behavior is a good indicator of future behavior. But past cooperation is not a perfect predictor of current or future cooperation

with anyone. Even if they've always "gone along with the program before" or are seeming to do so now, don't drop your guard.

10. Approach every suspect from the side or rear. Standing directly in front of him to talk, search, or pat him down is an invitation for a punch to the face, a headbutt to the nose, or a knee to the privates. Even in an FI stance, if you're face to face, you can raise his tension level by "violating his space." Offset yourself, especially during those moments right before you make hands-on contact for searching or cuffing.

11. With every suspect contact, expect to be resisted, assaulted, punched, or kicked. If it doesn't happen, fine, but if it does you won't be caught completely by surprise.

12. Similarly, until you know differently, expect every traffic violator *not* to stop for you. If he or she pulls over, go about your usual business. If not, you won't be completely surprised. As with #11, the moments you waste thinking, "Hey! I'm a cop and he's hitting me!" or "I'm a cop and she's not stopping!" won't be wasted in shock and disbelief.

13. Success while shooting or grappling with suspects relies plenty on your forearm and grip strength. You want to be able to hold people when you grab them. As you drive around, develop your gripping power by squeezing a racquet or tennis ball or similar exercise device. It kills time and may give you an edge in close quarters.

14. The closer you stand to suspects, the closer your gun should be to your body. Pointing your gun from a fully extended arm position at a suspect who is close enough to touch is to risk a disarming. Any touch to the slide of your pistol may cause it to malfunction. If he gets too close, back up and draw your gun toward your solar plexus. There are plenty of street idiots who think they can grab your gun before you can shoot it. Don't prove them right.

15. In a safe and private location, train yourself to fight back one-handed. Practice using your equipment with one piece in each hand: mace and baton, mace and nunchakus, gun and empty-hand, radio and gun, radio and mace, and so on.

16. Search the suspect's mouth, hat, socks, and shoes better than you do now.

17. Even in daylight, presearch the suspect's pockets with a small flashlight before you go jamming your hand inside.

18. Get into the habit of using your cordcuff for all arrests. It only takes a few seconds to put it around their waists, and it can help avoid kicked patrol car windows, twisting and turning, and possible escapes.

19. If you see a fire extinguisher in a car, make sure it's legitimate and not a phony filled with dope, a gun, or other contraband.

261

20. Check the condition of your "portable cover," otherwise known as your vest. Wash the covers frequently, and if the Kevlar is old and bedraggled, replace it.

21. Keep your finger out of the trigger guard until you're ready to fire. This small step would avoid nearly every accidental discharge caused by stress, the "startle" response, or involuntary muscle movements.

22. Don't get tactically complacent just because more cops than just you have now arrived. Studies show most police shootings happen when more than one officer is on scene. Keep your guard up no matter how many uniforms are with you.

23. Look harder for weapons that "print through" or show an outline in the suspect's pocket. Studies say that most crooks carry their guns unholstered (because leather gear costs too much) in their front or rear waistband. Frequent touches or adjustments by them to these areas may mean it's a gun.

24. Make more contacts from the passenger side during traffic stops. It may stop some yahoo from running you down and it gives you a tactical edge on most crook-drivers and crook-passengers, who may be expecting you to come to them in the usual way.

25. Ask and answer a very hard and soul-searching question: If I responded to a high-risk call involving a juvenile suspect using a firearm, will I have the ability to use deadly force? With the school shootings at Columbine High School and West Paducah, Kentucky, and baby-faced killer-gangsters armed with assault weapons, this issue is real. Cops who say, "I can't shoot at a kid" are forgetting that for a growing number of dead-eyed children, killing people with a gun is no big deal.

26. Buy some heavy bag gloves and use them. For a good fitness change of pace, practice hitting the heavy bag in your area station gym (or in your home garage if you're so equipped). Stand near the bag and determine where you need to strike it to create "suspect realism." Some officers will wrap duct tape rings around the bag to mark certain areas at the approximate head or body heights of their opponents.

27. Buy a lockable plastic firearms storage box for your in-state air travel plans. If you're flying and need to bring your weapon for personal or professional protection reasons, you'll need to check your unloaded firearm as baggage before you get on board. Don't make a big deal out of displaying your unloaded firearm when checking with the ticket counter personnel. Be very discreet. Crooks fly—and may even have jobs at the airport. You don't want to have your luggage rifled or stolen.

28. Check the conditions of your duty belt and off-duty holsters. Signs of

cracked leather, missing strapdown screws, worn thumb breaks, and frayed nylon should tell you it's time to get your holster repaired or, better yet, replaced. If it's loose for you, it's that way for a crook trying to grab it.

29. In domestic violence situations, your role may change quickly from the "protector" of the victim to the "aggressor," who somehow wants to "hurt" the suspect by arresting him or her. This change can take place in a split second and force you and your partner to deal suddenly with two hostile people instead of the original one.

30. In domestic violence, family squabbles, or other calls involving the presence of children, watch for suspects who use their kids as a shield or even a weapon when you try to arrest them. Many cops can tell stories of women who turned into she-wolves when it came time for Child Protective Services to take their kids away for abuse or neglect. Some disturbed women will try to get you into a tug-of-war with the child's arm. Some angry men will toss their child in the air toward you as they aim a kick at your groin. Get help and read the early-warning signs. Get the kids separated and away ASAP.

31. Some officers prefer discretion when off duty. They carry only their ID card and their weapon, rather than their badge as well. This makes sense when you consider it. If it ever comes time to get in the grease, the only people who need to know you're a cop are the responding officers. Carrying your badge and letting it show in your wallet makes it easy for savvy crooks to target you.

32. Anytime your stress level is high or your nerves are on edge, practice "combat breathing." This cycle involves inhaling for a count of four, holding your breath for a count of four, exhaling for a count of four, and resting for a count of four. This quick fix will keep your breath rate smooth, lessen your chances of tunnel vision, and help you focus on large-muscle actions and reactions when you need them.

33. Decide today what you will do when someone points a laser pointer at you. The hard questions you have to answer are these: Is this some nitwit kid with a $12 laser pointer he stole from an office supply store? Or is this a shooter focusing his sights on your ten-ring?

34. When in need, consider faking it. If it's one of those dark nights where you're on a traffic stop with a car filled with hoods or the creep that raises your neck hair, role-play it a little. Tell the suspect who comes out of his car, "Please stand by the hood of my car and face the windshield. It works better for the video camera that way." Shout out some fake German commands to your invisible canine partner or some English ones

to your invisible human partner. "Down, Rex!" or "I'll handle this, partner," works for either species.

35. During any contact, keep your awareness on your FI stance. If the suspect(s) shift around, you should shift around too. Always, always, always keep your gun side away from people who are not cops.

36. Practice putting your gun back in your holster without looking at it. After viewing stacks of videos of cops involved in high-risk situations where their guns are out, I still see too many of them breaking eye contact with their targets and looking at their guns and their leather when they reholster. Worse yet, they grab at their holsters with their "off hands" to help get their back guns inside. It's a bad habit that can turn deadly. You should be able to pull your gun, change magazines, and reholster without taking your eyes off the target.

37. When writing FIs for Asian gangsters, don't just ask them about their tattoos; ask if they have any symbolic or ritualistic burns on their skin.

38. If you're the Cover Officer, stay focused on the Big Three: Assault, Escape, or Disarmings. It's easy to get complacent when the situation seems "normal."

39. If, during a contact, you think you're about to lose what might euphemistically be called "tactical integrity," break it off. Better to let an FI or a ticket go and live to catch them another day.

40. Keep up a healthy stock of rubber gloves and flex cuffs. When you *really* need these items, you *really* need them. Don't get caught gloveless around bloody, oozing people or cuffless in a crowd-cuff situation.

41. Don't fight your instincts. If it doesn't "look" right, it's not. If it doesn't "sound" right, it's not. And, most importantly, if it doesn't "feel" right, it's definitely not right. Trust your intuitive organs: your gut, your heart, and your head. Act on your feelings; they've carried you this far.

42. Keep potential suspects guessing. Do what they don't expect. Come in through the back door of a bar if the fight is in the front. Park in the rear alley of the apartment building if people would usually expect you to park in the front lot. Don't automatically use your flashlight if an approach in darkness might be safer. Keep your partner in sight but stay "tactically away" from each other so one ambush shot doesn't get you both.

43. Think "lightning speed" when handcuffing. More problems start when you get only one cuff on one wrist. Cuff quickly! Try to get both cuffs on at the same time, rather then one first and then the other. If the suspect is mostly compliant, grab as many fingers on both hands as you can hold, position the wrists, and push the cuffs on. One cuff at a time often leads to a change of heart for crooks. This can lead to your slashed face or their escape.

44. Statistically, the majority of people who end up in the back of our cars are drug abusers, alcohol abusers, chronically psychologically disturbed, or all three. They don't think, reason, or cope as well as we'd like them to. You can't expect irrational people to think or act rationally. Adjust your expectations and instructions accordingly.

45. Know what's behind you if you have to back up. You don't want to fall over curbs, wet grass, etc. Practice backing up in a tactical "L"-shape, rather than in a straight line. The "L"-shape can help you keep your balance and control and move the suspect's momentum toward the ground.

46. Keep your radio on low during contacts. Not only is it distracting for all concerned, it can raise the suspect's fight or flight level, even if the statements he hears are not about him. Keep the information about him quiet until you're ready to take action. Saying, "Hear that? She's confirming your warrant right now" offers a gold-plated invitation to a smacked face or a chase.

47. Be prepared for the opposite reaction to your use of pepper spray. Tough guys may weep from their buckled knees. Violent fighters can become even more aggressive. And suspects who are supposed to put their hands behind their backs for handcuffing may spend all their time trying to rub their eyes.

48. Deadly force decisions can go from "Shoot!" to "No Shoot!" in microseconds. Your decision either way will be judged by which side of this double-edged coin came up for you. Long before you ever have to make a true deadly-force decision, think of how you will express, in words and on paper, any shoot-don't shoot scenario so it shows that you made a trained, conscious, and lifesaving choice.

49. Use the wall, Luke. As my recent experience will attest, the infamous "wall stun" will stop a fleeing or fighting street lizard in his tracks. Leaving a restaurant with my kids one afternoon, I saw a handcuffed suspect break free from sheriff's deputies near their substation parking lot. As he ran toward me, I realized I had to play street football. I kindly and gently plowed into his ribs as he came near. He bounced off my head and shoulder, careened off a bench, banked off the wall, and flopped face down on the pavement. As I crawled to his hard-breathing, newly prone position, I realized he had rolled onto my right pinkie and ring fingers, fracturing one and tearing ligaments in the other. No good deed goes unpunished.

50. Make an investment in your mental health and order the two-hour, two-tape audiocassette program *The Bullet-Proof Mind: What It Takes to Win Violent Encounters and After*. This program is narrated by former Army

Ranger Dave Grossman, who wrote the powerful book *On Killing* (Grossman, Little, Brown 1995). This audio course is designed specifically for cops and can help you condition your mind and body for the psychological trauma you may face following any critical incident.

Good luck and stay safe.

About the Author

Steve Albrecht retired in November 1999 from the San Diego Police Department, where he had worked since 1984, both as a regular officer and later as a reserve sergeant. For six years, he served as an investigator in the San Diego Police Domestic Violence Unit and handled more than 1,500 cases.

His other Paladin Press books include *Streetwork: The Way to Police Officer Safety and Survival* and *One-Strike Stopping Power: How to Win Street Confrontations with Speed and Skill.* He cowrote *CONTACT & COVER: Two-Officer Suspect Control* (C.C. Thomas Publishers) with Lt. John Morrison (San Diego Police, Ret.).

For 14 years, Steve wrote the "Streetwork" officer safety column for the award-winning San Diego Police Officers Association publication *The Informant.* In 1999, he won a San Diego Press Club award for "Streetwork," named the best column in a monthly newspaper.

He is the managing director for Albrecht Training & Development, a San Diego, California-based firm that provides training and consulting on workplace violence prevention and threat management, subjects on which he is a nationally recognized authority. His business books include *Crisis Management for Corporate Self-Defense, Fear and Violence on the Job,* and *Ticking Bombs: Defusing Violence in the Workplace.*

He holds a doctoral degree in business administration, an M.A. in security management, and a B.A. in English. He is certified as a Professional in Human Resources (PHR) by the Society for Human Resource Management (SHRM) and as a Certified Protection Professional (CPP) by the American Society for Industrial Security (ASIS). He is a member of the Association of Threat Assessment Professionals (ATAP) and the San Diego County District Attorney's Stalking Strike Force.

He can be reached at Albrechttd@aol.com.